Strategies for
Working with Families of
Young Children with Disabilities

Strategies for Working with Families of Young Children with Disabilities

edited by

Paula J. Beckman, Ph.D.
University of Maryland, College Park

Baltimore • London • Toronto • Sydney

Paul H. Brookes Publishing Co.
Post Office Box 10624
Baltimore, Maryland 21285-0624

Copyright © 1996 by Paul H. Brookes Publishing Co., Inc.
All rights reserved.

Typeset by PRO-IMAGE Corporation, York, Pennsylvania.
Manufactured in the United States of America by
The Maple Press Company, York, Pennsylvania.

The case studies described in this book are completely fictional. Any similarity to actual individuals or circumstances is coincidental and no implications should be inferred.

Library of Congress Cataloging-in-Publication Data
Strategies for working with families of young children with
    disabilities / edited by Paula J. Beckman.
        p.   cm.
    Includes bibliographical references and index.
    ISBN 1-55766-257-6
    1. Family social work.   2. Social work with handicapped children.
3. Parents of handicapped children—Services for.   4. Handicapped
children—Services for.   I. Beckman, Paula J., 1952–
HV697.S86   1996
362.4′083—dc20   96-9073
                                                                                    CIP

British Library Cataloguing-in-Publication data are available from the
British Library.

Contents

About the Authors

THE EDITOR

Paula J. Beckman, Ph.D., is a full professor in the Department of Special Education at the University of Maryland, College Park. She received her doctorate in 1980 from the University of North Carolina. Dr. Beckman began working with the families of infants and toddlers with disabilities at Meyer Children's Rehabilitation Institute in 1974. During her more than 20 years in early intervention, she has been involved in direct services and personnel preparation and has conducted numerous studies concerned with families of young children with disabilities. Dr. Beckman currently directs Project Assist, a project designed to provide support to families of infants and toddlers with disabilities, directs a personnel preparation grant for students specializing in work with families, and is an investigator on the Early Childhood Research Institute on Inclusion. She also has a family member with special needs.

THE CONTRIBUTORS

Deirdre A. Barnwell, M.A., has more than 10 years of academic and practical experience in early childhood and special education. She has worked in a variety of special education and early childhood settings, with families from diverse cultural and economic backgrounds, and with children with various disabilities. Ms. Barnwell developed a communitywide early intervention program for children with and without disabilities while a Peace Corps volunteer in Honduras. She has extensive experience in training and supervising early intervention personnel, including the development of training products and materials and ongoing program evaluation. In addition to working with Project Assist, she is a full-time doctoral student and faculty research assistant at the University of Maryland, College Park, where she is involved in a variety of activities such as research and the supervision of graduate students providing support to families of infants and toddlers with disabilities.

Lynn Brown, M.S., has provided support and assistance to parents of children with disabilities, on both an individual and a group basis, for many years. In the course of her 20 years in the field, Ms. Brown has worked in both home-based and center-based programs and has extensive experience in providing in-service and preservice preparation for students in special education. At the University of Maryland, College Park, Ms. Brown has facilitated support groups for families of infants and toddlers with disabilities and provided individual support to families as part of Project Assist. She has also supervised students in preservice programs who were going to be working with families, and she has participated in statewide in-service training efforts.

Monimalika Day, M.A., has worked with children and their families since 1989. She worked with homeless children in Calcutta, India, and is one of the founders of a drop-in center operated by Calcutta Rescue. Ms. Day also taught in a school for children with special needs and started a center-based program in a hospital in Calcutta. She has a master's degree in child development and a Certificate of Advanced Graduate Studies from Wheelock College in Boston. She worked as a volunteer at the Foundation for Children with AIDS in Boston. Ms. Day is a doctoral student in the Department of Special Education at the University of Maryland, College Park. She has worked with Project Assist, supervised students, and been involved in research on families of children with special needs since 1993.

Nancy Frank, M.S.W., a clinical social worker, has worked for the past 12 years with a variety of families. Since 1990, she has worked with parents of infants and toddlers with disabilities, has facilitated support groups, and has provided individual counseling and support services as part of Project Assist. Ms. Frank has also been involved in personnel preparation efforts at both the preservice and in-service levels. She has had considerable experience in running groups, conducting individual and family therapy, and assisting families as a service coordinator. She is the sibling of an individual with special needs.

Krista Kettler, M.A., is a Ph.D. candidate in the special education program at the University of Maryland, College Park. She received the B.S. in Special Education from Louisiana State University and the M.A. in Early Childhood Special Education from the University of Alabama. Since 1986, Ms. Kettler has taught children with and without disabilities in a variety of educational settings, including classroom-based, home-based, segregated, integrated, and fully included programs. While at the University of Maryland, she has worked with Project Assist, supervised students, and participated in both in-service and preservice personnel preparation activities. She works as a special educator and service coordinator for the Infants and Toddlers Program in Charles County, Maryland, where she serves infants and young children with disabilities and their families in both home-based and center-based settings.

Sandra Newcomb, M.A., has a master's degree in special education and is a faculty research assistant in the Department of Special Education at the University of Maryland, College Park. She has extensive experience in providing support to families of infants and toddlers, both in individual settings and in parent support groups, as part of Project Assist. She also has provided home-based early intervention services for children from birth to 3 years of age. Her experience also includes preservice and in-service personnel preparation and supervision. Ms. Newcomb is currently the coordinator of a family specialization training grant that prepares graduate students in early childhood special education to work with families who have young children with disabilities. She is also the parent of three children, one of whom has special needs.

Jennifer Smith Stepanek, B.A., is the parent of four children with complex health and developmental needs (three of whom are deceased). She is an author, editor, and international presenter on issues related to grief, health care for children, medical technology in the home, and family–professional collaboration. Ms. Stepanek is involved in both preservice and in-service personnel preparation in special education at the University of Maryland, College Park. In this role, she provides support to families who have young children with disabilities in both group and individual settings as part of Project Assist. She also currently serves as the Family/Professional Resource Specialist at the Association for the Care of Children's Health in Bethesda, Maryland. She has experience as a teacher and a service coordinator for families of infants and toddlers.

Foreword

Since its inception in the 1960s, early intervention has recognized the central role that families play in the lives of young children with disabilities. Through the 1990s, there has been a near-constant discussion about the implications of this fact for early intervention professionals. Researchers have described family needs, examined parent–child interactions, documented family–professional interactions, evaluated the family-related training and skills of professionals, and debated the efficacy of parent involvement. Legislation has replaced the individualized education program for infants and toddlers with the individualized family service plan. Various terms have been used to describe approaches to working with families, including *family-friendly*, *family-focused*, *family-centered*, *family-allied*, and *family-directed*.

Throughout the discussions, debates, and innumerable publications, one fact stands out: Working with families stands as both an important goal and a significant challenge for professionals who work with young children with disabilities. Research has documented that 1) preservice training programs spend relatively little time in preparing students for family-related roles; 2) practicing professionals believe that work with families is an important goal, but most perceive their skills in working with children to be greater than their skills in working with families; 3) early intervention professionals report significant discrepancies between typical and desired practices in working with families; and 4) the lack of family-centered practices is attributed to a complex array of variables that include real and perceived administrative barriers, family and professional attitudes, and professional skills.

The institutionalization of family-centered practices will continue to be a long, complex process. In the meantime, professionals need practical information to serve as a guide to the many different roles possible in working with families. Paula J. Beckman and her colleagues offer just such a resource. These authors first lay the theoretical and rational foundation for working with families and then proceed to provide concrete guidance in such topics as communicating with families, coordinating services, engaging in family assessments, involving families in team meetings, resolving conflicts with families, developing support groups, facilitating transitions, and supporting siblings. The authors recognize the diverse array of families who participate in early intervention programs. The book concludes with six case studies providing concrete examples of how project staff have worked with families, often in the context of complex and difficult situations.

The authors recognize that there are few set answers for working with families. If readers approach this book with the hope of finding a precise curriculum for working with families, they will be disappointed. What the authors provide is a framework, guidelines, and examples of successful interactions between parents and professionals. Practices that are successful with one family may not be successful with others. An examination of the *processes* used to arrive at successful solutions yields the true value of a family-centered approach.

Donald B. Bailey, Jr., Ph.D.
Director
Frank Porter Graham Child Development Center
University of North Carolina at Chapel Hill

Preface

There is little doubt that the move toward family-centered services for young children with disabilities is one of the most important changes that has occurred in early intervention. This change has created many challenges for professionals.

This book describes a variety of strategies that can be used by service providers to build positive working relationships with families. They are based, in part, on a growing body of literature that provides suggestions about effective practice. They are also based on the experience that the contributing authors have had with families of individuals with disabilities. Although all of the authors bring a diverse mix of professional experience, several authors also bring personal perspectives and experiences gained from having a child or family member with a disability.

One of the most valuable experiences shared by the contributing authors is their involvement with Project Assist, a project designed to provide support for families of infants and toddlers with disabilities in a large public school system. The strategies are also based on the cumulative experiences of the authors, both in intervention and in personnel preparation activities.

Although the strategies described in this book do not derive exclusively from Project Assist, this shared experience provided an opportunity to learn from families and examine many issues related to professional practice. A general overview of Project Assist is provided here because it offers a context for many of the strategies described throughout the book.

The Project Assist model is specifically designed to provide support to families who are receiving direct services for their children from a local infant and toddler program. Project Assist is available to families of children in the program and consists of three major components: a parent support group, individual support, and follow-up. Families are offered the option of participating in Project Assist by their service coordinator or by their child's teacher. Families who choose to participate are free to select those components that most meet their needs. These become part of the services identified on the individualized family service plan (IFSP).

The first component is a parent support group. The support group is facilitated by two individuals, typically a social worker and either a parent or a special educator who has had experience in facilitating support groups. Groups are held at a time that is most convenient for the majority of families and occur both during the day and in the evening. Each group meets on a weekly basis for 8 weeks and has closed membership. That is, once a group is established and begins, new members do not join that particular group. This structure permits the group to become a cohesive unit, allows families to develop friendships with one another, and prevents families from having to repeatedly explain their particular circumstances to new members. The agenda for group activities is determined by families. To facilitate participation in the support group, transportation and on-site child care are provided. Further information about this and alternative ways to organize support groups is available in Chapter 8.

The second major component of the model includes individual support, which is provided through such mechanisms as home visits and frequent telephone contact. These contacts are specifically intended to focus on the needs of families and are conducted in addition to visits from staff who provide direct services to children. Families that select this option often wish to have a source of support available who is not involved in direct services to their child, but who is knowledgeable about disability and experienced with the system. As such, the content and frequency of this service varies, and the agenda is determined by the family. Examples of individual support activities may include helping a parent prepare for an upcoming individualized education program or IFSP meeting, supporting a parent while their child is in the hospital, or working with the family to support siblings.

Because of the time-limited nature of the services, a follow-up component has also been established. This includes a follow-up group for parents who wish to have continued contact beyond the more intensive, 8-week support group. The follow-up group meets less frequently (typically about twice a month) and often includes a social component (e.g., potluck dinners, parties). Membership is also more fluid, with new families entering and other families coming less frequently as their needs change.

Although individual support visits are initially designed to last for approximately 3 months, they may extend past that time if parents express a need for additional support. The decision to continue individual support visits is made during an informal discussion that occurs at the end of the original 3-month period and is reevaluated at 2- to 3-month intervals thereafter. Although some families decide that additional individual visits would be helpful, others no longer feel the need for ongoing visits. Still others remain in casual telephone contact with the project and occasionally reinitiate contact when new events occur for which they would like support.

Several features are important in the Project Assist model. First, *family defines family*; that is, services are offered to anyone who cares for the child. In addition to biological parents, participants have included such individuals as foster parents and grandparents. Second, *the family determines the length of service*. The system of follow-up services permits families to decide for themselves when it is best to move on and when they need additional support. This accommodates a wide range of family needs. A third feature that family members have consistently viewed as favorable is that *group participants all have children of similar ages*. Families often find these age similarities supportive because, although the children have a variety of disabilities, they are frequently dealing with similar issues (e.g., finding appropriate services, adjusting to the child's diagnosis). Families also like *starting the group together*. Many families had tried other groups in the past. Some were intimidated by previous experiences, however, because they felt that they were entering an established group in which other members already knew each other. By starting together, families found it easier to connect with other participants. Finally, *family member checks* occur during special meetings to help ensure that the project continues to address the needs of families. During such meetings, past and present members are invited to formally provide feedback to project staff. This feedback forms the basis for modifications in the way that services are delivered.

Efforts to evaluate the project have occurred through the use of individual interviews, member checks, and paper-and-pencil evaluation measures. In general, families report several important benefits, including an increased sense of acceptance, a sense of reduced isolation, an increased sense of self-esteem and empowerment, and the availability of information and resources.

The Project Assist model is only one way to provide support for families. Many other excellent and creative examples are available throughout the United States. Practitioners may find that some elements of these models can be applied to their programs, whereas others cannot. Additional information regarding Project Assist is available elsewhere in the literature (Beckman, Newcomb, Frank, Brown, & Filer, 1993; Newcomb, Stepanek, Beckman, Frank, & Brown, 1994).

The purpose of this book is to describe specific strategies and skills that can help professionals build relationships with families in ways that reflect an understanding of the multiple factors that can influence family adaptation. Chapters 2, 3, and 4 focus on the process of developing working relationships with families and basic skills that can be used in a variety of situations with families. Chapters 5 and 6 describe basic skills involved in coordinating services, interviewing, and conducting planning meetings with families. After providing this base, Chapters 7 through 11 provide suggestions for handling more specific circumstances, including resolving conflicts, developing and implementing support groups, providing support during transitions, helping families support siblings, and supporting families through the loss of a child. In addition to concrete strategies for working with families, each chapter provides activities that service providers and students can use as a basis for discussion, practice, and self-reflection. Some of the activities in each chapter rely on the case studies that are included at the end of the book.

This book is an effort to provide a concrete resource for students and service providers who want to further develop their ability to work with families. It has been designed to integrate the literature pertaining to families and the philosophy of family-centered services with practical strategies that can be used by interventionists in their work. Although working in a more collaborative way with families can present service providers with many challenges, it also provides many opportunities for personal and professional development. We hope that the material provided in this book can contribute to the efforts of students and professionals who are trying to meet this challenge.

REFERENCES

Beckman, P., Newcomb, S., Frank, N., Brown, L., & Filer, J. (1993). Innovative practices: Providing support to families of infants with disabilities. *Journal of Early Intervention, 17,* 445–454.

Newcomb, S., Stepanek, J.S., Beckman, P.J., Frank, N., & Brown, L. (1994). Providing family support services as part of a comprehensive early intervention system. *ACCH Advocate, 1*(2), 21–24.

Acknowledgments

Many individuals have given generously of their time and their knowledge to make this book possible. I would like to thank the authors who contributed many lessons from their personal and professional experience. Their sensitivity, their willingness to learn, and their unfailing tendency to put the needs of children and families above other professional priorities has made working with each of them a privilege. The students who have participated, both in our direct work with families and in our training activities, have also contributed a great deal to this effort. They regularly challenged us with their energy, enthusiasm, and ideas. I would also like to express my deepest appreciation to Betty Pollins for the many hours she spent on this manuscript, for her continual willingness to stay late and pick up and deliver various drafts, and for the countless ways she goes out of her way to help. For me, as for many others, she is a constant source of support.

I am also grateful to several organizations that, over the years, have provided funding, both for our direct work with families and for our efforts to prepare personnel who work with families. These organizations include the Office of Special Education, U.S. Department of Education (Grant nos. H024H90009 and H029Q20102); the Maryland Infants and Toddlers Program; and the Ronald McDonald Foundation.

I would like to thank my family for their unwavering encouragement and support. I particularly want to thank my husband, Bob. His integrity, intelligence, and sense of humor can almost always put the events of my life in perspective and provide an ongoing source of strength and support.

Finally, and perhaps most important, all of us would like to thank the children and families with whom we have worked. We are repeatedly touched by their stories and are grateful for the lessons we have learned from them. They have challenged our thinking and enriched our lives.

*This book is dedicated
to the memory of Akila, Brandon,
Danny, Jamie, Justin, and Justin. We
would like to thank their families for
sharing their joys and sorrows and
for allowing us to be a
part of their lives.*

Chapter 1

Theoretical, Philosophical, and Empirical Bases of Effective Work with Families

Paula J. Beckman

As services for young children with disabilities have evolved, there has been a fundamental shift in prevailing views of recommended practice (Bailey, Buysse, Edmondson, & Smith, 1992; Dunst, Trivette, & Deal, 1988). Since the mid-1980s, researchers and practitioners have increasingly acknowledged the central role of families in early intervention. This shift has become known as a move toward *family-centered services.* Service providers are now expected to work collaboratively with families and to address the child's needs in ways that are consistent with the needs of the entire family.

The reasons for this philosophical shift have been described frequently in the literature (Bailey, 1987, in press; Bailey, Buysse, et al., 1992; Beckman & Bristol, 1991; Beckman, Robinson, Rosenberg, & Filer, 1994; Dunst, 1985; Dunst et al., 1988; Dunst, Johanson, Trivette, & Hamby, 1991; McBride, Brotherson, Joanning, Whiddon, & Demmitt, 1993; McGonigel & Garland, 1988; Raver & Kilgo, 1991). Unlike service providers, families affect and are affected by their children throughout the life span. Moreover, families offer unique information about the child in a variety of contexts that professionals are not able to obtain otherwise.

The shift toward a family-centered philosophy has implications for virtually all aspects of intervention, including assessment, decision making, family–provider relationships, and service delivery. In general, there are increasing expectations that practitioners will work more closely and collaboratively with families and that they will respect the family's right to a central role in decision making.

1

In the face of such shifts, service providers have expressed some concerns about implementing family-centered services (Bailey, in press; Bailey, Buysse, et al., 1992; Beckman et al., 1996). These concerns stem in part from an underlying uncertainty about the relative importance of their own role and the skills they bring to these new relationships. Some studies have found that providers were concerned about moving toward a more family-centered approach to services because they felt inadequately prepared (Bailey, Palsha, & Simeonsson, 1991; Mahoney, O'Sullivan, & Fors, 1989). For example, in their investigation of the concerns expressed by professionals, Bailey et al. (1991) reported that many participants were already familiar with the philosophy of family-centered intervention but felt they lacked adequate skills to implement the approach.

This awareness has led many advocates of a family-centered philosophy to argue for the importance of better training to work with families (Bailey, in press; Beckman et al., 1996). A substantial body of literature has emerged that provides students and service providers with an important philosophical grounding for a family-centered approach to services. To ensure that this philosophical shift is translated into practice, however, service providers need concrete strategies and skills for working with families.

This chapter briefly describes the theoretical basis of a family-centered approach to working with families and examines professional practices that can influence the ability of practitioners to work cooperatively with families. The intent is to provide a basis for the subsequent chapters in this book where specific strategies are described in more detail.

AN ECOLOGICAL APPROACH TO FAMILIES

In large part, the basis for the growing emphasis on family-centered services in early intervention has been the widespread acceptance of an ecological or systems approach to families. This approach is based largely on the work of Bronfenbrenner (1979), who described individuals as being part of a series of nested systems. This perspective begins by viewing a child as part of a family. Within each family are multiple subsystems (e.g., mother–child dyad, mother–father dyad) that exert influence over one another. The family is in turn part of an interrelated network of social systems that includes extended family members, friends, neighbors, and so on. These social systems are part of many other larger systems, which may include such organizations as the school or the church. These more formal organizations exist within an even larger overarching political, cultural, and economic context.

Implications of a Family Systems Approach for Intervention

Seeing the child and family as part of a larger social system has in many ways changed the lens through which researchers and service providers view families. Increasingly, this lens is being used to gain a new perspective on children with disabilities and their families. This perspective simultaneously clarifies issues that were previously puzzling and highlights the complexity of the issues confronting early interventionists. For example, in the past, interventionists were frequently puzzled when a parent (most frequently the mother) did not carry out an activity at home that had been designed to promote the development of the child. An ecological perspective encourages the interventionist to look beyond whether the activity was carried out to other factors that may have influenced the mother's actions. Such a view may reveal that the mother had worked long hours or was caring for two or three other children in addition to the child with a disability. From this perspective, it becomes easier to understand differences in priorities and to respect competing demands on the mother's time. The following sections discuss three implications of a systems perspective:

- Multiple influences affect families.
- Systems are dynamic and change.
- The service delivery system influences families.

Multiple Influences Affect Families The rather simple example described in the preceding paragraph illustrates one of the first and most important implications of viewing the family as part of a larger system; that is, there are *multiple influences* on the behavior of any individual within the system. From an ecological perspective, the complexity of a family system partly derives from the range of variables that can potentially exert an influence on the family at any given time. Outcome for a child or a family at a particular time depends on how these multiple influences converge.

As professionals have begun to appreciate the multiple influences on families, they have come face to face with the complex issues that often confront families. For instance, some service providers have become aware of how social and economic pressures can affect service delivery. It is easy to become overwhelmed by the complex array of issues that face families and perplexed about how to best provide services to children while supporting their families. By becoming aware of this complexity, however, practitioners have learned some essential lessons that can have an important impact on their ability to work with families effectively. An awareness of this complexity also allows practitioners to see the often rich and varied array of resources and strengths that families have available.

The impact of multiple influences is apparent in literature on family stress and coping. In an effort to explain the considerable variability between families in whether a stressful event becomes a crisis, some investigators (Hill, 1949; McCubbin & Patterson, 1983) have described what has been called the *ABCX* model of stress. The *A* in the model represents the stressor event; *B* represents the family's resources for coping with the event; and *C* represents the family's perception of the event. These three factors interact to determine *X*, the extent to which the family experiences a crisis. This model has been applied to the issues facing families of children with disabilities (Wikler, 1986) and helps explain variability in family adaptation.

Applied to families of children with disabilities, the *A* factor represents the child's disability; the *B* factor represents the resources the family has for coping with the disability; and the *C* factor represents the way in which the family perceives the disability. From this model, it is possible to anticipate very different outcomes for two families that have children with similar disabilities. Limited resources in the form of insufficient income, a lack of concrete help (e.g., no one to babysit, inadequate medical or educational services), or a lack of emotional support may combine with the disability itself to result in adverse outcomes for a particular family. In contrast, a family whose child has a similar disability, but that has a substantial amount of support, may have a very different experience.

Systems Are Dynamic and Change The complexity of any system partly lies in the fact that it continually changes. Adaptation and coping are dynamic processes. Over time, the multiple factors exerting an influence on families interact to produce ongoing changes in one another, a process described as *transactional* (Beckman, 1984; Sameroff & Chandler, 1975). As a result, *outcome* for families, however it is defined and measured, may often be different for the same family at different times. For interventionists, this suggests the importance of developing and maintaining ongoing relationships with families. Information based on "one-shot" or limited contacts is unlikely to generate a real understanding of the family's adaptation over an extended period. An awareness of the changes that may occur over time, as well as the recognition that a particular service provider will not always be available to a particular family, has led to an awareness of the importance of strategies that will work for families over the long term (Turnbull & Turnbull, 1990). Thus, it is important to provide support in ways that do not create dependence on an individual interventionist, but that instead enhance the family's ability to mobilize supports as they are needed (Dunst et al., 1988).

The Service Delivery System Influences Families A relatively unexplored implication of viewing the family from an ecological perspective lies in the importance of considering influences on families that derive from the service system and the larger contexts in which families function. An examination of the literature reveals that, for the most part, investigators are inclined to view influences on family functioning as factors that lie within the child or within the family itself (Beckman, in press). For example, investigators have studied the extent to which characteristics of the child and the parent have contributed to family stress. An ecological approach, however, leads to the conclusion that families may also be influenced by the service system and the professionals within it. Like other factors, there are multiple ways in which the service system may influence families. Moreover, its influence may change over time and may be either positive or negative.

Thus, although the service system is intended to provide support to children and families, its effect may not be uniformly positive. Indeed, the results of some studies in the 1990s suggest that the service system itself poses substantial barriers to the implementation of family-centered services (Bailey, Buysse, et al., 1992; Bjorck-Akesson & Granlund, 1995). To effectively provide services to families, it is important that providers have a clear understanding of the multiple ways in which the service system may influence families. It is only through an awareness of these issues that service providers can attempt to maximize the positive impact of the system while minimizing potentially adverse outcomes.

The next section of this chapter describes the potential influences of the service system and of the service providers who operate within it. Although the service system has unquestionably resulted in many positive outcomes for children and families, there are sometimes adverse influences as well. The point is not to suggest that the impact of the system is only, or even primarily, negative; rather, the point is to sensitize service providers to potential pitfalls that can occur as they deliver services. This sensitivity, combined with the specific skills and strategies described throughout this book, provides an excellent grounding for practitioners who want to "do the right thing." It can help alert service providers to pitfalls in the implementation of services for children and families and suggest more appropriate alternatives.

PROFESSIONAL PRACTICES THAT INFLUENCE FAMILIES

Many cultural and political factors have converged to produce an unprecedented system of services for young children with disabilities and their families. These services are intended to support children and families and are very often successful in that effort. In spite of the many positive changes that have occurred since the mid-1980s, it is in the context of concrete, day-to-day professional practices that services may or may not ultimately be viewed as family centered. Such practices can contribute either to the sense of support experienced by families or to a sense of dissatisfaction. Practices that are the source of dissatisfaction for families can interfere with the development of collaborative relationships. Some of these practices are the responsibility of individual service providers, and others are an outgrowth of the policies of particular programs. In either case, professionals make daily choices in their own actions and in the policies they establish that can influence families.

In this section, several practices are identified that, depending on the approach taken by professionals, can contribute to or detract from their ability to support families. This is not intended to be an exhaustive list of topics; rather, it is intended to illustrate the many ways in which professional practice influences families. By remaining aware of the impact of their practices, providers can work more effectively to develop positive relationships with families. These professional practices are discussed in the following sections and include:

- How providers listen
- Whether providers respect families
- How professionals characterize families
- Whether professionals are sensitive
- How services are obtained
- How meetings are conducted
- How multiple professionals interact
- How programs are structured
- How differences are resolved

How Providers Listen

One of the most important things that service providers can do is to truly listen to families. Service providers who listen effectively learn a great deal about the child's abilities, the resources that families have available to them, the child's needs, and other information that enhances their ability to provide intervention effectively.

Unfortunately, families frequently report that service providers fail to listen when they provide information or express concerns (Segal, 1985). Failure to listen works against the basic principles of family-centered services and can negatively influence the relationship between providers and families. Listening effectively requires more than simply hearing words. Seligman and Darling (1989) argued that it involves empathy and an understanding of the family members' points of view. This requires professionals to put aside their own biases and opinions, which can be difficult when professionals have their own agendas or are focused on their own opinions and needs.

Whether Providers Respect Families

Implicit within a family-centered philosophy is a fundamental respect for families. Many authors have argued that respect is an integral component in developing a positive and supportive relationship with families (e.g., Beckman, in press; Beckman & Bristol, 1991; Moeller, 1986; Seligman & Darling, 1989). For example, by recognizing the family's decision-making role, professionals demonstrate a respect for the right of families to make choices about the issues influencing their lives and the lives of their children.

A concern that is sometimes voiced by parents is the sense that they are not respected. Greig (1993) conducted a qualitative study of families of infants who were low birth weight. Among the most salient characteristics that influenced parent perceptions of the helpfulness of service providers was whether they felt respected. Parents felt respected when service providers conveyed the belief that the parent knew the child best, when they were honest, and when they respected the family's right to have information about the child.

Professionals demonstrate their respect for families on a daily basis in large and small ways. For instance, promptly providing promised information demonstrates that a professional takes a parent's request seriously and considers it important. In contrast, failing to listen when a family identifies a priority, expresses an opinion, or shares a concern is problematic because it conveys a lack of respect for the family.

How Professionals Characterize Families

An area related to respect involves how professionals characterize families. Characterizations can be both positive and negative. For instance, when a family seeks another opinion, one professional may view them as being "good health care consumers" and another may label them as being "in denial."

Several authors identified difficulties with making negative characterizations (Beckman, in press; Lipsky, 1985; Seligman & Darling, 1989). First, the way in which such labels are assigned may have more to do with the attitudes that the provider brings to the relationship than any real attributes of the family. Second, such characterizations are often overgeneralized, and thus the family member's behavior is interpreted negatively, regardless of what he or she does or the reasons behind these actions. Thus, the same professionals who describe a family in search of another opinion as "unable to accept the disability" or as "shopping" may label a family that does not question a controversial intervention as "naïve" or "unconcerned." Third, negative characterizations can be used to place the responsibility for disagreements on the family. Such attitudes can frequently interfere with the evolution of positive and supportive working relationships with families. For example, a provider who interprets a disagreement by suggesting that the parents are "hostile" or "difficult" implicitly shifts the responsibility away from him- or herself. Because both parties usually share some responsibility for the dispute, little can be accomplished when one participant characterizes another in such a negative light.

Whether Professionals Are Sensitive

Also at the heart of a family-centered philosophy, and linked to respect, is professional sensitivity to families. Professionals demonstrate their sensitivity to families by seeking and providing information, responding to family concerns, and including families in decision making. Such sensitivity is often the basis for strong positive feelings on the part of parents toward providers.

In contrast, insensitivity by the service providers can jeopardize their relationship with families. Although most practitioners are aware of the potential harm that can result from overt insensitivities such as making a derogatory statement about a child, there are many other, more subtle examples of insensitivity. For instance, relaying difficult information without warmth or compassion is one form of insensitivity that is often long remembered. Similarly, when professionals fail to return telephone calls, fail to provide information or materials that were previously promised, or do not think about the implications of their statements, they are engaging in insensitive behavior, even if unintentional. Moreover, they risk jeopardizing subsequent exchanges with families (Sokoly & Dokecki, 1992). Similarly, when professionals are evasive or withhold information, they are being insensitive to the families' need for honest information. Indeed, Greig's (1993) study of families whose infants had extremely low birth weights found that the perceived availability and quality of information received from professionals was a major criteria by which parents judged a service provider to be supportive. In contrast, information that was provided in an insensitive manner, was conflicting, or was provided in such a way that the parents did not understand it was a source of stress.

How Services Are Obtained

The many changes in programs for young children that have taken place since the 1970s have resulted in an ever-increasing array of services for children and families. In spite of the many changes in the early intervention system, some families still report difficulty gaining access to services that they view as important to their children. For example, half of the families of children who were medically fragile whom Thorp (1987) interviewed experienced difficulties obtaining services. These experiences included a lack of opportunity for inclusive educational programs, inadequate nursing coverage, and the need to supplement therapy provided by the schools with private therapy. There are several reasons that families may have difficulty accessing needed services: 1) funding and eligibility requirements based on factors such as income or disability level (Krauss, 1986; Upshur, 1991); 2) lack of awareness that needed services are available (Upshur, 1991); and 3) differences of opinion about the nature or intensity of services that the child needs. For instance, one provider may recommend physical therapy once a week and another may recommend physical therapy three times a week. Such disagreements can ultimately lead to formal disputes between parents and service providers.

How Meetings Are Conducted

The meetings and conferences that occur between parents and professionals are integral to the process of working with families collaboratively. When conducted with respect and sensitivity, they are an important mechanism that parents can use to understand the educational and therapeutic needs of their child. They are also a forum in which parents can assert their preferences and participate in decision making about their child's program. Moreover, they provide a structure in which providers can hear about the issues with which families are faced. When professionals approach these meetings as simply a legal requirement with which they must comply, however, meetings can become a source of stress rather than a source of support.

The concerns that parents have about these meetings are described extensively in the literature (Beckman, Boyes, & Herres, 1993; Brinkerhoff & Vincent, 1986; Harry, 1992). These concerns often include the parents' feeling that they were rushed through the meeting, that decisions were made by professionals before the meeting and that parents were simply expected to sign the individualized education program (IEP) or individualized family service plan (IFSP) document, that the entire focus was on the child's weaknesses rather than his or her strengths, and that they were treated rudely. Service providers who wish to establish positive working relationships with families need to implement strategies to make such meetings more family friendly.

How Multiple Professionals Interact

Children who receive multiple services are typically seen by several different professionals. For instance, parents may simultaneously interact with a teacher, physical therapist, occupational therapist, speech-language pathologist, physician, and psychologist. If the child has complex medical needs, there may also be an array of medical specialists involved in his or her care. The advantage of working with multiple professionals is that families have access to the skills and resources of many individuals.

Although access to the expertise of multiple service providers can often be advantageous, it also can create stress for families. One difficulty is that practitioners sometimes contradict one another (Beckman & Kohl, 1993). The sources of these contradictions vary and may include conflicting assessment and diagnostic information and conflicting recommendations about needed services. For instance, Segal (1985) asked 21 mothers whose children had disabilities and were between 3 months and 4 years of age about the most difficult problems for them. The major difficulty they reported was professional disagreements regarding the diagnosis.

Another frustration that can occur when parents work with multiple professionals is a lack of privacy. In her study of children with chronic illnesses, Thorp (1987) reported a substantial disruption in privacy because of the large number of professionals who came into the families' home. Other potential difficulties that parents face when working with multiple professionals were described by Beckman and Kohl (1993), including professional turf disputes and domination by one team member. Such problems can give families the feeling that they are caught in the middle. They may be forced to spend needed energy understanding the source of the difficulty and resolving the differences that the professionals have concerning their children.

How Programs Are Structured

Many positive changes have occurred since the mid-1980s in how services are structured for families. For instance, services that once were offered only at school or in hospitals may now be offered at home or in child care settings. With the emphasis on natural environments, the least restrictive environment, and inclusion, children are increasingly being served in the settings in which other children of their age are served and in neighborhood schools rather than in large, segregated settings.

At the same time, there are many ways in which the time and structure of programs work against the provision of truly family-centered services. A frequently used example occurs in home-based infant programs that operate only during the day and do not offer services on evenings or weekends. This structure limits the participation not only of many fathers but also of mothers who are employed. Although providing services in a child care setting is a way for service providers to visit the child and is more convenient for service providers, it does not meet the needs of a family that wishes to be more involved with their child's program or services.

Another example concerns the year-round delivery of services. Programs that are on the same schedule as school-based programs sometimes offer only limited services during the summer. This can result in a break in intervention of 2–3 months. Such practices can result in program disruptions for children who cannot afford such experiences. Parents may have to advocate actively to obtain extended school year services or summer school for their child.

Difficulty with time and structure of programs is not limited to education. Families that rely on clinics for health care may often have to wait several hours to see a health care provider. When caring for several children, it may be difficult for families with limited transportation and limited access to child care to manage such clinic visits.

These examples suggest that the time and structure of a program are often established without regard for the needs or preferences of families. Instead, they reflect the needs of the professionals or agencies that serve the families. Although such decisions may be unavoidable because of constraints on resources, it is important to acknowledge that these decisions are fundamentally *professionally centered* rather than *family-centered.* Moreover, such decisions can ultimately limit the use of these services by many families.

How Differences Are Resolved

The opportunity to express disagreement and, when necessary, to fight for different or additional services is an important and basic right that families retain. The reasons for disagreements between families and professionals vary and may include differences of opinion about the type and amount of services to be offered, placement, eligibility, assessment results, or specific goals for the child. The right to protest or disagree can be exercised in informal or formal ways. Families often experience conflict about exercising this right because they are challenging the very same people in whom they have invested their hope of receiving help for their children. It is important for professionals to understand that choosing to exercise this right is typically difficult for families, and there are many costs entailed in such a decision, including expenditures of emotional energy as well as time and money.

CONCLUSIONS

As a part of the larger system, an appreciation for the ways in which the service system can influence families is an important basis for understanding the importance of support.

Providing effective support to families of children with disabilities requires that service providers be aware of a complex set of factors that can affect families' lives. These include the programs and agencies that deliver services to families and the practices of professionals who operate within these programs. By being aware of professional practices that can have an impact on families, service providers can improve the likelihood of providing services in ways that strengthen and support families. Without adequate training and professional development, however, service providers must often depend on intuition and good intention in their exchanges with families.

The ability to work with families in a way that conveys respect and sensitivity is an ongoing process of personal and professional development. In addition to the skills and strategies identified throughout this book, developing good working relationships with families depends on the willingness of service providers to continually reflect on their own professional practices and to change these practices when necessary. Although challenging, this ongoing process is one that can be both personally and professionally rewarding.

ACTIVITIES AND DISCUSSION

1. Read Case Study I, the Barnes Family, and Case Study III, the Winger Family, and discuss the following questions:
   a. What issues, other than the child's special needs, faced each family?
   b. How do the issues confronted by each family fit into an ecological perspective?
   c. What implications does an ecological perspective have for intervention with each of these families?
   d. What is your personal reaction to each family? How do your own values and beliefs influence this reaction?
   e. What are the strengths of each of these families?
2. Brainstorm professional practices that might enhance the supportiveness of the system for the Winger family. Initially, try to engage in this process without evaluating how practical the practices would be. After generating a list, evaluate each practice in terms of the advantages that may accrue from implementing it. Then discuss the disadvantages that you associate with each practice. To what extent are the disadvantages you identify professionally centered?
3. With a partner, enact a scenario in which a professional used a negative label, such as "noncompliant," "hostile," or "uncooperative" to describe a parent. Then discuss the following questions:
   a. What negative label was used, and what was the basis for characterizing the parent in this way?
   b. How did the partner who heard feel when the label was used?
   c. What might be the adverse consequences of viewing the parent in this way?
   d. How did the partner who heard the label used respond?
   e. How might this person help his or her colleague reframe the characterization of the family?
4. Think of a service system with which you have been involved as a consumer. What policies did you observe that you felt supported families? How did these policies enhance your professional practice? What policies might have had adverse effects on families? How did these policies constrain professional practice?
5. Assume that another professional is describing a situation in which a parent did not follow through on a professional recommendation. What are some positive ways in which the pro-

fessional could characterize the situation? What are some negative ways in which you have heard such a scenario characterized?

6. Think about situations in which you have observed providers characterizing the actions of a family in a negative way. For each situation, think of a more positive explanation for the family's actions.

REFERENCES

Bailey, D.B. (1987). Collaborative goal-setting with families: Resolving differences in values and priorities for service. *Topics in Early Childhood Special Education, 7*(2), 59–71.

Bailey, D.B. (in press). Preparing early intervention professionals for the 21st century. In M. Brambring, H. Rauh, & A. Beelman (Eds.), *Early intervention: Theory, evaluation and practice*. Berlin: de Gruyter.

Bailey, D.B., Buysse, V., Edmondson, R., & Smith, T. (1992). Creating family-centered services in early intervention: Perceptions of professionals in four states. *Exceptional Children, 58*, 298–309.

Bailey, D.B., Palsha, S.A., & Simeonsson, R.J. (1991). Professional skills, concerns, and perceived importance of work with families in early intervention. *Exceptional Children, 58*, 156–165.

Beckman, P.J. (1984). A transactional view of stress in families of handicapped children. In M. Lewis (Ed.), *Social connections beyond the dyad* (pp. 281–298). New York: Plenum.

Beckman, P.J. (in press). The service system and its effects on families: An ecological perspective. In M. Brambring, H. Rauh, & A. Beelman (Eds.), *Early childhood intervention: Theory, evaluation and practice*. Berlin: de Gruyter.

Beckman, P.J., Boyes, G.B., & Herres, A. (1993). The IEP and IFSP meetings. In P.J. Beckman & G.B. Boyes (Eds.), *Deciphering the system: A guide for families of young children with disabilities* (pp. 81–100). Cambridge, MA: Brookline Books.

Beckman, P.J., & Bristol, M.M. (1991). Issues in developing the IFSP: A framework for establishing family outcomes. *Topics in Early Childhood Special Education, 11*(3), 19–31.

Beckman, P.J., & Kohl, F.L. (1993). Working with multiple professionals. In P.J. Beckman & G.B. Boyes (Eds.), *Deciphering the system: A guide for families of young children with disabilities* (pp. 21–38). Cambridge, MA: Brookline Books.

Beckman, P.J., Newcomb, S., Frank, N., Brown, L., Stepanek, J.S., & Barnwell, D. (1996). Preparing personnel to work with families. In D. Bricker & A. Widerstrom (Eds.), *Preparing personnel to work with infants and young children and their families: A team approach* (pp. 273–293). Baltimore: Paul H. Brookes Publishing Co.

Beckman, P.J., Robinson, C.C., Rosenberg, S., & Filer, J. (1994). Family involvement in early intervention: The evolution of family-centered services. In L.J. Johnson, R.J. Gallagher, M.J. LaMontagne, J.B. Jordan, J.J. Gallagher, P.L. Hutinger, & M.B. Karnes (Eds.), *Meeting early intervention challenges: Issues from birth to three* (2nd ed., pp. 13–41). Baltimore: Paul H. Brookes Publishing Co.

Bjorck-Akesson, L., & Granlund, M. (1995). Family involvement in assessment and intervention: Perceptions of professionals and parents in Sweden. *Exceptional Children, 61*(6), 520–535.

Brinkerhoff, J.L., & Vincent, L.J. (1986). Increasing parental decision-making at the individualized educational program meeting. *Journal of the Division for Early Childhood, 11*(1), 46–58.

Bronfenbrenner, U. (1979). *The ecology of human development: Experiences by nature and design.* Cambridge, MA: Harvard University Press.

Dunst, C.J. (1985). Rethinking early intervention. *Analysis and Intervention in Developmental Disabilities, 5*, 165–201.

Dunst, C.J., Johanson, C., Trivette, C.M., & Hamby, D. (1991). Family-oriented early intervention policies and practices: Family-centered or not? *Exceptional Children, 58*, 115–126.

Dunst, C.J., Trivette, C.M., & Deal, A.G. (1988). *Enabling and empowering families: Principles and guidelines for practice.* Cambridge, MA: Brookline Books.

Greig, D.L. (1993). *Extremely low birth weight infants (800 grams or less): Medical and developmental outcome at one to five years and social support needs of their mothers.* Unpublished doctoral dissertation, University of Maryland, College Park.

Harry, B. (1992). *Cultural diversity, families, and the special education system: Communication and empowerment.* New York: Teachers College Press.

Hill, R. (1949). *Families under stress.* New York: Harper & Row.

Krauss, M.W. (1986). Patterns and trends in public services to families with a mentally retarded member. In J.L. Gallagher & P.M. Vietze (Eds.), *Families of handicapped persons: Research, programs, and policy issues* (pp. 237–248). Baltimore: Paul H. Brookes Publishing Co.

Lipsky, D.K. (1985). A parental perspective on stress and coping. *American Journal of Orthopsychiatry, 55*(4), 614–617.

Mahoney, G., O'Sullivan, P.S., & Fors, S. (1989). The family practices of service providers for young handicapped children. *Infant Mental Health Journal, 10*(2), 75–83.

McBride, S.L., Brotherson, M.J., Joanning, H., Whiddon, D., & Demmitt, A. (1993). Implementation of family-centered services: Perceptions of families and professionals. *Journal of Early Intervention, 17*(4), 414–430.

McCubbin, H., & Patterson, J. (1983). Family stress process: A double ABCX model of adjustment and adaptation. In H. McCubbin, M. Sussman, & J. Patterson (Eds.), *Advances and developments in family stress theory and research* (pp. 7–37). New York: Haworth Press.

McGonigel, M.J., & Garland, C.W. (1988). The individualized family service plan and the early intervention team: Team and family issues and recommended practices. *Infants and Young Children, 1*(1), 10–21.

Moeller, C.T. (1986). The effect of professionals on the family of a handicapped child. In R.R. Fewell & P.F. Vadasy (Eds.), *Families of handicapped children: Needs and supports across the life span* (pp. 149–166). Austin, TX: PRO-ED.

Raver, S.A., & Kilgo, J. (1991). Effective family-centered services: Supporting family choices and rights. *Infant Toddler Intervention, 1*(3), 169–176.

Sameroff, A.J., & Chandler, M.J. (1975). Reproductive risk and the continuum of caretaking casualty. In F.D. Horowitz (Ed.), *Review of child development research* (Vol. 4, pp. 189–244). Chicago: University of Chicago Press.

Segal, M.M. (1985, December). *An interview study with mothers of handicapped children to identify both positive and negative experiences that influence their ability to cope.* Paper presented at the fourth annual conference of the National Center for Clinical Infant Programs, Washington, DC.

Seligman, M., & Darling, R.B. (1989). *Ordinary families, special children: A systems approach to childhood disability.* New York: Guilford Press.

Sokoly, M.M., & Dokecki, P.R. (1992). Ethical perspectives on family-centered early intervention. *Infants and Young Children, 4*(4), 23–32.

Thorp, E.K. (1987). *Mothers coping with home care of severe chronic respiratory disabled children requiring medical technology assistance.* Unpublished dissertation, George Washington University, Washington, DC.

Turnbull, A.P., & Turnbull, H.R. (1990). *Families, professionals, and exceptionality: A special partnership.* New York: Macmillan.

Upshur, C.C. (1991). Families and the community service maze. In M. Seligman (Ed.), *The family with a handicapped child.* Needham, MA: Allyn & Bacon.

Wikler, L. (1986). Family stress theory and research on families of children with mental retardation. In J.J. Gallagher & P.M. Vietze (Eds.), *Families of handicapped persons: Research, programs, and policy issues* (pp. 167–195). Baltimore: Paul H. Brookes Publishing Co.

Chapter 2

Evolution of Working Relationships with Families

Paula J. Beckman,
Sandra Newcomb,
Nancy Frank,
and Lynn Brown

Regardless of the particular model that early intervention programs adopt, service providers ultimately form some type of relationship with the families of the children they serve. It has even been argued that the basis for providing effective services in early intervention rests on the practitioners' ability to develop positive working relationships with families (Kalmanson & Seligman, 1992; Knafl, Breitmayer, Gallo, & Zoeller, 1992). Kalmanson and Seligman (1992) have suggested that, regardless of discipline, the provider–family relationship is critical to the outcome of intervention.

The concept that good working relationships serve as the medium for effective intervention is consistent with social work practice (Hepworth & Larsen, 1986; Hutchins & Cole, 1992; Shulman, 1992). Shulman (1993) describes a model of the helping process and provides evidence that a positive working relationship is a precondition for effective helping, regardless of profession (Shulman, 1978, 1992, 1993). Thus, whether providing intervention in a classroom, in a hospital, or at home, service providers need to establish and maintain positive relationships with families.

This chapter describes four typical phases in the evolution of positive working relationships with families. Common issues that frequently arise as professionals establish such relationships also are discussed. This is followed by an overview of some strategies that service providers can use to approach complex issues.

PHASES OF DEVELOPING RELATIONSHIPS WITH FAMILIES

As service providers work with families, they need to recognize that the emergence of positive working relationships is a process rather than a discrete event. Some lessons about this process can be derived from social work practice. Shulman (1992) believes that a common misconception among beginning social workers is that a relationship must be established before the work can begin. In his view, the relationship grows out of the work that the social worker and the client do together. As the process of working together progresses, the relationship solidifies. Shulman's perspective emphasizes the evolutionary nature of helping relationships and can be applied directly to the way in which relationships with families are established in early intervention.

Similarly, Walker and Singer (1993) have emphasized the dynamic and evolving nature of parent–professional relationships. They describe at least two major advantages that can be gained by viewing relationships from an evolutionary perspective. First, these authors suggest that such a perspective provides a framework for viewing the ups and downs of relationships in the context of a natural progression. Second, they suggest that it focuses attention on the growth of relationships that incorporate individual differences.

Based on an examination of the literature as well as practical experience, at least four general phases can be identified in the evolution of positive working relationships with families:

1. The initial phase
2. The exploration phase
3. The collaboration phase
4. The closure phase

As used here, these phases are primarily descriptive and are largely consistent with phases described by other authors who have outlined the process of developing helping relationships (Hepworth & Larsen, 1986; Shulman, 1992; Walker & Singer, 1993; Wasik, Bryant, & Lyons, 1990). These phases offer professionals guidelines for their actions and provide insights into the dynamics of individual relationships with families.

Initial Phase
The initial phase establishes a foundation for the relationship with the family (Shulman, 1992; Wasik et al., 1990). It provides the basis for establishing rapport, building trust, and developing a sense that working together will be worthwhile. This phase is consistent with

the "getting acquainted" stage of relationships with families described by Walker and Singer (1993), who pointed out that how practitioners initially respond to parental concerns is the basis that parents often use to determine whether the relationship is likely to be supportive. Moreover, the way in which service providers approach their initial contacts with families is likely to influence how interested the families will be in continuing to work with the providers. As a result, the initial phase lays an essential foundation for the relationship.

The initial phase begins when service providers and families exchange basic information. One task that needs to be accomplished during this phase is to provide information to the family about the program, available services, and additional options. It is also important for the service provider to obtain information about the child and the family and to identify the types of support that might be helpful. This exchange allows the family and provider to examine the match between available services and family concerns.

Another function of the initial phase is to establish preliminary goals for the relationship. These goals may revolve around such activities as obtaining necessary assessments, beginning a schedule of home visits, providing families with needed information, or helping families locate needed services. As a part of this process, both the provider and the family should have a clear idea of what the next steps in the working relationship will be.

In most instances, service providers develop relationships with families within the context of a discipline-specific role (e.g., teacher, physical therapist, nurse). Although contact with the family may often center around the provider's discipline-related responsibilities, he or she may often be called on to provide other types of support. For example, a home-based teacher typically visits for the purpose of implementing an educational program for a child. During these visits, however, the mother may describe her concerns about the reactions of siblings to the child's disability. It is important that the service provider convey to the mother that discussing the siblings' reaction is a legitimate use of time. Establishing a willingness to engage in such conversations sets a tone of openness for the entire relationship.

Exploration Phase

The exploration phase often involves further discussion of how resources and services can best be used to address the family's concerns and priorities. An important function of this phase is listening for additional family concerns and exploring such issues as they arise. Concerns may be expressed directly or indirectly. For example, although a mother may not specifically ask for respite care, she may comment that she and her partner have not spent time alone together in months. Exploring such information may reveal that child care is an issue for the family.

During this process, important goals for intervention can be generated, clarified, and expanded. This is also an opportunity to learn about the family's perception of the services available to them and the extent to which services match their current needs. Service providers should be prepared to review information, even if it has already been discussed during a previous visit.

An important goal of the exploration phase is to build trust. One way to build trust is to follow up on topics raised in previous meetings. For example, if a service provider has promised to make a referral, obtain specific information, or return a telephone call, it is critical that he or she follow through on these commitments. If he or she is unable to follow through within the time promised, it is important to contact the parent as soon as possible to explain the status of the commitment. It is important to remember that the family may be anxiously awaiting the promised information. Another way to build trust is to have a clear understanding of the family's wishes and to always secure parental permission before taking any action on behalf of a child or family. For example, parents should always be consulted before a referral is made to another agency or provider.

Families often make requests for instrumental support during this phase (e.g., information about equipment, assistance with day-to-day difficulties such as sleep or feeding problems, referrals for additional services). These requests provide an important opportunity to build trust. As commitments are honored and needs are addressed, trust is established and can become a foundation for the entire relationship.

As in all phases of the relationship, it is critical that the interventionist convey respect for the family. Specific strategies for communicating respect are described in detail in Chapter 3. In the process of communicating respect for the family and building trust, the service provider establishes a basis for providing emotional support, facilitating the family's use of resources, and developing an in-depth understanding of family concerns.

Collaboration Phase

During the collaboration phase, services are provided based on previously set goals. It is useful to relate each discussion to these previously established goals. This ensures that all participants have a common focus at the beginning of each meeting. For example, a service provider might say, "Last time we talked, you said that you would like to have additional information about respite care. I was able to find out that . . . ," or "Last week we talked about finger feeding; how did that go this week?" As issues are addressed, additional needs for services or other family concerns may emerge and the focus of the exchange may shift to these new concerns. Practitioners can validate the family's concerns by ensuring that adequate time is devoted to addressing them.

As in earlier phases, it is critical for providers to follow up on stated concerns and to determine if there are emerging issues or needs. Families' situations change over time; new issues arise and old ones are resolved. As a result, professionals cannot assume that families' priorities and concerns stay the same. Changes in the families' wishes can and should be discussed whenever necessary. Such discussions may result in a decision to change the nature of services, refocus priorities, provide additional services, or end the service.

During this phase, the foundation of respect and trust that has been established is reflected in many individual ways. Families may increasingly seek the service provider's advice in decision-making situations. They may show an increased willingness to share sensitive information or reveal their feelings about the issues affecting them and their children. The extent to which families signal their trust, however, is often influenced by culture (Harry, 1992; Lynch & Hanson, 1992). It is always important to interpret such signals within this broader context. Further information about the influence of culture is provided in Chapter 4.

Closure Phase

The closure phase represents the end of the working relationship. It is a natural part of the relationship that is prompted for a variety of reasons (e.g., the child goes to another program, the family no longer needs services, the school year ends). During this phase, it is important that the family and the provider review their shared experience and plan for future needs.

The process of ending the working relationship can be difficult. Working closely with an individual or group of individuals, particularly around emotionally laden or stressful issues, can result in strong emotional bonds. In many instances, the end of the relationship is associated with pride and a sense of accomplishment (Hepworth & Larsen, 1986). For example, the child may be moving out of special education into a general education placement or may no longer need intervention. Even though ending is an inevitable part of the relationship, it can also produce a sense of loss for all parties concerned (Hepworth & Larsen, 1986).

A critical skill during the closure phase is the ability to recognize when it is time to end the relationship (Hepworth & Larsen, 1986; Hutchins & Cole, 1992; Shulman, 1992). Although this occurs naturally in some settings because of the structure of the service system (e.g., end of school year), it may be less clear in other circumstances. For example, the family may no longer wish to continue their participation in a support group. In such instances, it is important to recognize when the service is no longer meeting a need.

Because this phase can often be difficult, Shulman (1992) believes it is important for both parties to acknowledge their feelings. One way to engage in such a discussion is to review what has been accomplished—the tasks as well as the process. It is also a good time to elicit specific feedback from the family about their experience with the program. Obtaining such information can help professionals reflect on their own efforts and build skills to enhance future relationships with families. Additionally, specific, positive feedback to the family about the changes and efforts that they have made is important at this time. For example, the service provider can discuss positive changes in the child or take note of particularly effective strategies used by the family.

It is also important for a service provider to note the significance of the time that he or she has shared with the family; in other words, to acknowledge the value of being in a relationship with them (Shulman, 1992). The provider can do this in many ways. For instance, the provider might comment on how much he or she enjoyed knowing the child or describe something specific that he or she learned from working with the family.

The service provider needs to ensure that the family has an ongoing sense of support. Previous efforts to provide support that is strength oriented, facilitates problem solving, and facilitates a sense of control and power contribute to the family's confidence as the working relationship ends (Hepworth & Larsen, 1986). It is helpful to anticipate needs or events that may arise for the family and to discuss how family members can continue to receive support if they need it (Shulman, 1992). For example, the interventionist can provide telephone numbers of helpful resources in the new program or community or can arrange an observation of the new program. Chapter 9 offers additional suggestions about supporting families during transitions.

Summary

In this section, four general phases were identified that are common in the evolution of the family–provider relationship. Although an awareness of these phases can help service providers understand the dynamics of relationships with families, it is also important that they recognize the variability that may occur across families. The evolution of any individual relationship is influenced by such factors as values, culture, the specific circumstances that confront each family, the characteristics of individual family members, the service provider's comfort in establishing relationships, and the family's history with service providers. Service providers cannot assume that all relationships with families will evolve in the same way or that the amount of time required to establish a working relationship will be the same with every family. Although the initial and closure phases are relatively fixed points, the exploration and collaboration phases can recur throughout the period of service. As a result, providers should anticipate variability and be flexible in accommodating individual needs.

ISSUES FOR SERVICE PROVIDERS

The process of working with families often can raise personal issues for service providers. These issues can be complex, often do not have one right solution, and therefore are not always easy to resolve. Service providers need to become aware of these issues and develop strategies for processing them as they arise.

Confidentiality

Confidentiality is an important issue because it provides a basis for establishing trust and for building the relationship with the family (Wasik et al., 1990). Service providers in each program need to work together to establish guidelines for ensuring confidentiality. These guidelines should also conform to applicable legal requirements. For example, under the Individuals with Disabilities Education Act of 1990 (PL 101-476), any personally identifiable information, evaluation results, assessments, and individual program plans are protected by confidentiality requirements. This information may not be shared without parental consent. In addition, service providers need to be familiar with requirements pertaining to their profession.

In addition to legal protections, providers need to develop strategies for other sensitive situations. Service providers frequently have questions about whether and when it is important to share information provided by families. For example, if a family shares information with one service provider on the team during a home visit, under what circumstances is it acceptable or necessary to disclose this information to others? What is an appropriate response if a parent discloses that he or she is experiencing difficulty with another member of the team?

Although answers to such questions are difficult, Wasik et al. (1990) provide at least two guidelines. First, the information should be *pertinent* to other members of the team. For example, if one member of the team is making recommendations that another member knows will not work, because he or she is aware of circumstances that will interfere, then sharing information is important. Second, the program's policies should be *clear to families*. For example, if information is routinely shared with another team member, parents should be informed of this policy from the outset. Developing policy statements about issues of confidentiality provides guidance for staff members, provides information for parents, and can prevent future misunderstandings.

Boundaries

Developing a warm and positive relationship with a family while maintaining appropriate professional boundaries can sometimes be difficult. Early interventionists are frequently in contact with families during some difficult and emotionally trying experiences. For example, the family may be concerned about their child's survival or may just be learning that their child has a disability. Being close to a family during such periods can be a powerful emotional experience, both for the family and the practitioner. In addition, service providers often encounter families that have extraordinary needs. The ability to assist during these periods can be extremely rewarding, and service providers often begin to feel important as well as personally responsible. Under such circumstances, appropriate boundaries are not always clear. Service providers may have difficulty knowing what actions are likely to be most appropriate. Wasik et al. (1990) suggested that establishing appropriate limits in intervention can be especially problematic for home visitors because they may feel that they are the major source of support for a family.

It is useful to ask several questions in such situations. Does the service provider have a personal need that is being met by this family? Does the situation empower the family or create unnecessary dependence? Does the service provider's involvement prevent the family from using a more natural support system? Is involvement with this family interfering with other aspects of the service provider's life? Does the service provider feel responsible for the family's situation? Wasik et al. (1990) emphasized that interventionists cannot be all things to all people and that their response to family needs must directly relate to their competence in handling the situation.

In this context, self-reflection is particularly important. Service providers need to examine their own needs and ensure that they are not using relationships with families to meet those needs (e.g., need for control, need to feel competent, need to feel special, need to feel part of a family). They also need to be aware of their own personal limits with respect to such factors as time, privacy, and involvement. It is also important to seek supervision for boundary-related issues. Strategies for developing a process for self-reflection and supervision are described in the next section of this chapter. By being self-reflective and seeking good supervision, service providers can be sensitive to circumstances in which appropriate boundaries are being violated.

Strategies for Approaching Complex Issues

The very nature of many of the dilemmas that confront service providers is such that resolution is difficult. Making good decisions about complex issues requires that professionals make judgments about their own practices. Three strategies that providers can use as a guide for working through the issues are 1) a guiding framework, 2) self-reflection, and 3) supervision.

Guiding Framework The importance of a guiding framework is emphasized by a number of authors and is implicit in the code of ethics established by major organizations (Reamer, 1982; Sokoly & Dokecki, 1992; Wasik et al., 1990). In discussing ethics in social service, Reamer identified guidelines that can be used by professionals in resolving ethical dilemmas. (These guidelines are also discussed by Wasik et al., 1990.) Such a framework can help service providers make important ethical decisions. One suggested guideline is that the basic well-being (e.g., life, safety, health) of an individual is more important than following rules to the letter. For example, a service provider may be required to violate standards of confidentiality because of ethical obligations to report suspected child abuse. In such cases, the child's safety and well-being take precedence over the family member's right to confidentiality.

It is helpful for intervention teams to develop a framework for guiding important ethical decisions. Such a framework should incorporate the ethical standards of the disciplines represented on the team. It also should provide a sound basis for exercising judgment in difficult and complex situations. Guidelines should address issues of confidentiality, provide for appropriate conduct, identify when particular values (e.g., that children are free from abuse and neglect) need to take priority over other values (e.g., the family's cultural traditions), and help staff members establish appropriate boundaries. Such guidelines provide a basis for exercising professional judgment about situations that frequently can create conflict for professionals, raise personal doubts, or elicit a sense of personal responsibility.

Self-Reflection A critical tool for all interventionists is the ability to use self-reflection. Self-reflection involves examining one's own actions and the context of those actions (Taylor & Valli, 1992). Several authors have argued that using self-reflection is an essential component of effective and ethical intervention (Beckman et al., 1996; Sokoly & Dokecki, 1992). Taylor and Valli (1992) argued that self-examination helps individuals create consciously driven professional actions rather than actions based on habit, tradition, or impulse.

The first step in self-reflection is for service providers to become actively aware of their own system of values, beliefs, and working styles. Questionnaires and activities that help providers examine personal attributes such as values, temperament, and learning style can be helpful. Such activities encourage staff members to think through these fundamental personal characteristics and provide a basis for personal and professional growth and for identifying circumstances that could create difficulties for practitioners.

Supervision Relationships with families often can raise questions for service providers regarding the most effective and appropriate ways to proceed. Individual families may elicit strong reactions from professionals because they challenge the professionals' values or working style. Even families that elicit positive feelings can pose dilemmas for service providers, such as how to maintain appropriate professional boundaries.

To provide support for individual staff members, intervention teams can build a process of peer supervision into their service model. Supervision helps practitioners integrate what they have learned about good practice with the day-to-day realities of their work (Chan & Leff, 1994; Fenichel, 1991). Such supervision can help staff members reflect on their own reactions to particular families or circumstances and find appropriate and ethical ways of handling these reactions. The supervision can be done individually or in the context of a team with an assigned mentor. It is important to create an atmosphere of trust during supervision in which staff members can share their feelings openly, without fear of reprisal. In seeking feedback, staff members should not have to worry that they will be viewed as ineffective. Senior staff members can facilitate an open atmosphere by modeling open and honest communication and self-reflection. Participants should convey the same respect and non-judgmental attitude with fellow staff members as they are expected to demonstrate with families.

These discussions can be facilitated by the development of guidelines for staff members to use for reflection and discussion. These guidelines can include factual information about the family and questions relating to both positive and negative ways in which staff members react to individual families. Whatever process a program decides to adopt for supervision should be constructed in such a way that the confidentiality of families is protected. In addition, families should be made aware that such a process exists and the purpose for it.

Summary

This section describes common issues that emerge for professionals who are establishing relationships with families. Two particularly important issues concern the exchange of confidential information and the provider's personal boundaries. Strategies that can be used to help professionals approach such complex issues also are described.

CONCLUSIONS

The process of developing positive working relationships with families can be simultaneously complex and rewarding. Such a process is central to early intervention and requires many specific skills. This chapter has described some general phases in the evolution of helping relationships and some common issues that arise for staff members during the development of such relationships. An awareness of the evolutionary nature of relationships with families can help professionals evaluate the effectiveness of their efforts and anticipate possible issues that may arise. Being aware of common issues that emerge for professionals during this process can help professionals avoid potential problems and recognize important issues.

ACTIVITIES AND DISCUSSION

1. Read Case Study I, the Barnes Family, and discuss the following questions:

    a. Describe phases of a relationship relative to this family and provider. What happened at each phase?

    b. In this case study, many issues identified by Beth are not directly related to David's needs; many are related to Jonathan's needs. How important was it to address Beth's concerns about Jonathan? Why? What did the provider's willingness to address the issues about Jonathan accomplish?

    c. In discussing Jonathan's behavior, what family considerations had to be addressed?

    d. What were the provider's personal reactions to the family? How did these change over time?

    e. How should the service provider handle giving suggestions she feels are reasonable if the family does not follow through?

    f. After meeting for 6 weeks, Beth begins to share how difficult she has found the move, loss of income, living with in-laws, her husband's injury, the baby's care and future surgery, and her husband's inability to help with child care. What did the service provider do to support her? Is there more that could have been done? If so, what?

2. With a partner, assume that one of you is a service provider and the other is a parent who is receiving services. Enact a scenario in which the parent approaches the service provider and inquires about another parent in the program who is experiencing a number of difficulties. The two parents know each other through their common participation in the program, and the parent who is inquiring seems genuinely concerned. Her questions suggest that she already knows some aspects of the other parent's situation. After enacting the scenario for a few minutes, discuss the following questions in a large-group format:

    a. How did the service provider handle this situation?

    b. What issues about confidentiality did this raise?

    c. How did each participant feel during the enactment?

    d. What would be good strategies for handling a situation such as this?

3. Imagine a situation in which you are making a home visit to provide intervention (e.g., speech or physical therapy, special instruction) for a little girl who is 30 months old. As you arrive, the mother tells you that she is out of diapers and needs to run to the store quickly while you are there. She suggests that you

go ahead and start working with her daughter, and she will be back. Discuss the following:

    a. What dilemmas does a situation such as this raise for the home visitor?

    b. Should the home visitor agree to the mother's plan? Why or why not?

    c. What boundary issues does this raise?

    d. What is the most appropriate way to handle such a situation?

4. Divide into groups of five or six participants. In each group, develop a policy about how your program will handle issues of confidentiality. For instance, what is the policy for talking to other members of the child's team about the family? Under what circumstances (if any) should you reveal information about which you are aware? What do you do if you feel that you need help to handle a particularly sensitive situation with a family? Each group should be able to defend the reasons for the policies it includes. After each group develops a policy, gather in the large group for discussion. Have a spokesperson from each group explain the policies that group identified for confidentiality and identify common points in your plans as well as those points that were different. What were the sources of differences?

REFERENCES

Beckman, P.J., Newcomb, S., Frank, N., Brown, L., Stepanek, J., & Barnwell, D. (1996). Preparing personnel to work with families. In D. Bricker & A. Widerstrom (Eds.), *Preparing personnel to work with infants and young children and their families: A team approach* (pp. 273–293). Baltimore: Paul H. Brookes Publishing Co.

Chan, J.M., & Leff, P.T. (1994). Educating students in providing humanistic care: The significant contribution of the health care professional. *ACCH Advocate, 1*(2), 37–45.

Fenichel, E. (1991). Learning through supervision and mentorship to support the development of infants, toddlers, and their families. *Zero to Three, 12*(2), 1–26.

Harry, B. (1992). Developing cultural self-awareness: The first step in values clarification for early interventionists. *Topics in Early Intervention, 12*(3), 333–350.

Hepworth, D.H., & Larsen, J.A. (1986). *Direct social work practice: Theory and skills.* Chicago: Dorsey Press.

Hutchins, D.E., & Cole, C.G. (1992). *Helping relationships and strategies.* Pacific Grove, CA: Brooks/Cole Publishing.

Individuals with Disabilities Education Act (IDEA) of 1990, PL 101-476. (October 30, 1990). Title 20, U.S.C. §§ 1400 et seq.: *U.S. Statutes at Large, 104*, 1103–1151.

Kalmanson, B., & Seligman, S. (1992). Family-provider relationships: The basis of all interventions. *Infants and Young Children, 4*(4), 46–52.

Knafl, K., Breitmayer, B., Gallo, A., & Zoeller, L. (1992). Parents' views of health care providers: An exploration of the components of a positive working relationship. *Children's Health Care, 21*(2), 90–95.

Lynch, E.W., & Hanson, M.J. (Eds.). (1992). *Developing cross-cultural competence: A guide for working with young children and their families.* Baltimore: Paul H. Brookes Publishing Co.

Reamer, F.G. (1982). *Ethical dilemmas in social service.* New York: Columbia University Press.

Shulman, L. (1978). A study of practice skill. *Social Work, 23,* 274–281.

Shulman, L. (1992). *The skills of helping: Individuals, families, and groups.* Itasca, IL: F.E. Peacock Publishers.

Shulman, L. (1993). Developing and testing a practice theory: An interactional perspective. *Social Work, 38*(1), 91–97.

Sokoly, M.M., & Dokecki, P.R. (1992). Ethical perspectives on family-centered early intervention. *Infants and Young Children, 4*(4), 23–32.

Taylor, N.E., & Valli, L. (1992). Refining the meaning of reflection in education through program evaluation. *Teacher Education Quarterly, 19*(2), 33–47.

Walker, B., & Singer, G.H.S. (1993). Improving collaborative communication between professionals and parents. In G.H.S. Singer & L.E. Powers (Eds.), *Families, disability, and empowerment: Active coping skills and strategies for family interventions* (pp. 285–316). Baltimore: Paul H. Brookes Publishing Co.

Wasik, B.H., Bryant, D.M., & Lyons, C.M. (1990). *Home visiting: Procedures for helping families.* Beverly Hills, CA: Sage Publications.

Chapter 3

Qualities and Skills for Communicating with Families

Paula J. Beckman,
Nancy Frank,
and Sandra Newcomb

As professionals have recognized the importance of developing a positive working relationship with families, there has been an increased interest in qualities that characterize effective helping relationships (Dunst, Trivette, & Deal, 1988; Walker & Singer, 1993). Based on a review of the literature, Dunst et al. concluded that helpgiving is most likely to enable and empower families when help is offered positively and proactively, maintains the family's decision-making power, reduces the family's need for services, and is consistent with the family's needs. Help should also promote the use of natural support networks, a sense of partnership, and the family's view of themselves as responsible for change.

Although many practitioners recognize the importance of developing helping relationships with families, many are uncertain about the best ways to foster these relationships. It is suggested in Chapter 2 that the relationship that develops over time is one that grows as the service provider gains a better understanding of the family and as the family gets to know and trust the service provider. Developing such relationships with families requires that service providers understand and practice many specific skills. For example, in an investigation of the factors that predicted positive outcome in social work practice, Shulman (1978, 1993) found that qualities such as empathy have been associated with the development of positive working relationships. Although many early interventionists have received excellent training within their respective disciplines, relationship skills frequently are not taught in a systematic way (Beckman et al., 1996; Leff & Walizer, 1992; Stepanek, 1995). This chapter describes qualities and skills that are important to developing positive and supportive relationships with families.

QUALITIES THAT SERVE AS BUILDING BLOCKS

The personal qualities that service providers bring to relationships with families can have a fundamental impact on how families view both the services offered and the individual professionals involved. These qualities include personal attributes as well as attitudes and serve as building blocks in the relationship. Three particularly important qualities are 1) respect for families, 2) a nonjudgmental attitude, and 3) empathy.

Respect for Families

At the heart of a positive working relationship lies a genuine respect for families. This means that professionals need to have a core belief that the family is the most important element in the child's life and to recognize that the family is managing their situation to the best of their ability. Hepworth and Larsen (1986) suggested that this is critical to establishing rapport.

The importance of respect has been highlighted by many authors (Beckman, in press; Hepworth & Larsen, 1986; Seligman & Darling, 1989; Turnbull & Turnbull, 1990). For example, in a review of literature concerned with systems-level sources of stress for families of young children with disabilities, Beckman (in press) concluded that a major source of difficulty for families in their interactions with service providers occurred when they felt that they were not respected.

Conveying respect is accomplished partly by recognizing potential differences in values and beliefs, acknowledging the family's expertise, and responding to family concerns. There are many ways for the service provider to convey respect. One way is to be sensitive to the family's desires when discussing difficult topics. For instance, a parent who is angry and frustrated about problem behaviors displayed by the child may be initially reluctant to discuss those feelings. A service provider who is willing to discuss such feelings without being intrusive can be a vital source of support.

Nonjudgmental Attitude

Davis (1993) suggested that being nonjudgmental involves thinking positively about families, regardless of their personal characteristics or situation. A nonjudgmental approach includes such key elements as being emotionally available, conveying positive regard, and being empathetic (Davis, 1993). Remaining nonjudgmental is important because it encourages the family to reach their own decisions without feeling that they must conform to the service provider's opinions. For example, a home visitor who either directly or indirectly expresses disapproval at the way a parent is managing some aspect of daily life may quickly lose the trust of the family.

Although most professionals understand the impact of negative judgments, it is easy to overlook the influence of positive judgments. For example, if the service provider continually reinforces a mother for being "so involved" in her child's program, the mother may feel pressure to maintain the same level of involvement even if it is having a negative impact on another aspect of family life.

Staying interested and involved while remaining nonjudgmental conveys a sense that the service provider has the family's best interests at heart. A genuinely nonjudgmental stance, in combination with empathy, offers the family the ultimate respect, for it communicates confidence that the family can manage their situation.

Empathy

Another building block in the relationship is empathy. Hepworth and Larsen (1986) described empathy as a two-dimensional process that involves both the ability to perceive another individual's feelings and the ability to communicate understanding of those feelings. Empathy requires that the service provider understand the family's experience while integrating his or her own history, training, and experience. In this sense, empathy involves being emotionally available to families and at the same time offering another perspective. It is the art of being able to understand and feel for a family without becoming part of the system. Seligman and Darling (1989) believe that families know immediately when they are in the presence of an empathetic listener because they feel understood.

In a review of literature concerned with helping, Shulman (1992) concluded that empathy is a core skill that applies to virtually all helping functions. Indeed, Shulman (1978, 1992) found that the ability to acknowledge feelings was one of the most powerful skills associated with effective helping for social workers. Subsequent work indicated similar findings in other professions as well (Shulman, 1992).

Turnbull and Turnbull (1990) suggested that service providers can tell whether they are demonstrating empathy effectively by the way the family responds. For example, when family members spontaneously share more personal matters or express feelings, this indicates an effective use of empathetic communication. In contrast, when family members respond by becoming more detached or changing the subject, their reactions may signal difficulties.

SKILLS

There are a number of skills that can help practitioners establish a relationship with families and communicate a sense of respect, acceptance, and empathy. This section describes several specific skills that can facilitate efforts to work with families:

- Join the family
- Use active listening
- Use questions effectively
- Reflect and clarify
- Provide information
- Reframe

Join the Family

One way in which service providers can demonstrate respect, acceptance, and empathy is through a process Minuchin (1974) called *joining*. This process of "joining the family" involves listening to the family's story without evaluating it in terms of some other external criteria. The initial task is to listen to the family, understand and respect their views, and offer support for the issues they identify. The service provider needs a genuine understanding of how the family views themselves, their child, and their circumstances. It is also important to understand how the family views themselves in relation to the larger community and culture. Minuchin (1974) regards joining as a helpful way to establish rapport and demonstrate respect. He considers it particularly useful in working with families from diverse cultures because it demonstrates respect for differing values.

Families may be more likely to take advantage of a professional's skills when they believe that the professional understands and accepts their view (Minuchin, 1974). The importance of this can be understood by considering the example of a family whose child has cerebral palsy and multiple disabilities. Although the program staff believe it is unlikely, the family expects the child to walk eventually. Under such circumstances, an interventionist may feel compelled to convince the parents that the child will not walk because the interventionist believes it is not realistic or the parents need to accept their child's disability. Regardless of who is correct, attempts to impose the interventionist's perspective can be unproductive.

The parents may feel that no one is listening and that their views are not respected. To promote a relationship that the family experiences as supportive, the professional needs to find ways to join the family in their view of their child. This is difficult if the service provider feels that he or she must help the family adjust or accept a certain view of the child. As an alternative, the interventionist could enter a discussion of what needs to happen for the child to walk. By joining the family in this way, some mutually acceptable goals may be identified (e.g., working on head control).

One way to join a family is to respect family roles (Hepworth & Larsen, 1986). For example, if one person (e.g., father, grandparent) is the acknowledged spokesperson for the family, it is critical to respect this individual's role. Another way to join the family is to use family expressions and nicknames, allow the family to pace exchanges, and mirror the family's interaction style.

Use Active Listening

A key skill in developing a relationship with families involves active and focused listening. According to Hutchins and Cole (1992), active listening is the basis for many aspects of good helping relationships and is a key skill for helpers. Good listening involves listening to what is said as well as *how* it is said and what is *not* said. Good, active listening, particularly in the context of helping relationships, involves several key elements, including interpreting, evaluating, and responding (Hutchins & Cole, 1992). *Interpretation* is the basis for understanding (or misunderstanding) the message. It can be influenced by such factors as cultural background or experiences. *Evaluation* is the process of deciding how to use the information that is provided. *Responding* involves both verbal and nonverbal acknowledgment of what has been said.

Hutchins and Cole (1992) also suggested listening for the relationship between thoughts, feelings, and actions. They note that additional skills such as reflection, silence, and the effective use of questions can contribute to the helper's ability to listen actively. Interventionists also can listen to both the content of what is said (e.g., parents' concerns about their child) as well as how the information is presented (e.g., body language, affect, tone).

Use Questions Effectively

Questions are important tools that can be used to elicit additional information, clarify something the family has said, and expand the conversation into other topic areas or into a more in-depth discussion of a particular issue (Friend & Cook, 1996; Hutchins & Cole,

1992; Shulman, 1992). At the same time, questions should be asked judiciously, so that the family does not feel they are being grilled for information.

Different kinds of questions elicit various types of information. Several authors (Friend & Cook, 1996; Hepworth & Larsen, 1986; Hutchins & Cole, 1992) distinguish between open- and closed-ended questions. Closed-ended questions typically can be answered with either a yes or no response or with short, two- to three-word answers. They elicit brief, limited answers and are most useful when the intent is to obtain factual information. Examples include questions such as "Do you have any other children?" "How many children do you have?" and "What time does your therapist come?" Interviews that begin with a series of closed-ended questions, however, can give the impression that the interviewer will initiate or control the entire discussion. As a result, the interviewer may obtain relatively little information, particularly with individuals who are not very verbal (Hutchins & Cole, 1992).

In contrast, open-ended questions encourage people to talk, invite expansion, and allow respondents freedom to express what is most relevant or important. As a result, requests such as "Tell me about your child" or "How did the visit to the pediatrician go?" can elicit much more information. When open-ended questions are asked, parents can describe an event or their feelings about the event in their own way.

In asking questions, Hutchins and Cole (1992) caution that care must be used in asking "why"-type questions. They believe that such questions may make respondents feel as if they have to justify what happened or how they feel. For example, a question such as "Why were you upset about the individualized education program meeting?" might, in some circumstances, create the impression that the parent must defend his or her feelings. Rephrasing the question as "What happened at the IEP meeting that upset you?" is more likely to elicit information about the event, without making the parent feel as if he or she must justify his or her response.

Other ways of asking questions can also be counterproductive and create barriers to communication. Hepworth and Larsen (1986) noted three such difficulties: 1) asking excessive closed-ended questions limits the information received; 2) stacking questions or asking several questions in succession can be confusing and distracting and can diffuse the focus; and 3) leading questions (e.g., "Don't you think that . . .") may convey a hidden agenda and prevent the respondent from sharing important information.

How the family offers information, their pacing and timing, also should be considered when asking questions. A professional can convey a respectful attitude by adjusting his or her pace to the family's communication style.

The systematic use of questions can help service providers more fully understand what families are trying to communicate. Hutchins and Cole (1992) described several different strategies depending on the information that is needed. One strategy is to focus on three dimensions of an event or behavior, which they described as thinking, feeling, and acting. Thus, when parents describe a particular event, the service provider may be able to better understand their perspective by asking what they did when the event occurred, how they felt about it, and what they thought about it. Another strategy is to focus on particular aspects of the situation through a series of who, where, and when questions. For example, if the parents express concern about the way their child is treated by other children, the service provider may obtain more specific information by asking who is typically involved, when the disturbing exchanges tend to occur, and where they tend to happen.

Finally, an important way to obtain relevant information is to follow up on content from a family member's previous statement (Hutchins & Cole, 1992). This helps to develop an understanding of the issue before the topic shifts. For example, it is possible to ask the parents for information about a particular topic, what they think about it, or how it makes them feel.

Reflect and Clarify

Interventionists can convey understanding by reflecting the key topics or concerns that the family has mentioned. An effective way to use reflection is for the provider to intertwine the family's words with his or her own when reviewing what the family has said. In so doing, it is important not to simply repeat the words that the family uses, but rather to incorporate both what is said and what is felt. It is helpful to make statements that feed back key information and, whenever it is comfortable or natural, to use the language and style of communicating that the family uses. For example, if a parent is describing a particular behavior on the part of the child, it may be helpful to use his or her descriptions of the child while exploring the topic further. This lets families know that their perspective has been heard and that their interpretation is respected.

In the process of developing a positive and supportive relationship with families, the service provider needs to clarify his or her understanding of a situation; clarify the family member's feelings, concerns, and priorities; and clarify any terms that are not clear. Even a familiar term used in an unusual way needs clarification to ensure a true understanding of the family's point of view. Both reflection and questions can be employed to clarify information. When a family member is describing a particular event, systematic questions can help the interventionist better understand what happened. For example, if the parent says, "I'm really upset with Maria's doctor," the interventionist can ask questions about what happened, how the parent felt when it happened, and what he or she did in response.

Similarly, reflection can be used to clarify meaning. Hutchins and Cole (1992) suggested that reflection organized around a thinking, feeling, and action framework helps focus the discussion and helps the provider understand an individual's concerns. For example, if a parent goes to an appointment and comes back describing the appointment as "horrible," clarification can be used to establish what was horrible (e.g., did the child do poorly? Were the evaluators insensitive?).

In addition to clarifying messages received from family members, it is important that professionals are clear in their efforts to communicate. Practitioners need to be careful about using professional jargon and need to clarify terms that may be unfamiliar to the family. It is also important to clarify any plan of action that has been agreed upon, as well as to clarify such issues as whether the family wants specific information to be shared with other service providers.

Provide Information
Relationships with families require that service providers offer information and feedback to families. Shulman (1992) believes that sharing information is an important step in building a working relationship. He points out that if an individual senses that a help giver is withholding information, it may adversely affect the relationship. This perspective is consistent with literature specifically focused on families of children with disabilities. One of the most important family needs described in the literature is for honest information (Bailey, Blasco, & Simeonsson, 1992; Beckman, in press; Greig, 1993). Greig (1993) found that the criteria by which families judged the support they received from service providers were related to the quality and availability of the information that was provided.

An interventionist can provide information in a way that fits into what the family already knows and believes (Davis, 1993). The information can expand their view by building on existing knowledge and perceptions, creating a sense of synchrony and providing information that makes sense and is congruent with the family's view. This approach supports the family's competence by highlighting their understanding and giving them additional information. Knowledge is a powerful tool in helping families feel in charge of their lives. Service providers need to offer information and feedback in a way that enhances this sense of competence. It is important that information *not* be offered in ways that highlight what the family does not know or that make the family feel less able to deal with their situation (Dunst et al., 1988).

To present information and feedback in an enhancing manner, the service provider needs to recognize the family's functioning or coping style. By understanding how a family typically manages issues, the service provider can tailor information so that it is easily available and so that the family does not have to make adaptations just to use the information. For example, the family may process information and make decisions by discussing the issue with extended family members. In such cases, providing copies of reports or materials that the family can share with others may be helpful. However, written information would be less useful if the family member could not read or the information were not in the family's native language.

Determining the family's information-processing style can be accomplished by being aware of the family's strengths, the needs they describe, and how they handle various situations. Open-ended questions about how the family has processed information in the past can help interventionists understand this style.

It is important to recognize the power implicit in having knowledge and information (e.g., about various types of disabilities, the service system, strategies for interventions). A collaborative working relationship requires that professionals use their knowledge in ways that are ethical and that respect the family's ultimate right to make decisions on behalf of their child (Sokoly & Dokecki, 1992). For example, it is important to distinguish between the provision of accurate information and the attempt to persuade or win over a family member to a particular perspective. Using information to try to persuade families can become a problem because it conveys a lack of respect and carries an implicit hidden agenda. As a result, the family may feel the need to weigh the helper's information to determine if such a hidden agenda exists (Shulman, 1992).

Shulman (1992) also suggested that information is most useful when it is connected to the recipient's immediate areas of concern.

He argued that the attraction that people feel toward ideas and information is related to how useful they find them at the time.

Reframe

Another skill that service providers can use when working with families is reframing. Shulman (1992) defined *reframing* as the process of viewing something in a new and more helpful way. Similarly, Hepworth and Larsen (1986) described reframing as a way of redefining problems to put them in a fresh perspective and suggest constructive actions. Turnbull and Turnbull (1990) noted that reframing involves two steps: 1) differentiating situations that can be changed from those that are beyond his or her control and 2) acting on situations that are alterable and redefining those situations that cannot be changed to make them more acceptable.

Turnbull and Turnbull (1990) suggested that there are two ways for families to redefine their perceptions of the child's exceptionality. The first is to use positive comparisons, in which individuals consider the problems of others and conclude that, by comparison, their own do not seem so bad (Pearlin & Schooler, 1978). Families may do this spontaneously when they meet another family whose child has a more severe disability and decide that their child's disability is somehow less difficult. Turnbull and Turnbull (1990) suggested that positive comparisons can be used indirectly by indicating that a particular phenomenon is not uncommon. They cautioned against violating the confidentiality of another family as a way to facilitate positive comparisons, however.

The second way is the use of selective attention and selective ignoring. In this approach, attention is focused on the positive aspects of the situation with less attention directed to the negative aspects. For example, a parent might attend to the positive ways in which the child has contributed to the family. Perhaps a child's disability influenced the career direction of a family member, developed the parent's advocacy skills, or brought family members closer.

Reframing can be useful in many ways. For example, if a parent negatively describes a characteristic of a child, reframing can put the characteristic in a more positive light. Thus, if a child is described as "stubborn," the service provider might reframe this by noting that it sounds as if he is "persistent." When the service provider uses reframing, he or she acknowledges the characteristic while describing it in a way that may be perceived more favorably.

When using the strategy of reframing, the service provider should not inadvertently discount negative feelings. Professionals can monitor whether this is occurring by making certain that reframing is not used to make themselves more comfortable. Reframing involves more than simply shifting from a negative to a positive perspective. For example, if a mother is expressing feelings of frustration about feeding problems and says the child "does not like anything I give him because he spits everything out," it is possible to reframe without minimizing her feelings of frustration. One way to reframe this is by saying something such as "He may spit this out because of his involuntary tongue thrust; maybe we can see if it would help to change his position, or modify his spoon." By responding in this way, the service provider acknowledges the difficulty while providing an alternative explanation and a way to explore solutions.

COUNTERPRODUCTIVE COMMUNICATION

As professionals practice the basic skills involved in developing relationships with families, they need to be aware of counterproductive practices. Such communication patterns inhibit the flow of information and can have a negative impact on the helping process. Even when there is no direct conflict, the family may prematurely withdraw from services or the evolution of the working relationship may stop. Hepworth and Larsen (1986) identified counterproductive ways of communicating, including both nonverbal and verbal ways of responding.

Nonverbal Behaviors

According to Hepworth and Larsen (1986), nonverbal communication can either confirm or deny verbal messages. These authors noted that if there is a discrepancy between nonverbal and verbal messages, most people discredit the verbal before they discredit the nonverbal messages. For instance, the authors pointed out that a shocked facial expression may convey much more to the family than anything the practitioner says.

Nonverbal signals that are extremely important are those involving physical attention. A service provider who looks at a watch, looks out the window, or yawns may inadvertently send the signal that he or she is disinterested or uncomfortable or does not view the family's communications as important. When culturally appropriate, Hepworth and Larsen (1986) recommend facing the individual, making eye contact, and leaning forward slightly.

The recommendation about maintaining eye contact raises another important way in which practitioners need to be sensitive to nonverbal cues. Individuals from different cultures interpret nonverbal signals such as eye contact in different ways. In some cultures, making eye contact with someone in authority is considered disrespectful, while in other cultures eye contact communicates sincerity and trustworthiness (Hepworth & Larsen, 1986; Lynch & Hanson, 1992). Similar differences in the meaning of nonverbal cues exist for such signals as gestures, facial expressions, body position and posture, proximity, and touching (Lynch & Hanson, 1992). Practitioners who are unaware of such cultural differences may inadvertently block the development of a relationship with families. Thus, it is important to become familiar with cultural differences and incorporate this knowledge into interactions with families. This issue is further discussed in Chapter 4.

Verbal Barriers

There are also a number of verbal barriers to communication during the helping process that have been identified by Hepworth and Larsen (1986). Some of these barriers are particularly relevant to work with families of children with disabilities. The first of these includes moralizing. Moralizing involves the frequent use of "should" or "ought" statements, which elicit guilt or obligation in the other person (e.g., "You *should* take him to the preschool program."). Such statements also imply criticism and convey distrust in the individual's judgment.

A second verbal barrier identified by Hepworth and Larsen (1986) is the attempt to prematurely offer advice. These authors note that service providers who engage in this practice may do so because they feel pressure to provide solutions. Often, however, they do not have enough information (e.g., What has the family already tried? What were the circumstances that led to the present situation?). Moreover, unsolicited advice frequently ignores strengths in the family, inadvertently conveys an attitude of superiority, and encourages dependence. This can result in both resentment and resistance on the part of the recipient. Hepworth and Larsen suggest that professionals refrain from offering advice and instead encourage mutual participation in generating solutions.

A third barrier to communication identified by Hepworth and Larsen involves efforts to persuade or instruct. Efforts to convince another person frequently ignore the individual's feelings and perspectives. As a result, they are likely to elicit defensiveness, resentment, and hostility. For example, a health care professional who insists that a child must get a specific number of calories without first identifying factors that interfere with feeding may elicit resentment from the parent.

Similarly, Hepworth and Larsen (1986) pointed out that judging, criticizing, or blaming can elicit defensiveness because these behaviors are essentially evaluative and convey a lack of respect. As a result, they can diminish confidence and elicit resistance, withdrawal, and/or counterattack — for example, a teacher who gives a family activities to carry out at home and then responds negatively if the family has been unable to follow through. A judgmental attitude is not always conveyed verbally, but also can be conveyed nonverbally.

Labeling also can result in defensiveness and/or resistance (Hepworth & Larsen, 1986). For example, when a practitioner labels a family's effort to obtain another opinion as *denial* or *shopping*, the family may feel that their efforts and concerns are being discounted. They may feel a need to explain or to defend themselves. Such practices are counterproductive, because they frequently oversimplify more complex issues and tend to stereotype the individual about whom the remark is being made.

Efforts to provide reassurance or to console can also be counterproductive (Hepworth & Larsen, 1986; Shulman, 1992). Hepworth and Larsen noted that, although well-timed reassurance can be perceived as supportive, it should be directed at the individual's capabilities. They caution that, when used inappropriately, reassurance can leave the impression that the helper did not really understand the individual's concerns. This is a risk when individuals face extremely difficult circumstances, particularly when no solution or relief is possible.

Hepworth and Larsen (1986) also recommended exercising great care in the use of humor. They noted that, although humor can be an important tool, it sometimes can be used to avoid important issues, particularly when used inappropriately or excessively. Personal styles often vary considerably and attempts to use humor may be interpreted in many different ways.

Threats or counterattacks are also unproductive ways of communicating (Hepworth & Larsen, 1986). This may be especially tempting when a practitioner is faced with someone who is angry or hostile or who challenges the practitioner's integrity, competence, or motives. Threats or counterattacks typically only escalate the situation, however, and may produce more resistance.

Inappropriate or excessive interruptions also interfere with the helping process. Hepworth and Larsen (1986) noted that interruptions can divert the conversation, annoy the other person, stifle spontaneous exchanges, and generally hinder the exploration of concerns.

Finally, Hepworth and Larsen (1986) noted that a tendency to dominate interactions is a barrier to effective communication and can happen in several ways. Some of the barriers previously mentioned, such as giving advice, presenting lengthy arguments, and interrupting, are all behaviors that contribute to dominating the discussion. Talking too much or excessively asking closed-ended questions also creates an atmosphere in which the practitioner dominates. It is particularly important for practitioners to watch this tendency when involved with a quiet or nonassertive individual.

CONCLUSIONS

This chapter has identified a number of important skills that facilitate development of effective working relationships with families and has also reviewed a number of barriers to the process of communicating with families. An understanding of these barriers can help service providers avoid inadvertently inhibiting the development of a positive, constructive working relationship. When committed and caring professionals are aware of and consistently use good skills during their interactions with families, they can effectively establish relationships that are meaningful to both the practitioner and the family.

ACTIVITIES AND DISCUSSION

1. Read Case Study I, the Barnes Family, and discuss the following:
    a. What behaviors and/or actions on the part of the service provider reflect the three qualities identified in this chapter as "building blocks" (respect, a nonjudgmental attitude, and empathy)?
    b. Give examples of ways in which Carrie used the following skills to help develop a relationship with Beth Barnes:
        • Joining
        • Active listening
        • Open-ended questions
        • Closed-ended questions
        • Reflecting
        • Clarifying
        • Providing information
        • Reframing

    c. What questions might Carrie ask to explore other family needs?

2. With a partner, have one person state a problem or a feeling. Have the other person respond. Demonstrate joining, empathy, and reflection in this response.

3. With a partner, have one participant think about a personal experience (e.g., a visit to a doctor, entering the hospital). The other partner's task is to find out information by:
- Asking three closed-ended questions
- Asking three open-ended questions
- Using three clarifying questions
- Using three reflection remarks

At the end of the exercise, have each person describe how he or she felt, what the experience was like, and what would have made it better. (This activity may be audiotaped or a third person could observe.) How much information was obtained using each strategy?

4. In a group, have each participant make a personal statement or repeat one he or she has heard a family make. Is this a statement that could be reframed? How might this be reframed?

5. Videotape yourself interviewing another individual. Observe the interview and identify the following:
- Positive aspects of your style
- Ways in which different phrasing of questions might have produced a different response
- Places in which you did not follow up on an issue about which the other person expressed concern
- Nonverbal cues that you used. What do you think these cues reflected (e.g., nervousness, interest)?
- Nonverbal cues used by the interviewee. What did these reflect?
- What would you change about your style if you could do the interview again?

REFERENCES

Bailey, D.B., Blasco, P.M., & Simeonsson, R.J. (1992). Needs expressed by mothers and fathers of young children with disabilities. *American Journal on Mental Retardation, 97*(1), 1–10.

Beckman, P.J. (in press). The service system and its effects on families: An ecological perspective. In M. Brambring, H. Rauh, & A. Beelman (Eds.), *Early childhood intervention: Theory, evaluation and practice.* Berlin: de Gruyter.

Beckman, P.J., Newcomb, S., Frank, N., Brown, L., Stepanek, J., & Barnwell, D. (1996). Preparing personnel to work with families. In D. Bricker & A. Widerstrom (Eds.), *Preparing personnel to work with infants and young children and their families: A team approach* (pp. 273–293). Baltimore: Paul H. Brookes Publishing Co.

Davis, H. (1993). *Counseling parents of children with chronic illness or disability.* Leicester, England: British Psychological Society.

Dunst, C., Trivette, C., & Deal, A. (1988). *Enabling and empowering families: Principles and guidelines for practice.* Cambridge, MA: Brookline Books.

Friend, M., & Cook, L. (1996). *Interactions: Collaboration skills for school professionals.* New York: Longman.

Greig, D.L. (1993). *Extremely low birthweight infants (800 grams or less): Medical and developmental outcome at one to five years and social support needs of their mothers.* Unpublished doctoral dissertation, University of Maryland, College Park.

Hepworth, D.H., & Larsen, J.A. (1986). *Direct social work practice: Theory and skills.* Chicago, IL: Dorsey Press.

Hutchins, D.E., & Cole, C.G. (1992). *Helping relationships and strategies.* Pacific Grove, CA: Brooks/Cole Publishing.

Leff, P.T., & Walizer, E.H. (1992). *Building the healing partnership: Parents, professionals, and children with chronic illnesses and disabilities.* Cambridge, MA: Brookline Books.

Lynch, E.W., & Hanson, M.J. (Eds.). (1992). *Developing cross-cultural competence: A guide for working with young children and their families.* Baltimore: Paul H. Brookes Publishing Co.

Minuchin, S. (1974). *Families and family therapy.* Cambridge, MA: Harvard University Press.

Pearlin, L.I., & Schooler, C. (1978). The structure of coping. *Journal of Health and Social Behavior, 19,* 2–21.

Seligman, M., & Darling, R.B. (1989). *Ordinary families, special children: A systems approach to childhood disability.* New York: Guilford Press.

Shulman, L. (1978). A study of practice skill. *Social Work, 23,* 274–281.

Shulman, L. (1992). *The skills of helping: Individuals, families, and groups.* Itasca, IL: F.E. Peacock Publishers

Shulman, L. (1993). Developing and testing a practice theory: An interactional perspective. *Social Work, 38*(1), 91–97.

Sokoly, M.M., & Dokecki, P.R. (1992). Ethical perspectives in family-centered early intervention. *Infants and Young Children, 4*(4), 23–32.

Stepanek, J.S. (1995). *Moving beyond the medical/technical: Analysis and discussion of psychosocial practices in pediatric hospitals.* Bethesda, MD: Association for the Care of Children's Health.

Turnbull, A.P., & Turnbull, H.R. (1990). *Families, professionals, and exceptionality: A special partnership.* Columbus, OH: Charles E. Merrill.

Walker, B., & Singer, G.H.S. (1993). Improving collaborative communication between professionals and parents. In G.H.S. Singer & L.E. Powers (Eds.), *Families, disability, and empowerment: Active coping skills and strategies for family interventions* (pp. 285–316). Baltimore: Paul H. Brookes Publishing Co.

Chapter 4

Providing Support to Diverse Families

Deirdre A. Barnwell and Monimalika Day

Since the mid-1980s, families in the United States have become increasingly diverse. Typical families no longer consist of a nuclear family with two biological parents and their children. Social and economic changes within the United States have resulted in an increased number of families headed by single parents, foster parents, and same-sex parents (Hanson & Lynch, 1992; Hanson, Lynch, & Wayman, 1990). Moreover, many ethnic groups consider other relatives or friends to be part of the family (Anderson, 1989; Harry, 1992).

Families who are served by the early intervention system come from diverse backgrounds. To intervene successfully, practitioners need to understand that the values and experiences of these families may be very different from their own. The meaning of disability, the goals that parents have for their children, and the way they address those goals depend greatly on the cultural background of the family.

As noted elsewhere in this book, the needs of the family are dynamic; new experiences or changes in family structure can lead to changes in the needs of the family. Service providers need to understand and respect the transitional nature of the family's needs (Lieberman, 1990). Families who live in a culture that is different from their culture of origin may undergo change due to acculturation (Harry, 1992). Individuals and families vary in the extent to which they identify with the culture of origin and the larger culture in which they operate.

Diversity among families requires interventionists to broaden their perspectives and to look at larger family issues. A broader perspective can often be difficult to achieve, because professionals may have little preparation for working closely with families from diverse backgrounds (Christensen, 1992).

This chapter provides an overview of issues related to the increasing diversity found within the United States. The chapter begins with a discussion of the importance of achieving cross-cultural competence. Several areas in which the family's cultural perspectives may influence services to children and families are then identified, including the meaning of disability, child-rearing practices, communication styles, support networks, and the influence of these factors are also discussed. Strategies are then provided to help professionals evaluate their cultural competence and become more culturally sensitive. Guidelines and activities are suggested for professionals working with culturally diverse families.

THE IMPORTANCE OF CROSS-CULTURAL COMPETENCE

During the early 1990s, at least three important changes increased professionals' awareness of the need for cross-cultural competence (Lynch & Hanson, 1992b): 1) the changing demographic patterns in the United States, 2) the underutilization of services by culturally diverse families, and 3) the implementation of the Individuals with Disabilities Education Act (IDEA) of 1990. This section provides an overview of these trends and describes their importance to early intervention.

Changing Demographics

Since the 1980s, the population of the United States has changed dramatically. The number of ethnic and cultural groups has increased along with the population in several of these groups. A report by the Annie E. Casey Foundation (1992) concluded that the percentage of the population under 18 years of age of minority background rose from 26.2% in 1980 to 31.1% in 1990. Individuals of Asian background represent the fastest-growing group, followed by people of Hispanic/Latino background (people of Hispanic origin may be of any race) (U.S. Census Bureau, 1993). It has been projected that, by the end of the 21st century, no one racial or ethnic group will comprise a majority in the United States. People of color will be the majority in 53 of the largest U.S. cities by 2000, when one of every three Americans will be African American, Asian/Pacific Islander, Middle Eastern, or Hispanic/Latino (Richie, 1991).

Demographic studies indicate that the United States is becoming a richer mix of cultures, and this diversity is reflected among young children with special educational needs. Edmunds, Martinson, and Goldberg (1990) reported that children of color are the most rapidly increasing population group and the largest group at risk for disabilities. African American and Hispanic American children are more likely than Anglo-American children to live in poverty, which makes them more vulnerable to disabling conditions and learning problems.

Although poverty in and of itself is not a cultural attribute, people of color are affected disproportionately by poverty (Edmunds et al., 1990). According to the U.S. General Accounting Office (GAO) (1994), there have been dramatic increases in the number of infants and toddlers living in poverty. In 1990, infants and toddlers in poverty were about twice as likely to be immigrants or linguistically isolated. In addition, these infants and toddlers were more likely to be immigrants and live in 1) households where no person over the age of 14 spoke English well, 2) single-parent families, 3) families where parents had low educational attainment, or 4) families where the parents did not work (GAO, 1994).

The changes in family composition and the increased ethnolinguistic diversity among families in the United States have had a major impact on family structure and functioning. For example, the increase in the proportion of single-parent families and dual–wage earner families has influenced families' patterns of interactions (Hanson & Lynch, 1992). Given that children from minority backgrounds and those who live in poverty are at a higher risk of having disabilities (Edmunds et al., 1990) and that the minority population is increasing (U.S. Census Bureau, 1993), the proportion of children from these groups is likely to increase in the early intervention system. The diversity found among families and the demographic shifts previously mentioned serve as a reminder for new and varied directions in service delivery planning and implementation.

Service Utilization
Although there has been an increasing emphasis on family participation in systems that serve persons with disabilities (Beckman, Robinson, Rosenberg, & Filer, 1994; Turnbull, Summers, & Brotherson, 1984; Turnbull, Turnbull, Summers, Brotherson, & Benson, 1986), there is evidence that many minority families do not become involved in service delivery systems and treatment programs. For example, in a study by Lynch and Stein (1987), African American and Latino parents reported less involvement in the assessment pro-

cess than did Anglo-American parents and offered significantly fewer suggestions at their child's individualized education program meeting. African American and Hispanic/Latino parents also knew significantly less about what services their child was receiving than did Anglo-American parents. In a study of families of persons with developmental disabilities, Mercer and Chavez (1990) found that ethnic minorities and persons from low socioeconomic backgrounds tended to participate less in community advocacy groups than did well-educated nonminority families with high incomes.

There are a number of hypothesized explanations for this pattern of underutilization. Research on service utilization patterns has documented that ethnicity, income, geographic location, and disability status place an individual at risk for underutilization of services (O'Connell, Minkler, Dereshiwsky, Guy, & Roanhorse, 1992; Palfrey, Singer, Walker, & Buttler, 1987; Sontag, Schacht, Horn, & Lenz, 1993). A study by Arcia, Keyes, Gallagher, and Herrick (1992) concluded that 10% of all young children and 20% of families of all young minority children may underuse early intervention services, partly because of poverty and maternal employment. If a child is a member of an ethnic minority group, poor, and living in a rural area and has disabilities, the risk of not obtaining the early intervention services is quadrupled. In their 1993 study, Sontag and Schacht asked families why they were not receiving a particular service. The most frequent response indicated that families either did not want or felt that their child did not need the service. This response suggested that parental choice and child characteristics played a role in the type of services the family was using. Other reasons included not having any information about the service and not being eligible for the service. In some instances, this may have been the family's perception as opposed to an actual agency determination of ineligibility.

Sontag and Schacht (1993) argued that if Part H is to result in an equitable service system throughout the United States, service providers must be aware of service utilization patterns. These patterns can be influenced by factors such as parental preference, child characteristics, financial resources, ethnicity, age of the child, geographic location, professional preference, and service availability. Professionals need to disseminate information clearly about the support services that exist in each family's community. This information should include the types of benefits, the family's rights to use these services, and the cost of these services (Florian, 1987).

A lack of understanding of cultural differences can lead to inappropriate efforts that can sometimes result in underutilization of services. Lynch and Stein (1987) suggested that service systems are designed based on the middle-class value system. For example, McGoldrick (1982) noted that Anglo-Americans typically emphasize self-reliance, self-control, and self-determination. These values tend to be promoted in social service settings. In contrast, the values of Hispanic/Latino families, such as cooperation and interdependence, are often intertwined with a strong emphasis on the extended family. If the family's value system is ignored during the process of delivering services, it may create barriers to developing a positive working relationship.

Early Intervention Legislation

The ability to serve families from diverse backgrounds has become a major interest and concern as states plan and implement services under IDEA. One of the underpinnings of infant–toddler services is the focus on enhancing family capabilities by helping families gain access to resources and acquire skills that will help them meet the needs of their children. To work closely and build a relationship with a family requires respect, knowledge, and awareness of the family's cultural, ethnic, and linguistic heritage.

Part H of IDEA requires states to focus efforts on populations that typically have not been involved in early intervention services (Bernstein & Stettner-Eaton, 1994). This requirement is designed to enhance the capacity of state and local agencies to identify, evaluate, and meet the needs of underrepresented populations, particularly minority, low-income, inner-city, and rural populations, and to provide access to culturally competent services within their local geographic areas.

Parents who do not speak or understand English or who come from cultures where procedural safeguards do not exist may have difficulty exercising their rights. This problem can be exacerbated by sometimes complex and legalistic procedures, such as due process, used in some schools. These families may need additional support and a more simplified method to exercise their rights. For example, some families may not be aware of mainstream philosophical movements and legislative mandates that legitimize parents' rights and involvement (Chan, 1992). Procedural safeguards are an asset only when they are understood and used. Professionals who demonstrate sensitivity to and respect for the cultural values and customs of families are more likely to be successful in implementing the mandates of IDEA.

CULTURAL PERSPECTIVES

No two families "fit" precisely the same way into any cultural model or along any cultural continuum (Anderson, 1989). Culture is only one influence on families' reaction to having a child with a disability. Other influences, such as financial status and intactness of the family support system, must also be considered (Dunst, Trivette, & Deal, 1988). Individual families and family members demonstrate their own style based on their unique experiences, which may be partly determined by their education and length of stay in the United States. Professionals are responsible for respecting the differences that may exist, both within and between cultures. This section describes sources of variability in families that are frequently influenced by culture and that can have an impact on the life of a child with a disability. These include the meaning of disability, beliefs about the cause of the disability, beliefs about health and illness, the role of the family, child-rearing practices, and communication styles.

Meaning of Disability
The birth of a child with a disability has different meanings in various societies throughout the world. Even within a single complex society, this event can have a variety of meanings that are shaped by cultural values and beliefs (Seligman & Darling, 1989). The view that many culturally diverse families hold concerning the cause of their child's disability often contrasts strongly with the dominant view held in the United States (Harry, 1992). For example, many cultures emphasize the role of fate in determining a person's future. *Divine intervention* is a term often used in the Mexican culture to refer to the belief that it is God's will that the parent should have a child with a disability. Belief in divine intervention is exhibited in many ways, such as the view that God is punishing the parent, is testing the parent, or has selected the parent for an unknown reason (Mardiros, 1989). In Vietnamese culture, the belief is that an individual has little power to escape fate (Green, 1982).

Leonard's (1985) study of parent–family reaction to childhood disability in families from three ethnic minority groups demonstrated how the country and culture of origin may affect families' coping responses. Often families from diverse cultures are required to make cultural adaptations in response to contemporary advances and changes in early intervention practice. Some families may not be familiar with current trends in the service delivery system, such as family-centered practice and inclusion. Home visits may be viewed as an intrusion into the private lives of family members. Professionals need to make cultural adaptations to work more effectively with these families (Lynch & Hanson, 1992a; Mardiros, 1989). As Mardiros suggested, these adaptations require that professionals understand parents' perceptions of the disability, why it exists, what caused it, the kind of support needed, who should provide that support, the treatments that are expected and acceptable, and what outcomes of treatment are sought. These questions apply to both formal and informal support systems and provide understanding of how the parents cope with the child and the disability.

Beliefs About the Cause of the Disability

Beliefs about what caused a particular disability can greatly influence an individual's views of intervention. For example, a fatalistic perspective is likely to result in acceptance of fate and reliance on inner strength (Hanson et al., 1990). Some parents of children with disabilities may be expected to accept their fate and lifelong burden as principal caregivers (Chan, 1986). For some families, no action is seen as appropriate, because things cannot be changed or helped.

Families that attribute the cause of their child's disability to transgressions of family members are more likely to avoid seeking help (Seligman & Darling, 1989). If they do seek help, it is likely to come from within the family or from a larger-community extended family network rather than from outside agencies (Hanson & Lynch, 1992). For example, Chan (1986) described how important it is for professionals to be sensitive to Asian American families' need to save face. He further noted that the professional's aim of encouraging parental participation and involvement may be strange and discomforting to certain families.

Mardiros (1989) examined the concept of disability among Mexican American parents. The causes of childhood disability as described by the parents were classified in terms of two discrete views: 1) a biomedical perspective and 2) a sociocultural, or folk, view. Responses to the question "What is the cause of the disability?" were identified as biomedical whenever a biological basis for the disability was identified. These responses were often prefaced with phrases such as, "The doctor said . . . ," or "I looked it up in a book and it said. . . ." This view coincided with the label used by the professionals working with the child. Mexican American parents also used informal supports, including cultural prescriptions and traditional healing practices, as well as advice from professionals. Formal supports were used when the causes were attributed to biomedical factors such as a genetic problem, prematurity, or infection. Formal systems typically consisted of professionals, the organizations they represented, and the specific services provided.

Mardiros (1989) found that informal supports were used by parents who attributed the cause of disability to sociocultural factors such as past transgressions and difficulty within the marriage. Informal support consisted of a set of contacts through which parents maintained a social identity and received emotional support, material aid, services, and information. The most frequently cited sources of informal support were all Mexican American and included the spouse, the husband's mother, the wife's grandmother, and elderly female neighbors. Selected members of the parents' church were also identified as supportive. People were more likely to seek support from individuals of the same cultural background.

Native Americans, like other ethnic groups, may hold folk beliefs about various childhood disabilities. Some Navajo families believe a child's illness is caused by a taboo broken by the mother during pregnancy (Kunitz & Levy, 1981). Family members may use tribal healers or practitioners to enhance treatment while continuing to take their child to physicians or other specialists.

Depending on their degree of identification with the traditional culture, families may attribute disability to spiritual causes and consult with healers, elders, or persons with special powers or knowledge for information and treatment (Seligman & Darling, 1989). In some cases, families may not want to share this information with professionals because of their concern about the professionals' reaction.

Beliefs About Health and Illness

In early intervention, the health care system is often the first entry point at which families are exposed to their child's disability. The World Health Organization has defined *health* as "a state of complete physical, mental and social well-being and not merely the absence of disease" (Spector, 1985, p. 16). This definition supports the idea of primary health care as emphasizing prevention and early detection. In many cultures, however, *health* is defined by the absence of disease, which leaves no room for preventive practice (Niederhauser, 1989). Culture influences, defines, and gives meaning to the experience of illness. For instance, Anderson (1986) described the differences between American health care workers' approach to illness and that of a family of Chinese immigrants. The family's child was chronically ill and was sent home with instructions for the parents to conduct various home treatments. Typically, U.S. health professionals focus on returning a client to as typical a life as possible. Caring for a child with a long-term illness was a new experience for the Chinese family, however, because most children with that illness in their country would have died. Also, in the Chinese value system, caring for this child meant fostering daily happiness and contentment. The rehabilitation procedures meant inflicting pain, which their value system rejected. This family was labeled by the health care workers as noncompliant because they did not carry out the instructions as expected.

Western views of medicine and healing typically are focused on preventive education and interventions through prescriptive drugs, surgery, and testing, with very technical equipment and methods. This contrasts with both Hispanic/Latino and Asian/Pacific Islander cultures, where physical and emotional well-being are seen as linked (Green, 1982). For example, Green identified two types of disruptions to the balance between physical and social factors in the Mexican culture: 1) *mal ojo* and 2) *mal puesto. Mal ojo* (evil eye) is believed to be the result of excessive admiration or desire by another person. Mothers may isolate their children for fear of having one become a victim of *mal ojo. Mal puesto* is an evil hex or illness willfully put on someone by a *curandero* (healer) or a *brujo* (witch). When a child is born with a disability, someone in the family or someone close to the family who is at odds with the family may be viewed as the cause. For example, one mother believed that her child was born with Down syndrome because her husband's family put an evil eye on the child (Gonzalez, 1991). Parents may take a child with a disability to a *curandero* to seek a cure. Professionals need to acknowledge and respect such belief systems rather than ridicule or disregard them so that they do not misinterpret the family's motives. Professionals should also recognize that these belief systems reflect the family's concern for their child and their need for some type of intervention. Thus, even if parents and professionals have different perspectives about health, they share a need for some type of intervention. To understand the family, professionals need to consider the underlying rationale for the family's actions. Ensuring the child's safety can often be accomplished through sensitive questioning of the family without putting them on the defensive (Hanson & Lynch, 1992).

The Role of the Family
All cultures distinguish between individuals who are considered related to one another and those who are not. However, the composition of the family and the degree of its importance vary from culture to culture. In the mainstream culture of the United States, small nuclear families are the norm, and value is placed on making one's own way in life (Anderson, 1989; Hanson et al., 1990). In other cultures, families are extended, and many relatives are included within the closely knit family group. However, extended families may consist of not only blood relatives but also neighbors and

friends. Personal sacrifices for the sake of one's family often are expected, and, in turn, the family serves as the individual's major support network. A Mexican American family, for example, may be a large, close-knit group, including both lineal and collateral relatives. Ties beyond the nuclear family are likely to be strong and extensive. These ties link grandparents, aunts, uncles, and cousins in relationships characterized by frequent material and emotionally supportive exchanges (Schreiber & Homiak, 1981).

Another example is found in the Navajo community, where the concept of *family* refers to immediate family members, extended family, or even the entire tribe (Malach, Segel, & Thomas, 1989). This broader view of the family is especially relevant when a single parent is the head of the household. In some circumstances, the single parent may have a support network that consists of people not necessarily living in the same household (Willis, 1992).

Although the extended family is often the primary source of help and social support for many Hispanic/Latino families, they also may approach professionals whom they know well. Ghali (1977) suggested that many Hispanic/Latino families do not confide in anyone until *confianza*, or a familial type of trusting relationship, is established. As a result, it may be helpful for professionals working with such families to establish a personal bond with their clients (Ghali, 1977).

Recent immigration or the conditions under which immigration occurs can strongly affect many families. For example, the conditions under which many immigrants leave their homelands force them to leave family members behind. At a time when there is the most need for the support of an extended family, recent immigrants may be alone. The impact of this may be particularly critical for an immigrant raised in a family where the extended family is especially important (Honig, Gardner, & Vesin, 1987).

Child-Rearing Practices

Child-rearing practices reflect the parents' perspectives about skills that the child needs to participate as a member of his or her cultural group (Norton, 1990). Parents set goals for their children based on their views of reality. Child rearing is influenced by factors such as who serves as the primary caregiver, procedures for disciplining, and group expectations for children of a certain age. Child-rearing practices vary considerably from culture to culture. Many families who immigrate to the United States leave their children in the care of extended or adopted families in their homeland. Such actions are acceptable to these families and are not interpreted as lack of interest or parental neglect (Harry, 1992).

Many cultures strongly value age and experience in raising children. In certain communities, biological parents seek the advice of elder family members, and responsibility for child care may be shared among extended family members (Malach et al., 1989). How the family views a child determines how the child is treated. For example, some Asian American families view children as "gifts to be treasured" (Hanson et al., 1990, p. 117). African American families also may be indulgent with their children, but, unlike Asian Americans, they promote individuality rather than conformity (Hanson et al., 1990).

Differences between the professional's and the family's view of specific child-rearing practices may emerge as the professional learns about the family. To understand the family's perspective, it is important for the professional to build a relationship with the family. This relationship can be facilitated by understanding and learning about how culture influences communication styles.

Communication Styles

The process of communication involves the use of verbal and nonverbal cues. Different cultures vary in the extent to which they emphasize these forms of communication (Hall, 1983). Cultures can be described in terms of the level of context involved in communication. A low-context culture is characterized by direct verbal communication, with an emphasis on direction, speed, and getting the work done (Hanson et al., 1990). For example, when conversing by telephone, a person from a low-context culture may immediately bring up the topic that is the point of the call after only a brief greeting. This is markedly different from high-context cultures, which emphasize the context of the communication. A person from a high-context culture may indulge in small talk before plunging into a discussion on a specific topic. For example, in India, a high-context culture, many languages use the same word (*kul*) for *yesterday* and *tomorrow*. The meaning of the word can be interpreted only in the context of the whole sentence. The Japanese axiom "What is left unsaid is rich as flowers" (Chan, 1992, p. 181) reveals the importance of the context of communication in their culture.

In high-context communication, greater emphasis is placed on the setting, values, and nonverbal messages than in low-context communication. For example, African Americans use shared experiences, signals, nonverbal cues, and the situation itself as a part of the communication process (Willis, 1992). Members of low-context cultures may not process gestures, environmental clues, and unarticulated moods that are crucial to effective communication in high-context cultures. Therefore, communication between high- and low-context cultures may lead to misunderstanding and frustration for both parties.

In some cultures, the aim of the communication process is "to achieve mutually satisfactory and face saving outcomes" (Chan, 1992, p. 232). Members are often reluctant to "contradict, criticize, disappoint or otherwise cause unease or discomfort in another" (Chan, 1992, p. 232). Thus, a nod may be interpreted as an agreement or it may be a gesture that indicates the individual does not wish to offend the speaker. Similarly, in certain cultures, the listener is expected to look down and not ask many questions. In these cultures, silence is an important component of the communication that allows the person to reflect on the content of the talk. It may be helpful for professionals to observe family communication patterns to become more aware of the level of context the family uses and to adapt to a style that is comfortable for the family.

Furthermore, all cultures have some rules about with whom the family can share information. For example, in many Native American cultures, it may not be appropriate to share the family's concern with someone from the same tribe. Choosing an interpreter from the same tribe may lead to a serious communication barrier (Malach et al., 1989). According to Anderson (1989), members of different cultures can speak different languages or use the same language to communicate different meanings. Language also can be useful in understanding attitudes and beliefs about disabilities.

In addition to using language to obtain information, many cultures place more importance on the interpersonal process involved in the communicative interaction. The time and effort the professional spends building a relationship with a family will lead to more meaningful and valid communication, which will greatly affect the overall benefit and success of the early intervention services.

STRATEGIES FOR BECOMING MORE CULTURALLY SENSITIVE

Communication is an important issue when working with families because it is linked to all aspects of service delivery. Communication is especially critical when the family speaks a different language and has limited English ability. In addition, professionals may need simple strategies and recommendations for improving communication and overall services for culturally diverse families. This section provides strategies for enhancing cross-cultural communication and service delivery for culturally diverse families and for becoming more culturally competent.

Enhancing Cross-Cultural Communication

Working with families who speak a different language can often cause problems with cross-cultural communication. A translator or interpreter can facilitate communication but can also cause some dilemmas. Ideally, an interpreter should be trained in early childhood education, proficient in both languages, trained in cross-cultural interpretation, and able to understand and respect the cultures of both the family and the professional (Randall-David, 1989).

It is important for professionals to be cautious about using family members as interpreters, especially those of a different age or sex from the parent involved. Children, for example, may be embarrassed to discuss intimate matters about their parents with professionals, and being asked to interpret may place the child in an uncomfortable position. Murillo (1978) described how this affected a Mexican American family when, during a doctor's visit for her sick infant, the mother's older son was asked to translate. In this example, the doctor told the mother she should not have waited so long to obtain medical attention for the sick infant. The boy serving as the translator found it impossible to convey such a message to his mother, fearing he might appear rude and disrespectful. At the same time, he could say nothing to the doctor, who was viewed as an authority figure. The son deliberately misinterpreted what the doctor said. Thus, in an attempt to escape his difficult position, he failed to communicate some important medical information (Murillo, 1978).

This example illustrates the importance of remaining sensitive to the parents' right to privacy and their choice of interpreters. There also may be problems if the interpreter is of a different social class, educational level, age, or sex (Randall-David, 1989). Confidentiality is always a concern, especially if the interpreter comes from the same community as the family.

During an interaction, it is important for professionals to look at and speak directly to the parent, not the interpreter. The professionals also should verify the parent's understanding and the accuracy of the translation by asking the parent to repeat the information in his or her own language. The translator can assist with this process of clarification. Even when using an interpreter, it is still possible to be involved in the communication process. Randall-David (1989) suggested the following strategies for professionals to facilitate communication.

First, follow the family's lead to determine proper social etiquette for this family. For example, in some cultures, people look straight in the eye of the listener while talking, whereas in others it is considered disrespectful or impolite. It is helpful for service providers to observe the family when they are talking or listening to gather cues regarding appropriate eye contact.

Second, it is helpful to allow family members to choose seating to establish comfortable body space. In some cultures, close body space is viewed as appropriate, whereas in others greater distance between people is more comfortable. In the family's home, professionals should wait to sit down until a family member indicates where to sit.

It is also helpful to avoid overt gestures and body language that may be misunderstood. Body movements have different meanings in different cultures. For example, some cultures consider finger or foot pointing disrespectful, whereas others consider vigorous hand-shaking a sign of aggression. Professionals can observe the family members' interactions with others to determine what gestures are acceptable and appropriate in the culture. When in doubt, ask.

The fluency of family members who speak English should be determined informally. This can be done by asking some simple, open-ended questions such as, "What does your child like to do?" Notice whether the person uses single words, simple sentences, or detailed descriptions.

Avoiding slang, professional jargon, and complex sentences also can facilitate communication. For example, slang descriptions such as, "He's a cool kid," may be confusing. Service providers should be careful about using technical terminology unless it has been determined that the family understands the meaning of such terms.

It is also helpful for service providers to adjust their speech rate and style so that they are understandable to the child or family. Professionals may find it helpful to record a conversation with a friend or colleague. Listening to the tape can provide a basis for reflection on the rate and clarity of their speech. Another strategy is for the professional to ask colleagues and friends to provide feedback about the rate and clarity of his or her speech.

Learning the proper forms of address in the family's language also can help establish a good relationship. In some cultures, the use of titles conveys respect for the family and demonstrates the service provider's willingness to learn about the family's culture.

If another family member (such as a grandparent) appears to have an important role in the family, this role should be acknowledged. For instance, even if the service provider is communicating in English with the parents and the grandparent does not speak English, the provider can acknowledge the grandparent's role by making eye contact with the grandparent during the conversation. However, the appropriateness of this strategy depends on the extent to which eye contact is viewed as respectful in a particular culture.

Finally, it is also helpful for the provider to learn basic words and sentences in the family's language. The professional also should 1) become familiar with special terminology in other languages, 2) use a positive tone of voice, 3) try not to be patronizing or judgmental, 4) repeat important information more than once, 5) always give a reason for suggestions to the family, and 6) reinforce verbal interaction with material written in the family's language and with visual aids.

Becoming More Culturally Competent

Florian (1987) suggested that professionals should evaluate their services by questioning whether they are 1) realistic, 2) culturally sensitive, 3) in agreement with the family's values and beliefs, 4) excessively demanding of resources (e.g., money, transportation), and 5) delivered by supportive and respectful practitioners. An ideal strategy is for a person who is bicultural and trained in child development issues to be on the service delivery team (Anderson & Fenichel, 1989). If such a professional is not available, however, staff or community members can be contacted to assist with communication or to obtain information on child-rearing practices. Knowledge of sociocultural factors that affect health and cross-cultural understanding is also essential for practitioners who work with diverse families.

It is helpful for service providers to develop a philosophy statement in which the purpose and procedures for achieving cultural sensitivity are clearly defined. It is important for families from diverse backgrounds to participate in this process to identify their expectations of the program and to develop criteria to evaluate effectiveness. Some additional ways to improve the cultural sensitivity of a program are identified in Tables 1 and 2.

Families are not defined by their culture alone, and culture is not a static phenomenon (Harry, 1992). Other factors such as socioeconomic status, education, experiences, reason for immigration, and time spent in the United States influence the family's outlook. The degree of acculturation and where the family functions from a transcultural perspective—that is, the degree to which they identify with their original culture or that of the U.S. mainstream culture—are also important influences. Although various frame-

Table 1.   Strategies to improve the cultural sensitivity of a program

- Take time to establish a relationship with the family.
- Establish contacts with different community groups, local colleges, and organizations to locate and recruit bicultural staff.
- Ensure valid communication by using bilingual and bicultural staff whenever possible.
- Provide materials for the family in their primary language.
- Use alternative strategies such as tape recording, diagrams, or pictures if the primary caregiver is unable to read.
- Give the family choices about whether to participate or how much they want to participate in the intervention process. For example, explain what the intervention process entails and let the family know they can decide to what extent they wish to participate.
- Respect families' decisions.
- Discuss with the family who should be involved in the process—for example, grandparents, baby sitters, neighbors, friends, relatives, or community members (advocates).
- Ask families what location would be the most convenient and comfortable for the assessment and for intervention.
- Ensure that information about child-rearing practices from the family's community has been collected and shared with all team members.

works have been used to describe the process of acculturation (Ramirez & Castaneda, 1974), professionals need to remember that this process is continuous and dynamic.

CONCLUSIONS

Demographic and legislative changes that have occurred in the United States since the 1980s have created a need to provide culturally sensitive services to families and young children. Professionals working with young children increasingly meet families whose values and beliefs are different from their own. This chapter identified ways in which culture may be important to early interventionists and provided strategies for professionals on working more effectively with culturally diverse families. Each family is unique, however, and general characteristics do not apply to all families of a specific culture. Differences may also exist in views and approaches between individual family members. Professionals should remember that there is no way to know everything about all cultures and should not feel embarrassed about asking relevant questions. Seeking information shows an interest in learning about the family's culture.

Service providers need to develop self-awareness because, unless professionals can understand the influence of their culture on

Table 2. Learning about cultural groups in the community

- Identify the different cultural groups in your region.
- Read about these cultural groups.
- Consult with a bicultural team member or professional who has worked with this community.
- Participate as an observer in religious events, community meetings, and gatherings. Notice similarities as well as differences from the mainstream culture in how the community participates in these events.
- Visit local businesses patronized by the different communities represented in your program.
- Develop relationships with key persons (community leaders, clergy, teachers, leaders of community groups) and organizations.
- Try to learn the language or at least a few sentences spoken by the families in your agency.
- Avoid making assumptions; take time to reflect on the information you have collected.

attitudes, beliefs, and values, it is difficult to fully appreciate other cultures (Chan, 1986; Hanson et al., 1990). Harry (1992) suggested that professionals openly discuss differences in cultural values and practices with families as a way of forming a collaborative relationship. A collaborative relationship with families is critical in delivering meaningful intervention services that are truly family-driven.

The effectiveness of early intervention services to diverse families depends largely on the cultural sensitivity of the service providers. In learning to be sensitive to a family's culture, providers need to begin by exploring and examining personal values and biases. Awareness of personal beliefs, values, and practices is the first step in developing a mutually respectful relationship with families (Wayman, Lynch, & Hanson, 1990).

ACTIVITIES AND DISCUSSION

1. Read Case Study V, the Singh Family, and discuss the following:
   a. Describe the composition of this household.
   b. What is the role of the child's grandmother? To what extent would it be important to include her in program planning and service delivery? How might this be accomplished? How might it be important to signal the professional's understanding that the grandmother's role is important?
   c. What is the family's understanding of the child's disability? What strategies can the professional use to discover the fam-

ily's beliefs about disability in general? What questions might elicit this information?

d. What issues exist concerning communication with this family? How might communication be facilitated?

2. Learn about your own culture. The process of self-reflection and values clarification (Hanson et al., 1990; Harry, 1992) should be ongoing as professionals encounter new and different experiences. Answering the following questions and completing the values clarification activity can help you begin this process.

a. How would you describe your ethnic and cultural background?

b. How are decisions made in your family?

c. If you have a crisis or problem, do you more frequently seek family support or professional assistance?

d. How would you describe the perfect family?

e. Which ethnic, cultural, or socioeconomic group would you most prefer to work with? Why?

f. To what extent do you think families should assimilate into the dominant culture? Can they maintain their traditional customs and beliefs?

g. Can you accommodate the priorities and concerns of the family even when your personal values conflict with theirs?

3. Identify health beliefs and causes of disability. The following group activity is designed to help you identify the underlying reasons for your beliefs about the causes of different disabilities. You can then reflect on how your beliefs may contrast with those held by some families.

a. List some of the causes of common disabilities.

b. Discuss Mardiros' (1989) framework for causation of disability: sociocultural and biomedical. Would the causes identified in 3a. be considered sociocultural or biomedical?

c. Identify your source of information about each cause. Where did you learn about the causes of disability (e.g., schools, family members, media)?

d. Think about ways in which each of the causes you identified can be a possible area of disagreement.

4. Clarify values. Values are an important component of culture. The culture in which one is raised greatly influences attitudes, beliefs, and values. Values play an important part in the kind of work that you do. The following activity has been adapted from Edelman (1991). Use this activity to better understand your own values and the values of the families with whom you work.

a. Write down five things that you value above all else in life (e.g., independence, family, religion).
b. Study the five values you chose. You can keep only two of them and must give up the other three. You will have to live without the ones you give up.
c. Was this an easy decision? How did this feel? Could anyone else have selected these values for you?
d. Now that you have examined your own values, think about the families you serve. Do you respect their values as you want your values to be respected? Or is it assumed that, because they have a child with a disability, are from another country, or are from a different socioeconomic class, they cannot determine their values for themselves?

REFERENCES

Anderson, J.M. (1986). Ethnicity and illness experience: Ideological structures and the health care delivery system. *Social Sciences Medicine, 22*(11), 1277–1283.

Anderson, P.P. (1989). Issues in serving culturally diverse families of young children with disabilities. *Early Childhood Development and Care, 50,* 167–188.

Anderson, P.P., & Fenichel, E.S. (1989). *Serving culturally diverse families of infants and toddlers with disabilities.* Arlington, VA: ZERO TO THREE/ National Center for Clinical Infant Programs.

Annie E. Casey Foundation. (1992). *Kids count data book.* Washington, DC: Center for the Study of Social Policy.

Arcia, E., Keyes, L., Gallagher, J.J., & Herrick, H. (1992). *Potential underutilization of Part H services: An empirical study of national demographic factors.* Chapel Hill, NC: Carolina Policy Studies Program.

Beckman, P.J., Robinson, C.C., Rosenberg, S., & Filer, J. (1994). Family involvement in early intervention: The evolution of family-centered service. In L.J. Johnson, R.J. Gallagher, M.J. LaMontagne, J.B. Jordan, J.J. Gallagher, P.L. Hutinger, & M.B. Karnes (Eds.), *Meeting early intervention challenges: Issues from birth to three* (pp. 13–31). Baltimore: Paul H. Brookes Publishing Co.

Bernstein, H.K., & Stettner-Eaton, B. (1994). Cultural inclusion in Part H: Systems development. *Infant-Toddler Intervention: The Transdisciplinary Journal, 4,* 1–10.

Chan, S. (1986). Parents of exceptional Asian children. In M.K. Kitano & P.C. Chinn (Eds.), *Exceptional Asian children and youth* (pp. 36–53). Reston, VA: Council for Exceptional Children.

Chan, S. (1992). Families with Asian roots. In E.W. Lynch & M.J. Hanson (Eds.), *Developing cross-cultural competence: A guide for working with young children and their families* (pp. 181–258). Baltimore: Paul H. Brookes Publishing Co.

Christensen, C.M. (1992). Multicultural competencies in early intervention: Training professionals for a pluralistic society. *Infants and Young Children, 4*(3), 49–57.

Dunst, C., Trivette, C., & Deal, A. (1988). *Enabling and empowering families: Principles and guidelines for practice.* Cambridge, MA: Brookline Books.

Edelman, L. (1991). *Getting on board: Training activities to promote the practice of family-centered care.* Bethesda, MD: Association for the Care of Children's Health.

Edmunds, P., Martinson, S., & Goldberg, P. (1990). *Demographics and cultural diversity in the 1990's: Implications for services to young children with special needs.* Minneapolis, MN: Pacer Center.

Florian, V. (1987). Cultural and ethnic aspects of family support services for parents of a child with a disability. In D.K. Lipsky (Ed.), *Family supports for families with a disabled member* (pp. 37–52). New York: World Rehabilitation Fund.

Ghali, S.B. (1977). Cultural sensitivity and the Puerto Rican client. *Social Casework, 58,* 459–474.

Gonzalez, G. (1991). Hispanics in the past two decades, Latinos in the next two: Hindsight and foresight. In M. Sotomayor (Ed.), *Empowering Hispanic families: A critical issue for the 90's* (pp. 1–19). Milwaukee, WI: Family Service America.

Green, J.S. (1982). *Cultural awareness in the human services.* Englewood Cliffs, NJ: Prentice Hall.

Hall, E.T. (1983). *The dance of life: The other dimension of time.* New York: Doubleday.

Hanson, M.J., & Lynch, E.W. (1992). Family diversity: Implications for policy and practice. *Topics in Early Childhood Special Education, 12,* 283–306.

Hanson, M.J., Lynch, E.W., & Wayman, K.I. (1990). Honoring the cultural diversity of families when gathering data. *Topics in Early Childhood Special Education, 10,* 112–131.

Harry, B. (1992). Developing cultural self-awareness: The first step in values clarification for early interventionists. *Topics in Early Childhood Special Education, 12*(3), 333–350.

Honig, A.S., Gardner, C., & Vesin, C. (1987). Stress factors among overwhelmed mothers of toddlers in immigrant families in France. *Early Childhood Development and Care, 28*(2), 37–46.

Individuals with Disabilities Education Act (IDEA) of 1990, PL 101-476. (October 30, 1990). Title 20, U.S.C. §§ 1400 et seq.: *U.S. Statutes at Large, 104,* 1103–1151.

Kunitz, S.J., & Levy, J.E. (1981). Navajos. In A. Harwood (Ed.), *Ethnicity and medical care* (pp. 337–396). Cambridge, MA: Harvard University Press.

Leonard, C.J. (1985). Brief outlines of the parent/family reaction to childhood disability in families from 3 ethnic minority groups. *International Journal for the Advancement of Counseling, 8,* 197–205.

Lieberman, A.F. (1990). Infant-parent intervention with recent immigrants: Reflections on a study with Latino families. *Zero to Three, 12*(3), 8–11.

Lynch, E.W., & Hanson, M.J. (Eds.). (1992a). *Developing cross-cultural competence: A guide for working with young children and their families.* Baltimore: Paul H. Brookes Publishing Co.

Lynch, E.W., & Hanson, M.J. (1992b). The importance of cross-cultural effectiveness. *Caring Magazine, 14,* 14–19.

Lynch, E.W., & Stein, R.C. (1987). Parent participation by ethnicity: A comparison of Hispanic, black, and Anglo families. *Exceptional Children, 54,* 105–11.

Malach, R.S., Segel, N., & Thomas, T. (1989). *Overcoming obstacles and improving outcomes: Early intervention services for Indian children with special needs.* Bernalillo, NM: Southwest Communication Resources.

Mardiros, M. (1989). Conception of childhood disability among Mexican-American parents. *Medical Anthropology, 12,* 55–68.

McGoldrick, M. (1982). Ethnicity and family therapy: An overview. In M. McGoldrick, J.K. Pearce, & J. Giordano (Eds.), *Ethnicity and family therapy* (pp. 3–30). New York: Guilford Press.

Mercer, J.R., & Chavez, D.J. (1990). *Families coping with disability: Study of California families with developmentally disabled children.* Unpublished monograph, University of California at Riverside.

Murillo, N. (1978). The Mexican American family. In C.A. Haug, J. Marsha, & N. Wagner (Eds.), *Chicanos: Social and psychological perspectives* (2nd ed., pp. 2–14). St. Louis, MO: C.V. Mosby.

Niederhauser, V.P. (1989). Health care of immigrant children: Incorporating culture into practice. *Pediatric Nursing, 15,* 569–574.

Norton, D.G. (1990). Understanding the early experience of black children in high risk environments: Culturally and ecologically relevant research as a guide to support for families. *Zero to Three, 10*(4), 1–25.

O'Connell, J.C., Minkler, S., Dereshiwsky, M., Guy, E., & Roanhorse, T. (1992). Identifying unique challenges to the provision of rehabilitation services on the Navajo reservation. *Rural Special Education Quarterly, 11*(2), 13–19.

Palfrey, J.S., Singer, J.R., Walker, D.H., & Butler, J. (1987). Early identification of children's special needs: A study in five metropolitan communities. *Journal of Pediatrics, 111,* 651–659.

Ramirez, M., & Castenada, A. (1974). *Cultural democracy, bicognitive development, and education.* New York: Academic Press.

Randall-David, E. (1989). *Strategies for working with culturally diverse communities and clients.* Bethesda, MD: Association for the Care of Children's Health.

Schreiber, J., & Homiak, J.P. (1981). Mexican Americans. In A. Harwood (Ed.), *Ethnicity and medical care* (pp. 264–336). Cambridge, MA: Harvard University Press.

Seligman, M., & Darling, R.B. (1989). *Ordinary families, special children: A systems approach to childhood disability* (pp. 183–208). New York: Guilford Press.

Sontag, J.C., & Schacht, R. (1993). Family diversity and patterns of service utilization in early intervention. *Journal of Early Intervention, 17*(4), 431–444.

Sontag, J.C., Schacht, R., Horn, R., & Lenz, D. (1993). Parental concerns for infants and toddlers with special needs in rural versus urban counties. *Rural Special Education Quarterly, 12*(1), 36–46.

Spector, R.E. (1985). Culture, health, and illness. In *Cultural diversity of health and illness* (pp. 1–77). Norwalk, CT: Appleton-Century-Crofts.

Turnbull, A.P., Summers, J.A., & Brotherson, M.J. (1984). *Working with families with disabled members: A family systems approach.* Lawrence: University of Kansas, University Affiliated Facility.

Turnbull, A.P., Turnbull, H.R., Summers, J.A., Brotherson, M.J., & Benson, H.A. (1986). *Families, professionals and exceptionality: A special partnership.* Columbus, OH: Charles E. Merrill.

U.S. Census Bureau. (1993). Current Population Reports: Series (P25-1092, P25-1095). Suitland, MD: U.S. Department of Commerce, Bureau of the Census.

U.S. General Accounting Office (GAO). (1994). *Infants & toddlers: Dramatic increases in numbers living in poverty.* Washington, DC: Author.

Wayman, K.I., Lynch, E.W., & Hanson, M.J. (1990). Home-based early childhood services: Cultural sensitivity in a family systems approach. *Topics in Early Childhood Special Education, 10*(4), 56–75.

Willis, W. (1992). Families with African American roots. In E.W. Lynch & M.J. Hanson (Eds.), *Developing cross-cultural competence: A guide for working with young children and their families* (pp. 121–150). Baltimore: Paul H. Brookes Publishing Co.

Chapter 5

Coordinating Services and Identifying Family Priorities, Resources, and Concerns

Jennifer Smith Stepanek,
Sandra Newcomb,
and Krista Kettler

Although still evolving with respect to special education, coordinating services for children and families is not a new concept. From the post–World War I Progressive Era to the implementation of the Americans with Disabilities Act of 1990 (PL 101-336), services for individuals with disabilities have changed from institution-based to community-based programs. Community services have often been accompanied by the designation of case managers to help clients gain access to an array of appropriate services (Bailey, 1989; Zipper, Weil, & Rounds, 1993).

Traditionally, case management has been recognized and provided as a service in fields such as nursing and social work, where professionals work with clients who have multiple needs. In 1986, Part H of the Education of the Handicapped Act Amendments (PL 99-457) recognized the need to coordinate services in early intervention. Part H was reauthorized in subsequent legislation, the Individuals with Disabilities Education Act (IDEA) Amendments of 1991 (PL 102-119).

Coordinating services among several providers, disciplines, and agencies requires working collaboratively with a variety of professionals. Because of the central role of the family in a child's life, service coordination also necessitates forming partnerships with family members (Dinnebeil & Rule, 1994; Shelton & Stepanek, 1994; Zipper et al., 1993). Collaboration is the cornerstone of quality family-centered services.

This chapter explores the concept of service coordination for young children with disabilities and their families. Specifically, it focuses on types of service coordination and activities involved in service coordination. Strategies that can assist professionals in collaborating with families as they gather and elicit information about family concerns, priorities, and resources also are identified.

COORDINATING SERVICES

Service coordination can be performed by personnel from a variety of disciplines. Part H defines *service coordination* as the activities carried out

> to assist and enable a child eligible under this part and the child's family to receive the rights, procedural safeguards, and services that are authorized to be provided under the State's early intervention program. (Early Intervention Program for Infants and Toddlers, 1993, p. 40,904)

Types of Service Coordination

Several approaches to service coordination have been explored and can be placed in three broad categories. These are approaches that use dedicated service coordinators, integrated service coordinators, and interim service coordinators. This section describes these three types of service coordination and examines the advantages and disadvantages of each.

Dedicated Service Coordinator An individual whose job is dedicated to service coordination and who provides no other service to the family is often referred to as a *dedicated service coordinator.* One advantage of using a dedicated service coordinator is that he or she is often in the best position to advocate for the family, because there is no conflict of interest if the family disagrees with the recommendations of professionals. Additionally, because a dedicated service coordinator provides specialized services, he or she has the opportunity to work with many different families. This experience provides more opportunities to develop the skills necessary for effective service coordination, such as the ability to interview families and resolve conflicts. Moreover, by regularly dealing with many different agencies, dedicated service coordinators can develop an in-depth knowledge base about many different service agencies. Dedicated service coordinators also may have more time for families who have multiple, complicated needs, because they are not responsible for providing some type of direct service to the child.

A disadvantage of this approach is that it adds one more person to an already wide array of professionals with whom families must collaborate. For example, a family whose child has multiple needs may already be working with a teacher, a physical therapist, a home nurse, several physicians, a medical equipment company, and an insurance "gatekeeper" on a daily or weekly basis. Finding the time, energy, and patience to collaborate with one more professional who does not provide a direct service to the child may be undesirable for some families.

Integrated Service Coordinator An *integrated service coordinator* provides direct services and also coordinates other services for the child and family. For example, a teacher who provides early intervention services also may function as a service coordinator. The major advantage of an integrated service coordinator is that this person already has a relationship with the family and maintains regular contact with them. As a result, he or she may have a better understanding of the family situation and of family concerns and priorities.

One disadvantage of this model is that the coordinator may be influenced by his or her specific discipline or agency and thus potentially be less open-minded about individual family priorities. Moreover, service coordination tasks can be time-consuming for some families—for example, for a family whose child has multiple medical needs that require follow-up and coordination. The provider may feel that the time needed to coordinate services interferes with his or her availability for direct services.

An integrated service coordinator can come from any number of professional or paraprofessional fields, which can be either an advantage or a disadvantage. When a variety of people from multiple disciplines provide service coordination, there may be many different interpretations of the role. For example, a teacher functioning as a service coordinator may be more interested in developing comprehensive educational and therapeutic plans for a child and give less emphasis to gaining access to community resources. A social worker functioning as service coordinator, however, may give more attention to addressing financial and social support concerns and give less attention to medical and educational aspects.

Interim Service Coordinator A third type of service coordinator is the *interim service coordinator.* Such an individual typically manages incoming referrals until a permanent service coordinator is appointed. This type of service coordination is useful because, at the time of referral, it is not always clear who will best serve the needs of the family. As concerns, needs, and priorities are identified, it becomes easier to designate an individual to provide service coordination who will best meet the needs of the family. Additionally, over time, families gain an increasing knowledge of the service system and thus are better able to provide input into personally choosing a service coordinator.

A disadvantage of interim service coordination is that the switch to a permanent service coordinator may be disruptive to the family. If the family has developed a rapport with the interim coordinator and then must work with a new coordinator, the process of building a trusting relationship must begin again. This can be difficult for both family members and professionals.

ACTIVITIES OF A SERVICE COORDINATOR

The activities of a service coordinator are described for infant and toddler services under Part H of the IDEA amendments. These activities include coordinating child and family assessments, gaining access to and monitoring entitlement services (e.g., therapy, intervention, respite), and helping families identify and gain access to appropriate linkage services (e.g., health insurance, food, family support services). Although service coordination is not mandated for preschoolers under IDEA, many of the same tasks must be performed. For example, activities such as assessing children's needs, collaborating with families, and monitoring of programs occur for children receiving preschool- and school-age services as well for infants and young children. Thus, even though service coordination currently is not mandated for preschool children and their families, many of the same functions are often needed when working with older children and their families. Professionals who work with children older than the age of 3 also benefit when comprehensive services are coordinated, used, and monitored for all children and families.

Coordinate Evaluations and Assessments

Service coordinators ensure that children receive all assessments necessary to determine eligibility for intervention and plan appropriate services. The service coordinator does not necessarily perform the assessments, but works with the family to see that they are scheduled and performed promptly. This may involve determining what assessments are needed, arranging the time and place of evaluations, and explaining the purpose of various assessments (Zipper et al., 1993).

Under Part H of IDEA, the individualized family service plan (IFSP) must be developed within 45 calendar days from referral, necessitating that a multidisciplinary assessment of the child's needs be coordinated quickly. Additionally, reassessment must be coordinated annually, both to determine continued eligibility and to plan ongoing programming needs. A child also may need medical evaluations, such as a vision or hearing screening. It is the function of the service coordinator to see that these are scheduled as well.

Children served under Part H of IDEA also must be evaluated (6 months before their third birthday) to determine transition needs. Regardless of whether a child will make the transition into Part B services for children ages 3–21 or into community-based programs because he or she is not eligible for Part B, the service coordinator ensures that necessary evaluations are completed and that the transition process is smooth for children and families.

Facilitate and Participate in IFSP Development
Once eligibility is established, a service coordinator ensures that an appropriate plan of intervention is developed with the family. In addition to completing assessments and evaluations related to the child's needs, family concerns, priorities, and resources must be determined. These data are documented in the IFSP.

The IFSP includes a statement of the child's strengths, needs, and current functioning across six developmental domains. It also contains statements of family-identified concerns, priorities, and resources related to enhancing the child's development. These family statements, like the child assessment results, are translated into outcomes for intervention on the IFSP. Determining family concerns, priorities, and resources is another major task of service coordination and is the cornerstone of collaboration. As such, it receives more attention later in this chapter.

Necessary services for achieving child and family outcomes are also documented in the IFSP. The service coordinator is responsible for bringing together the team—family and professional members—that develops the IFSP, thus ensuring that the plan is appropriate for the child and family (Zipper et al., 1993).

There is a parallel need to coordinate services for preschool children, even though service coordination currently is not mandated over age 3. The individualized education program (IEP) must reflect the child's current functioning and must state long- and short-term goals to meet the child's needs. One difference between an IFSP and an IEP is that the IFSP explicitly identifies family concerns, priorities, and resources. The IEP is still intended to be the product of collaboration between families and professionals, though. Even without a service coordinator, someone on the team must put all the recommendations together into a plan of service delivery and intervention. This requires the ability to work with other team members to coordinate recommendations and develop a plan.

Help Families Identify Service Providers
Once the IFSP has been developed and the services needed by the child and family are delineated, the service coordinator helps families find the needed services. This can be a significant and time-consuming component of service coordination. Services to infants and toddlers are handled on an interagency basis and require collaboration between health, education, and social services. Service coordinators need to be familiar with the services offered by the various agencies in the local jurisdiction to best help families gain access to the services their children need.

Part B services are specific to special education, with related services provided as needed. Under Part B, the child's services typically are provided through education. Once eligible, gaining access to special education services is not usually an issue for families with children older than 3. It is the availability of related services (e.g., speech, occupational, or physical therapies) that more often becomes an issue for families and Part B providers.

Coordinate and Monitor the Delivery of Services
Under Part H, services may come from a variety of sources (e.g., education, speech, nutrition, parent counseling) and can be provided in a variety of settings (e.g., school, outpatient clinic, child care center, home). It is the job of the service coordinator to monitor services and ensure that all services to which the child is entitled are being delivered as stated on the IFSP. This typically necessitates maintaining contact with the family and with service providers through informal telephone calls and formal meetings (Zipper et al., 1993). Additionally, it involves generating ideas and helping families gain access to appropriate linkage services.

Under Part B, special education and related services are usually offered in a school setting. The child's teacher often performs many of the tasks previously assumed by the service coordinator, such as managing the child's schedule.

Inform Families of the Availability of Advocacy Services
One function that service coordinators can perform is to inform parents of their rights in the system and of the availability of services to help them advocate for their children. Sources may include par-

ent education programs, advocacy organizations, additional state and national resources, and national parent advocacy groups (Zipper et al., 1993).

Coordinate with Medical and Health Providers

The service coordinator also coordinates the child's early intervention services with necessary medical services. Many young children with disabilities also have significant health needs, so it is important that the two be coordinated. This does not mean that all of the linkage services (e.g., home nursing for a child who is a technology user) are provided under Part H; rather, a service coordinator helps families gain access to and organize medical evaluations and services.

For children served under Part B, there also may be a need to coordinate with medical providers. Often it is the parent or the teacher who bridges these services and ensures that health and education work together to benefit the child. Although not all children have health conditions that affect their educational needs, if a child does have such a condition, it is critical that someone coordinate these services.

In addition to collaborating with health care providers to obtain necessary evaluations and treatments, the service coordinator may also help some families obtain necessary immunizations for their children. This may include arranging transportation to a clinic or accessing community resources that provide free immunizations.

Facilitate Development of Transition Plan

The service coordinator ensures that the child has the evaluations needed to establish eligibility for Part B services. For children who are eligible for Part B, the service coordinator works with the local education agency (LEA) to schedule the necessary meetings to review the child's strengths and needs, to determine eligibility for services, and to prepare for a transition in service delivery. The service coordinator also works with the family to prepare for the transition and to obtain the necessary signed consent forms to transfer information from Part H to Part B so that services are not interrupted. If eligible for Part B, the service coordinator then works with the LEA and the family to develop a new plan, the IEP, for the child in preschool.

For those children who are not eligible for Part B services or who are no longer eligible for Part H services, the service coordinator is responsible for connecting the family with appropriate community programs (e.g., Head Start, preschool, library programs, parenting groups). If the child is not eligible for Part H or Part B services, the service coordinator can link the family with available resources but does not necessarily have to ensure that the child is accepted into another program.

In summary, service coordination emphasizes a collaborative relationship with families. The cornerstone of collaboration is communication, the mutual exchange of information between and among families and professionals (Shelton & Stepanek, 1994; Turnbull & Turnbull, 1990; Walker & Singer, 1993; see also Chapter 3 of this book). The remainder of this chapter discusses strategies for determining family concerns, priorities, and resources. Understanding family preferences and goals is part of the IFSP process. For more information on any specific issues (e.g., transition, conflict management, grief, siblings, developing relationships), refer to other chapters in this volume.

GATHERING INFORMATION

Part H of IDEA indicates that the IFSP must contain a statement of the family's concerns, priorities, and resources related to enhancing the development of the child (PL 102-119). Although not required, such information is also useful in developing IEPs. This section focuses on strategies for determining family concerns, priorities, and resources and using this information to develop intervention plans for children with disabilities in collaboration with their families.

Since the mid-1980s, the role of the early interventionist has shifted from that of an expert who merely dispenses information to that of a partner who also gathers information from the family about their concerns, priorities, and resources (Winton & Bailey, 1990; Zipper et al., 1993). Because of this shift in roles, service providers need to be able to talk to families face-to-face and gather sufficient information. Eliciting family input can be achieved with appropriate professional training and support. Good interviewing skills can help professionals identify family needs that are relevant to the child's development. Such information, in turn, can facilitate comprehensive and appropriate family-driven intervention plans.

The family interview may occur at the beginning of a relationship with a family or may occur throughout the intervention process as the child's and family's needs change. The relationship with the family is the context for gathering information from and sharing information with the family. (See Chapters 2 and 3 for more information about skills necessary to form a working relationship with families.) This section describes the use of interviews to learn more about individual families.

Preparing for the Family Interview

In preparation for a family interview, professionals can use the skill of "tuning in" (Shulman, 1992). *Tuning in* involves recognizing any feelings and concerns the family may bring to the interview based on their experience. Being familiar with the family's history is one way to tune in. Another is to ask the family questions before making assumptions about what they need or want. For example, if this is an initial interview, the provider can ask if the family has received a diagnosis. If so, how are they feeling and what do they need first? Another example might be a child who has been receiving intervention for several years and is functioning at very close to his or her age level. This family might come to the discussion with questions regarding options for general education.

In making an effort to tune in, it is important that interventionists not make assumptions about what families feel. That information should come from the family. Tuning in does not guarantee that the service provider will know what the family wants to discuss. It can prepare the provider to better receive the family's direct and indirect communications during the interview, however.

Another purpose of tuning in is to recognize how the process of gathering information may affect the family. Some families feel comfortable sharing their priorities and concerns, whereas other families may regard the presence of professionals as intrusive or as another way to judge their parenting skills in a difficult situation. In a study of families who participated in a university affiliated early intervention program, Slentz, Walker, and Bricker (1989) found that one of the most threatening and uncomfortable aspects of early intervention services reported by the families occurred when the process of determining family needs was approached like an assessment. It is not a typical practice for any family to share sensitive and personal information with relative strangers. Furthermore, the process of assessment can carry the covert message that because the child needs specialized services, the family must have problems as well (Slentz & Bricker, 1990).

At an interview, families need to be in control of what information is shared, what topics are covered, and what aspects of their lives they wish to discuss. When a practitioner requests additional information, the reason for the request should be directly related to enhancing the child's development. Even then, it should be clear to the family that information is shared only at their discretion. It is important that the family not be pressured, either directly or indirectly, to share additional information. Families are typically willing to talk about their priorities and their concerns for their children, which is the purpose of gathering information. Sensitivity and respect should guide the interview process.

Another helpful way to prepare for an interview, particularly an initial interview, is for the coordinator to review national, state, and local requirements related to early intervention and/or special education. This allows the professional to answer questions that the family may ask about the system and services. Coordinators also need to be familiar with the availability and eligibility requirements of community resources (Healy & Lewis-Beck, 1987) to provide parents with the information needed to make informed decisions.

Types of Interviews

Some professionals use paper-and-pencil surveys to determine family concerns and priorities (Minke & Scott, 1993) or use surveys about general family needs. Parents have been asked to complete checklists covering topics such as financial, child care, information, and basic needs. Some interviewers use surveys or lists of questions to ask the family about their concerns and priorities. Others have conversation-type discussions with families to get the same information (Kaufmann & McGonigel, 1991).

The use of formal instruments, questionnaires, or checklists also may be beneficial in specific situations. Hanft (1991) suggested using formal guidelines and checklists with family members as conversation starters and to discuss unaddressed topics. When using any formal measure, service providers need to know what each scale or questionnaire is intended to measure and how that information may be important or beneficial to the family. Such knowledge involves an understanding of how a measure has been used in the past, any research associated with the measure (e.g., information about reliability and validity of the measure), and reports of how it has been received by families in the past. Any measure chosen should respect cultural and linguistic differences within and across families. It also is important to maintain respect for family privacy and confidentiality.

However, approaching families with a battery of surveys that cover a variety of areas of need can send mixed messages or create false assumptions about the purpose and nature of services that the professionals intend to provide. For example, if a questionnaire includes questions about general family functioning, families may assume that early intervention services will include efforts to improve family functioning, when in fact many community-based programs do not and cannot provide such services (Whitehead, Deiner, & Toccafondi, 1990). Family members also may question the need to provide personal information when the presumed purpose of the program is to facilitate the child's development.

In a study using consumer focus groups (Summers et al., 1990), there was strong consensus about the importance of using informal methods to gather information. Open-ended conversations and informal approaches were preferred to structured interviews or paper-and-pencil surveys. Although it clearly is important that interventionists have adequate information about the family to provide appropriate services, it is important not to grill the family with numerous questions, particularly ones that are irrelevant or redundant. Ultimately, to keep the interview process family-driven, it is often helpful for professionals to provide choices to families about how to proceed with the interview. It is also helpful to let individual families decide whether written or verbal methods of sharing relevant information are most comfortable for them.

Professional Behavior During an Interview
During an interview, service providers communicate respect for the family by what they say, how they say it, and how they listen. Both the verbal and nonverbal behaviors of the professional communicate many things to the family (see also Chapter 3). Does the interviewer look away or change the subject if certain topics are mentioned? Does he or she attend to all participants? Professionals may want to examine their own style by videotaping an interview or by having a peer accompany them on an interview. For example, after reviewing her videotape, one teacher discovered that she became anxious when the family discussed how difficult the child's medical problems had been. The teacher noticed that she began rocking in the rocking chair every time this subject was mentioned. Another service provider noticed that when she felt uncomfortable about a family's questions, she began to give rambling responses.

Verbal and Nonverbal Communication Effective communication means speaking simply so that the other individuals in the interview can hear and follow the conversation and information. These skills are covered extensively in Chapter 3, along with a review of barriers to communication. Professionals need to speak clearly with an even tempo and pitch. Jargon should be avoided, or, if used, it should be defined. Check with the family to see if they understand what is being said. For many families, English may be a second language, necessitating a language interpreter for communication.

Nonverbal communication skills include looking alert, interested, and nonjudgmental as information is exchanged. Leaning forward slightly, being relaxed yet professional with posture, using affect congruent with content, and using appropriate eye contact and gestures all convey openness and comfort. Some body movement is natural, but it is important to avoid such activities as finger-pointing, fidgeting, excessive nodding, yawning, and covering the mouth when speaking. Appropriate physical proximity and social distance needs to be maintained, and professionals and family members should sit at eye level together, without artificial barriers such as a desk between them. Note taking during the interview should be done only as necessary, and it is important for families to know what is being written and why it needs to be recorded.

The significance attached to nonverbal communication varies considerably across cultures. For instance, the meaning of eye contact or the appropriate amount of physical distance varies from culture to culture. Service coordinators and service providers need to be familiar with the meaning of various forms of nonverbal contact. (For more information about cultural issues, refer to Chapter 4.)

Scheduling Interviews
Ideally, family interviews should be conducted when and where it is most convenient for the family. Offering choices about scheduling can help ease stress and make the interview process smoother. It also conveys an important message of respect for the family's preferences. Although interviews are often done in the home, not all families are comfortable with having a professional come into their home. Interviews also can be conducted in an educational, developmental, or health care facility or in another setting such as a coffee shop or a community center.

Beginning the Family Interview
The professional sets the tone and parameters for the interview. Introductions and small talk (e.g., weather, traffic) need to be followed closely by stating the purpose of the interview, for example, "Today I would like to explain our program to you and talk with you about your child, your concerns about him, what you feel he needs, and what supports your family needs to help your child"; or, "I want us to talk today about how you think your child is doing, what progress he's made, and other things you think are important to his development. I also want to share some of what we are seeing in school

and hear about how things are going at home." Goals and objectives for the meeting can be clarified at the outset, along with any questions that family members may have.

In addition, a statement about the scheduled time frame is useful at the beginning of the interview. (For example, "I can only stay about an hour today, but if we need more time, we can schedule a follow-up interview on another day.") It is important for families to know that they are welcome members of their children's educational team and that they can be effective advocates for their children. This is communicated by listening and respecting their input and by providing adequate time for discussion and information exchange.

At the beginning of an interview, service providers need to ensure families of their privacy and confidentiality and present them with information about their rights as families in the system (e.g., the right to copies of records, the right to request mediation or due process). Although service providers and school districts are required to inform parents of their rights under the law, parents do not always have this information. Florian and Greig (1993) reported that, in 1989, both a Harris Poll and the National Council on Disability found that parents frequently were not aware of their rights. Professionals can help remedy this situation by taking time to explain those provisions in the law that affirm parental rights and by making sure families understand their rights. In addition to explaining the law and its provisions, professionals can offer resources for families who want additional information about services or state law and policies. Offering addresses and telephone numbers of local and national organizations allows families to keep abreast of any amendments to the law or of changes in regulations.

Conducting the Interview

It is helpful for the service provider to follow the family's lead during the interview rather than adhere strictly to a professional agenda. If a family member brings up a topic, it should be addressed as completely and sensitively as possible. Even the most well-informed professional, however, is unlikely to have all the answers to all families' questions. Competent professionals are honest with families; they let them know when they really do not have an answer and how they will follow up on the families' questions or concerns after the interview.

Information About the Child Families have many things to share with professionals about their child and about their life with the child. It is often helpful to talk about the strengths and needs of the child first. One strategy is for the provider to ask the family to describe a typical day with their child at home. Comparing a child's typical behavior at home with behaviors that are noted in other settings—from a medical or educational appointment to a trip to the grocery store, park, or neighbor's house—can reveal important information about issues that need to be addressed during intervention. Asking a family to describe how they think others view their child, including spouses, other immediate family members, extended family members, family friends, playmates, child care providers, and other professionals involved in the child's care, is another useful strategy for helping families describe their child.

In general, it helps to have a repertoire of questions to guide a conversation with family members and to identify their concerns, priorities, and resources. Table 1 provides some questions that can be used in a parent interview. These questions should be used only as a general guide, however, not as part of a rigid set of questions that must be answered by the family. It is important to follow the family's lead to determine the most appropriate and useful questions for the interview.

Information About the Family Discussing characteristics of the child can provide a context for families to begin describing their overall needs. Additionally, as families discuss their wishes and dreams for their child, their preferences for involvement with relevant services and programs often become apparent. This is a good

Table 1. Sample questions about the child

- Tell me about your child.
- How did you first learn about your child's diagnosis or need for specialized services and supports?
- What types of things does your child enjoy doing?
- What is your child like at home and outside of your home?
- What is challenging for your child?
- What types of things does your child avoid?
- What concerns you about your child?
- What is the most difficult part of caring for your child?
- What types of changes have you noticed recently about your child?
- What concerns do you have about how your child's needs are being handled?
- What makes your child happy and content?
- What are your dreams and goals for your child's future (short- and long-term)?
- What types of services and supports do you and your child need to meet your goals and outcomes?
- How did you learn about the early intervention system, and how do you hope it will benefit your child and family?

point for families to describe their personal resources to meet their child's needs and their priorities and concerns for the child and family.

Family members need to first understand what is meant by *family concerns, priorities*, and *resources*, and how sharing such information will benefit their child. Professionals can explain that the process of obtaining information about family concerns and priorities is intended to identify supports that may be helpful to the family related to enhancing the child's development.

Questions about family resources can be used to build on existing strengths and to determine where new services may be useful. One way to obtain such information is to ask families to describe individuals who are supportive or to identify other possible sources of support. Family members also may be asked to think about their own coping strategies. Sample questions are provided in Table 2. Every family has strengths, talents, and personal resources, but sometimes it takes some creative brainstorming to begin identifying and articulating these resources.

Categories of Information   Beckman and Bristol (1991) cited several types of family concerns that can serve as a framework when interviewing families. Family concerns may relate only to the child and his or her disability, such as concerns about specific services (e.g., frequency or intensity of services, transportation to and from services). Other family concerns may relate to the day-to-day functioning of the family because there is a child with a disability (e.g., need for respite care, need for sibling or parent peer support). Still other family concerns may be more general and unrelated to the child with a disability. For example, the family may need housing or transportation. Beckman and Bristol (1991) cautioned that, although these areas may need probing, as professionals move further away from questions about the child's development, they run an increasing risk of becoming intrusive.

Some service coordinators find it helpful to organize the concepts of resources and concerns into categories, such as financial, physical, social, emotional, medical, developmental, and informational (Bailey, 1987). Resources and concerns can then be further defined. For example, a father may initially indicate that he would like more information about his child's disability. After further discussion, he may share that, in addition to general professional information about his child, he really would like information from another parent who has a child with the same diagnosis. Naming a resource or concern imposes structure on it, which allows for an organized way to understand and address family priorities.

Table 2. Sample questions about the family

- How has life changed since the birth or diagnosis of your child?
- What gives you the most satisfaction when caring for your child?
- What is your family like (number of people; do they live in the home; where are they from; what types of jobs, skills, and talents do they have; etc.)?
- Who is available when you need to talk or take a break?
- Who do you get support from (emotional, physical, financial, etc.)?
- What type of support do they provide?
- What are your dreams and goals for you and your family?
- What are three major goals and needs of your family right now?
- What special resources and strengths help your family meet your goals and their needs?
- What are some of the barriers interfering with your dreams and goals?
- What would make it easier to work toward your dreams and goals?
- What types of information and assistance have you and your family previously sought?
- What type of information and help is most beneficial to you and your family?
- How would it be best for you and your family to work with the professionals caring for your child?
- How do you and your family generally tackle problems?
- Is there anything else you would like us to know?
- Do you have any questions, concerns, or comments?

Honoring Family Preferences Honoring family preferences for the amount of information and time they can handle in any one meeting is important (McGonigel, Kaufmann, & Johnson, 1991). If more time is needed to finish the interview or to discuss further any particular resources, concerns, or priorities, additional meetings should be scheduled by the end of the current meeting, if possible. Whether additional family members or professionals should be invited to attend future meetings also needs to be addressed.

Summarizing Content At the end of the meeting, all topics need to be summarized clearly. Reframing or paraphrasing what family members have said, commenting on discussion topics, reviewing areas that were covered, and highlighting some of the key discussion points are all beneficial ways to summarize and clarify perceptions. Professionals should check their interpretations with family members to ensure that they are accurate. Family members can then clarify or modify any misinterpretations. After this debriefing, notes of needed follow-up activities can be made and reviewed with families to ensure that all participants have a similar understanding of the tasks to be completed. Professionals need to continue to convey respect and appreciation for family involvement and information sharing throughout the debriefing. Finally, service providers need to convey respect for parents and other family members so that they do not feel judged as a result of exploring their needs and concerns or as a result of decisions they make regarding their children's services and care.

CONCLUSIONS

The long-term success of IDEA ultimately depends on the extent to which states can ensure that professionals working in early intervention and special education systems are adequately prepared to serve children and their families through both preservice and in-service training. Professional training should include basic competencies and strategies that lead to collaboration and communication between families and professionals and that enhance service coordination. IFSP and IEP documents can then be written in ways that honor families' concerns and priorities while meeting the diverse needs of the child within the family context (Hanson & Lynch, 1989).

There is no single right way to coordinate services for children and families or to facilitate a family interview. There are, however, strategies that, when used appropriately, can foster communication and collaboration in family–professional partnerships. These strategies involve understanding diverse family systems and interview styles and a sincere respect for the central role of families. Successful service coordination and family interviews are more likely to occur when professionals view parents as parents and families as families rather than as parents and relatives of children with disabilities (Shelton & Stepanek, 1994). This ultimately benefits the children being served as well as the families and professionals caring for them.

ACTIVITIES AND DISCUSSION

1. Read Case Study II, the Martínez Family, and Case Study III, the Winger Family, and discuss the following:
   a. What were each family's concerns and priorities?
   b. What strengths and resources did each family have?
   c. What would you, as a service coordinator, do after the initial interview?
   d. Discuss possible IFSP outcomes for each family.

    e. Is there more information you would need? If so, what?

    f. What do you think your personal reaction might be to each family?

    g. How would you create a climate of acceptance and concern to build trust and develop a positive relationship with each family?

    h. What follow-up is needed?

    i. What larger issues should be considered when working with each family?

2. Identify five persons to participate in the following role-playing exercise. Participants should assume the roles of Elsie Mercer (grandmother), George Williams (family friend), Vicki (the service coordinator), a teacher, and a therapist. Enact the following steps in the process:

    a. An interview with this family.

    b. Initial meeting to address the issues raised by this family.

Base your role playing on the following information: Elsie Mercer, grandmother of Lisa, just gained custody of her granddaughter. Lisa has Down syndrome and is 24 months old. Elsie feels she was tricked into taking Lisa. Lisa's mother, Tracey, had pretended to talk to Child Protective Services on the telephone and said that she could not handle Lisa and wanted to place her in foster care. When Elsie heard this, she said she would take Lisa temporarily to give Tracey a break so that Lisa did not go into foster care. This was 6 months ago, and there are no signs that Tracey is ready to take Lisa back. Elsie suspects that Tracey is using drugs again and would not trust her to take proper care of Lisa. Elsie is engaged to be married to George Williams. George recently has expressed concerns because he has never lived with children. He is embarrassed to go out with Lisa because he feels that she does not listen and behave. Lisa is currently attending a center-based program 2 days a week. This is the same program she was in when she lived with Tracey. Elsie likes the program but cannot visit the center, because she works. She wants some help to understand Lisa's behaviors and to know how to discipline a child with a disability. She also wants to know how to help George cope with Lisa. She also has concerns about finding a baby sitter for Lisa so that she and George can go out sometimes. "Raisin' a baby was not what I had in mind for my retirement!," she said.

Use the following questions as a basis for group discussion:

a. What issues emerged for this family as the scenario was enacted?

b. How well did Vicki understand the family situation?

c. Describe the problem-solving process. Were the solutions practical, accessible, and affordable? Did the actions meet the needs of the family? Did the actions fit the constraints of the system? Are they realistic?

d. How can Vicki help the family gain access to the services they want and need?

3. Read the following scenarios. Assume that you are the service coordinator and that each situation occurs while the family is receiving early intervention services. Brainstorm possible actions you might take as the service coordinator. What would you do? Detail the information you would need and the steps you would take to serve each family. With what issues do you think each family is coping? How might these issues affect your actions?

Scenario A: Sally is 8 months old and has Down syndrome. This is the first time she has received intervention services. She receives home-based education and physical therapy once each week. Although her mother, Betty Jo, has told you that Sally has Down syndrome, the referral source has told you that she refuses to accept the diagnosis. You ask Betty Jo if the hospital has given her any information about Down syndrome. She said, "They gave me a book, but I haven't read it. I skimmed over it." The evaluation results are somewhat lower than Betty Jo expected. Initial assessment results indicate that Sally does not respond to a bell and a rattle to the right, but she does to the left. Sally has not had her vision and hearing screened. Betty Jo asks if you think that Sally will learn quickly. She wants Sally to sit alone, to hold her bottle, and to reach for toys.

Scenario B: At 27 months, J.R. has microcephaly, cerebral palsy, and fevers of unknown origin. He lives with his father, Tim (19 years old), and mother, Dorothy (20 years old), on a military base. J.R. has been receiving services for approximately 1 year, about the length of time the family has been in the area. He is functioning in the 6–9 month age range in most areas of development. He has a new teacher. You ask how things are going. Dorothy says that J.R. has been running fevers lately and that they have been to the doctor numerous times without being given a diagnosis. When J.R.'s new teacher came the day before, Dorothy felt bad for J.R. because he kept arching and fussing and his teacher kept right on with her activities. Dorothy knew that he did not feel well, but she did not want to interrupt the teacher. When he fusses, it is only a soft sound, so it is hard to know that he is unhappy. She can tell, but others often do not know.

REFERENCES

Americans with Disabilities Act of 1990 (ADA), PL 101-336. (July 26, 1990). Title 42, U.S.C. §§ 12101 et seq.: *U.S. Statutes at Large, 104*, 327–378.

Bailey, D. (1987). Collaborative goal-setting with families: Resolving differences in values and priorities for services. *Topics in Early Childhood Special Education, 7*, 59–71.

Bailey, D.B. (1989). Case management in early intervention. *Journal of Early Intervention, 13*(2), 120–134.

Beckman, P.B., & Bristol, M.M. (1991). Issues in developing the IFSP: A framework for establishing family outcomes. *Topics in Early Childhood Special Education, 11*(3), 19–31.

Dinnebeil, L.A., & Rule, S. (1994). Variables that influence collaboration between parents and service coordinators. *Journal of Early Intervention, 18*(4), 349–361.

Early Intervention Program for Infants and Toddlers with Disabilities; final regulations, 34 C.F.R. § 6303 (1993, July). *Federal Register, 58*(145), 40,958–40,989.

Education of the Handicapped Act Amendments of 1986, PL 99-457. (October 9, 1986). Title 20, U.S.C. §§ 1400 et seq.: *U.S. Statutes at Large, 100*, 1145–1177.

Florian, L., & Greig, D. (1993). Entitlements and rights: The promise of the Individuals with Disabilities Education Act. In P.J. Beckman & G.B. Boyes (Eds.), *Deciphering the system: A guide for families of young children with disabilities* (pp. 7–19). Cambridge, MA: Brookline Books.

Hanft, B. (1991). Impact of federal policy on pediatric health and education programs. In W. Dunn (Ed.), *Pediatric service delivery* (pp. 273–284). Thorofare, NJ: Slack.

Hanson, M.J., & Lynch, E.W. (1989). *Early intervention: Implementing child and family services for infants and toddlers who are at-risk or disabled.* Austin, TX: PRO-ED.

Healy, A., & Lewis-Beck, J.A. (1987). *Improving health care for children with chronic conditions: Guidelines for social workers.* Iowa City: Division of Developmental Disabilities, University of Iowa.

Individuals with Disabilities Education Act Amendments of 1991, PL 102-119. (October 7, 1991). Title 20, U.S.C. §§ 1400 et seq.: *U.S. Statutes at Large, 105*, 587–608.

Kaufmann, R.K., & McGonigel, M.J. (1991). Identifying family concerns, priorities, and resources. In M.J. McGonigel, R.K. Kaufmann, & B.H. Johnson (Eds.), *Guidelines and recommended practices for the individualized family service plan* (2nd ed., pp. 67–78). Bethesda, MD: Association for the Care of Children's Health.

McGonigel, M.J., Kaufmann, R.K., & Johnson, B.H. (1991). *Guidelines and recommended practices for the individualized service plan.* Bethesda, MD: Association for the Care of Children's Health.

Minke, K.M., & Scott, M.M. (1993). The development of individualized family service plans: Roles for parents and staff. *Journal of Special Education,* *27*(1), 82–106.

Shelton, T.L., & Stepanek, J.S. (1994). *Family-centered care for children needing specialized health and developmental services.* Bethesda, MD: Association for the Care of Children's Health.

Shulman, L. (1992). *The skills of helping: Individuals, families and groups.* Itasca, IL: F.R. Peacock Publishers.

Slentz, K.L., & Bricker, D. (1990). Family guided assessment for IFSP development: Jumping off the family assessment bandwagon. *Journal of Early Intervention, 16*(1), 11–19.

Slentz, K., Walker, B., & Bricker, D. (1989). Supporting parent involvement in early intervention: A role-taking model. In G.H.S. Singer & L.K. Irvin (Eds.), *Support for caregiving families: Enabling positive adaptation to disability* (pp. 221–238). Baltimore, MD: Paul H. Brookes Publishing Co.

Summers, J., Dell'Oliver, C., Turnbull, A., Benson, H., Santelli, E., Campbell, M., & Siegel-Causey, E. (1990). Examining the individualized family service plan process: What are family and practitioner preferences? *Topics in Early Childhood Special Education, 10*(1), 78–99.

Turnbull, A.P., & Turnbull, H.R. (1990). *Families, professionals and exceptionality: A special partnership.* New York: Macmillan.

Walker, B., & Singer, G.H.S. (1993). Improving collaborative communication between professionals and parents. In G.H.S. Singer & L.E. Powers (Eds.), *Families, disability, and empowerment: Active coping skills and strategies for family interventions* (pp. 285–316). Baltimore: Paul H. Brookes Publishing Co.

Whitehead, L.C., Deiner, P.L., & Toccafondi, S. (1990). Family assessment: Parent and professional evaluation. *Topics in Early Childhood Special Education, 10*(1), 63–77.

Winton, P., & Bailey, D. (1990). Early intervention training related to family interviewing. *Topics in Early Childhood Special Education, 10*(1), 50–62.

Zipper, I.N., Weil, M., & Rounds, K. (1993). *Service coordination for early intervention: Parents and professionals.* Cambridge, MA: Brookline Books.

Chapter 6 ──────────────────────

Facilitating Collaboration
in Meetings and Conferences

Paula J. Beckman
───────────────────── **and Jennifer Smith Stepanek**

The meetings and conferences between parents and service providers are important components of all working relationships with families. Although most formal meetings are held to discuss the individualized family service plan (IFSP) or the individualized education program (IEP), other meetings also may occur throughout the year. The quality of the parent–professional relationship can both influence and be influenced by these exchanges (Dinnebeil & Rule, 1994; McGonigel, Kaufmann, & Johnson, 1991; Minke & Scott, 1993; see also Chapter 2 of this book). Therefore, it is in the best interests of all participants to ensure that meetings and conferences are a positive experience for families.

This chapter focuses on strategies for creating family-friendly planning meetings. First, it discusses the family's role in these meetings, and then it considers a number of professional practices that can be counterproductive. Remaining sections of the chapter identify practical strategies that can be used before, during, and after meetings to create an atmosphere of collaboration, partnership, and support.

FAMILY ROLES IN IFSP/IEP MEETINGS

Early interventionists are shifting away from traditional views of professionals as experts who are in charge of the services provided to a child. There has been a growing appreciation that families can make an important contribution to the planning and implementation of services for young children and that they have a right to assume a decision-making role. This shift is formally reflected in the requirements for the development of IFSPs in Part H of PL 102-119, the Individuals with Disabilities Education Act Amendments of 1991. The emphasis has changed from viewing the family as passive recipients of information from professionals to emphasizing collaborative decision making (Bailey, 1987; Beckman et al., 1996; Beckman, Robinson, Rosenberg, & Filer, 1994; Dunst, Johanson, Trivette, & Hamby, 1991; McGonigel & Garland, 1988; Shelton & Stepanek, 1994).

The family's role has been changed by the Part H requirements in at least four ways that may influence planning meetings. First, the focus of intervention has broadened to include the family's concerns, priorities, and resources. Interventionists now have to consider the potential impact of interventions on the entire family and a wider range of potential services than they did in the past.

Second, as a result of this shift in focus, it is increasingly important that service providers receive information from family members. The family provides a rich source of information for the entire team as the team works through issues concerning the child's capabilities, the areas in which the child needs assistance, the services that are needed, and the most effective strategies for addressing objectives. Families provide information on the child's medical and educational history, the child's abilities and preferences, contextually based behavior differences, and family needs. They also provide information about events, activities, people, and objects that motivate, excite, and frighten their children. Although such information has always been important, it often has not been solicited systematically.

Another role that parents assume over the life span is as the ultimate coordinators of the services that their child receives (Lash & Wertlieb, 1993). Parents frequently communicate with medical, educational, and therapy teams, as well as with other individuals involved in some aspect of their child's life. Moreover, the family typically mediates the child's participation in the service delivery system. Thus, the family's perspective is often much broader than that of individual service providers, encompassing a longer time span and a range of current and potential needs.

Finally, the family has a decision-making role. Making decisions about services for their child involves more than a signature on the final IFSP or IEP document; rather, it includes active participation in discussions concerning service options. This aspect of the family's role may be difficult for service providers, particularly if their training or experience has cast them as experts who prescribe interventions. The emerging emphasis on the parents' role as decision makers, however, does not diminish that of the service provider, but rather results in a new balance between the service provider's expertise in a discipline and the family's decision-making authority and responsibility. It has been suggested elsewhere (Beckman et al., 1996) that a process for informed decision making may provide the basis of this balance. In such a process, the parents and the professional integrate the parents' unique knowledge of the child and family with the service provider's knowledge of the service system and his or her discipline. To achieve this balance, it is critical that service providers be aware of the aspects of planning meetings that are sometimes a source of concern for families.

SOURCES OF CONCERN ABOUT MEETINGS

Most studies that have evaluated the concerns that family members have about planning meetings have focused on the IEP. Although such meetings provide a formal mechanism that parents can use to exercise their rights, the literature suggests that, when not conducted with respect and sensitivity, these meetings can be difficult for families (Beckman, Boyes, & Herres, 1993; Brinkerhoff & Vincent, 1986; Gill, 1993; Turnbull & Strickland, 1981; Turnbull & Turnbull, 1990). Understanding the potential sources of difficulties that can occur in planning meetings is necessary to avoid such long-term effects as diminished trust, lack of participation, lack of follow-through, and the potential for adversarial contacts. Turnbull and Turnbull (1990) concluded that, although the literature does not suggest that parents are always actively disgruntled with IEP meetings, parents often are relatively passive participants.

For example, Vaughn, Bos, Harrell, and Lasky (1988) reported that parent interactions in IEP meetings accounted for only 14.8% of the conference time. Similarly, Lynch and Stein (1982) found that only 14.6% of the parents in their study expressed opinions or wishes. Limited participation, however, does not necessarily reflect parental preferences (Harry, 1992a; Turnbull & Turnbull, 1990). Harry (1992a) has argued that it is safer to assume that some parents do not know how to participate in the manner expected by service providers than to assume that they do not wish to be more actively involved.

Several factors may discourage parents from assuming an active role in planning meetings. In some cases, families are unclear about their rights or may not have the information and resources needed to effectively advocate for their children (Brinkerhoff & Vincent, 1986; Fish, 1990; Strickland, 1983; Turnbull & Strickland, 1981). Studies have shown that when parents are given training and materials concerned with such topics as their legal rights, strategies for IEP participation, and terminology, they participate more than parents who do not receive such support (Brinkerhoff & Vincent, 1986). For example, Brinkerhoff and Vincent (1986) found that participation in IEP meetings can be increased by training both staff members and parents. Staff members in an experimental group were trained to recognize the importance of parental contributions, and parents were given information on how to participate effectively. When compared with a control group, parents in the experimental group contributed more information, generated more goals, and made more decisions.

Many authors have noted that one factor influencing parent participation in IEP meetings is the number of professionals who participate in the meeting (Harry, Allen, & McLaughlin, 1995; Turnbull & Strickland, 1981; Turnbull & Turnbull, 1990). Some parents may interpret the participation of many professionals as an indication of interest in their child; however, other parents feel outnumbered and experience difficulty asserting their views. The adverse effects of being outnumbered have been described in the literature as "the power of the group" (Gliedman & Roth, 1980; Harry et al., 1995). This phrase reflects a phenomenon in which parental views are overpowered by the opinions of a larger number of professionals. Harry et al. (1995) argued that the structure of parent–professional meetings often can undermine parents' efforts to be advocates. The authors found that, although professionals frequently were sympathetic to parents' discomfort in meetings, the power structure frequently interfered with attempts to make parents feel more comfortable.

Other factors that substantially influence parent participation include culture, ethnicity, and social class. These factors often can mediate the role of parents in early intervention. For example, culture can influence perspectives on disability, approaches to child rearing, views of authority, views of medicine and healing, and language (Harry, 1992a, 1992b; Lynch & Hanson, 1992; see also Chapter 4 of this book). Lynch and Stein (1982) found that the number of suggestions offered by parents on the IEP was influenced by culture (e.g., Latino families offered fewer suggestions than African-American or Caucasian families). Lynch and Stein (1982) also found that communication and logistical issues frequently prevented families from being more active participants. Moreover, Harry and Kalyanpur (1994) noted that many individuals from nonmainstream cultures tend to view experts as a source of unquestioned knowledge and do not expect to be collaborators or decision makers. These authors note that

> difficulty arises when the cultural beliefs underlying professional judgments are very different, and parents are caught in a conflict between expecting to have faith in professional judgment, doubting or not understanding the premises from which such judgments proceed, and then finding that they are expected to play a role in that judgment. (p. 153)

Harry et al. (1995) reported the results of a qualitative study on the participation of African American families in special education. They found that, although almost all parents attended IEP conferences the first year, there was a marked decrease in subsequent years. The explanations given for this change in participation included conflicts with work schedules, late receipt of notices, limited time for conferences, lack of influence over meetings, use of jargon, and that the school "would send the papers to sign anyway" (p. 370). Harry et al. (1995) concluded that schools emphasized documents and compliance rather than real participation.

Another factor that may influence family participation in planning meetings involves the sensitivity with which meetings are conducted. Petr and Barney (1993) reported that parents in their study found the IEP process insensitive. Many relatively common examples of insensitivity, although rarely intentional, have been reported in the literature (Beckman et al., 1993; Leviton, Mueller, & Kauffmann, 1992). For instance, insensitivity occurs when family members are not introduced to individuals present at the meeting or when someone talks about the family member as if she or he were not present (e.g., "Does mom agree with this plan?"). Leviton et al. (1992) believe that referring to parents as "mom" or "dad" immediately defines the relationship as unequal. Another aspect of planning meetings that can upset parents is an overemphasis on the areas in which the child is not developing. Beckman et al. (1993) quoted one mother as saying:

> Even when I get all of the services I want for my son, I never fail to leave the meetings with a lump in my throat. It is still so hard to hear about all of the things he *can't* do that other children his age can do. (p. 86)

Another source of concern for parents is the feeling that professionals somehow blame them for the child's disability (Turnbull & Turnbull, 1990). In a survey of 243 parents, Witt, Miller, McIntyre, and Smith (1984) found that one major factor contributing to parent satisfaction with meetings was the extent to which the parents felt they were blamed by school personnel for their children's difficulties. This is consistent with the work of Petr and Barney (1993), who found that parents perceived professionals as critical and blaming. Although this reaction was reported by families of children with a variety of disorders, it was particularly prevalent among families of children with behavioral disorders. Thus, many authors (Beckman, in press; Seligman & Darling, 1989; Turnbull & Turnbull, 1990) emphasize the importance of refraining from making any comments that either explicitly or implicitly could be construed as blaming. Turnbull and Turnbull (1990) also recommended highlighting positive aspects of the parents' contribution.

A number of other practices that can be sources of stress for parents during planning meetings have been identified in the literature. For example, families may feel frustrated by time constraints placed on the meeting (Beckman et al., 1993; Harry et al., 1995; Souffer, 1982; Witt et al., 1984). This can occur if one or more of the professionals must leave before the end of the meeting or if the meeting must end because another is scheduled. Harry et al. (1995) found that the time allowance for most annual conferences was approximately 20–30 minutes. In the case of one team that they studied, the meeting was always over before the allotted time, regardless of the status of the discussion. Parents were told to take up final discussion with the teacher. The teacher often was unavailable, however, because there was no one to cover the teacher's classes. Such experiences are frustrating for parents if their questions have not been addressed or if they need further information about their child's services.

Other problems identified (Beckman et al., 1993) include references to information that is new to the parent or that has not been previously explained, excessive use of professional jargon, and the absence of some service providers who play critical roles in the child's program. Another identified problem is the sense that critical decisions about placement and programming have been made by professionals before the meeting. This is supported by Salett and Henderson's (1980) finding that 52%–75% of IEPs were developed by school staff before the meeting. It is also confirmed by Mehan, Hartwick, and Meihls (1986), who found that many meetings simply involved ratification of actions that occurred at an earlier step in the referral-to-placement process.

Although it is unlikely that professionals intend planning meetings to be stressful for families, service providers need to recognize the potential impact of their practices on families. This recognition is an important basis for implementing alternative strategies that respect the family's decision-making role and are sensitive to the family's feelings. The remainder of this chapter describes skills and strategies that may facilitate truly collaborative efforts with families.

STRATEGIES FOR FACILITATING COLLABORATION

In conducting planning meetings with families, the skills involved in developing a relationship and communicating with families are critical tools (see Chapter 3). These skills can be used throughout the process of planning, implementing, and following up planning meetings. In addition, a number of specific strategies can help create a supportive and positive atmosphere during meetings. Using strategies that make families feel welcome on traditionally professional turf can lead to increased family participation and satisfaction. Service providers need to remember that families have been invited to the professional domain and may feel intimidated by both the service providers themselves and the setting. Professionals can help families feel wanted and useful by listening to them and implementing strategies that facilitate family participation. When professionals show that they value family perspectives and expertise, families are more likely to participate in the team process. In turn, families may become more invested in implementing goals or in negotiating obstacles, because they have been involved in the decision-making process. This section describes some strategies that can be used to promote a warm, collaborative atmosphere during planning meetings.

Before the Meeting

Respect for families is communicated as much by how things are said and done as by what is accomplished. In planning for meetings that involve families, practitioners can respect the family's time, effort, and input by holding meetings at a time and place convenient for both the family and the professional members of the team (Leviton et al., 1992; Walker & Singer, 1993). It often may be as difficult for a family member to take off another day of work or to find respite care and transportation as it is for service providers to meet at the family's home or to hold the meeting during early evening hours.

Professionals also can help families prepare for upcoming team meetings by providing as much information as possible in advance. This may include assessment results as well as recommendations that will be addressed at the meeting. Families can then be encouraged to make notes about their concerns and priorities to help them prepare for the meeting. Although providing this information may require extra effort by service providers, it places the family in a position more nearly equivalent to that of the service provider. Service providers have this information in advance and have had the opportunity to think through their recommendations based on this information. It is difficult for families to receive assessment information and make appropriate decisions without having adequate time to process the information. Family members also can be encouraged to bring a support person to an IFSP or IEP meeting to provide a second ear, to help with note taking, or to provide moral support during a potentially stressful time.

During the Meeting

In addition to taking steps to promote full family participation before the meeting, there are several steps that providers can take during the meeting. It is important that providers demonstrate their interest in the family's equal participation throughout the meeting.

Setting the Stage   The process of communicating respect and establishing a collaborative atmosphere begins when the facilitator of the meeting introduces him- or herself. Participants should introduce themselves by name and clarify their role on the team (e.g., Mary Smith, physical therapist). Service providers who work together on a daily basis may all know each other; however, parents may have had only brief contacts with some team participants. In the midst of what can be a confusing, intimidating, or emotional contact with service providers, it is helpful if family members do not have to remember the names and roles of persons that they have met only briefly. Several authors (Beckman et al., 1993; Leviton et al., 1992) recommend using name tags on which participants indicate both their names and their respective roles. This is especially important if there are many professionals involved in the meeting and if the parent does not know all of the participants (e.g., the first IEP meeting, when one or more members of the team are unfamiliar to the family).

Consistency across individuals in how they are addressed throughout the meeting also conveys respect. For example, it conveys unequal status to refer to the physician as "Dr. Jones" and to address the parents by their first names. Either everyone present is comfortable with first names, or everyone is addressed formally.

After each participant has been introduced, the facilitator should clarify the purpose of the meeting and address any potential time constraints. The facilitator can indicate the amount of time scheduled and make it clear that, if the discussion is not finished, a follow-up meeting can be arranged. Some service providers may be concerned about this recommendation because they have numerous IEPs or IFSPs to complete in a relatively short time. A frequent concern of parents, however, is the sense that they were rushed through the meeting, that professionals were not truly interested in their input, and that professionals view IEP meetings as formalities that must be conducted to comply with legal requirements (Beckman et al., 1993; Harry et al., 1995; Witt et al., 1984). By making it clear that service providers are willing to spend the necessary time to obtain substantive input from family members, address their concerns, and answer their questions, service providers can help establish a positive and collaborative atmosphere during the meeting. It is also important that all service providers involved in the planning process attend the meeting. If a service provider must leave the meeting early, this should be explained at the outset so that the family can address any concerns or issues specific to that individual. If the expertise of that team member is needed for a group decision after he or she has left, it should be made clear that it is possible to schedule another meeting so that his or her input can be included.

Sharing Information A critical component of planning meetings revolves around the mutual sharing of information (Beckman et al., 1994; McGonigel & Garland, 1988; Minke & Scott, 1993). An ongoing mutual exchange of information respects the central role of the family by providing information and creating a reciprocal atmosphere during meetings. Petr and Barney (1993) found that parents commonly expressed frustration about the lack of information provided by school staff during the IEP process. They also felt that their own wishes often were not considered. Service providers can use the planning meeting to discuss assessments and share information about progress on previously established goals, future placement options, and recommendations. Parents, in turn, can share information regarding progress at home, recent contacts with professionals who are not present (e.g., the pediatrician), family concerns, and other information that can provide the team with a broader perspective of the child and family.

To ensure a sense of equality and collaboration, it helps to provide family members with the same information that other team members have before the meeting (e.g., copies of reports, recommendations, medical records, rights and responsibilities of team members). This allows family members to prepare and to generate their own questions (Leviton et al., 1992). Although sharing information in advance may require additional time, it can enhance a sense of equality and partnership.

Discussing Assessment Results If parents have received assessment information before the meeting, service providers can ask if family members have any questions and if they have a preference regarding where they would like to begin. If they have not received information, the results of any assessments should be reviewed, and the family should be given an opportunity to respond to the results. It is important to ask family members if the results seem consistent with what they see in other settings. Questions such as "Does this match what you see at home?" or "Is there anything your child is doing that is different from what we saw during our assessment?" can help elicit such information. Moreover, these questions reflect the service provider's sensitivity to the many ways in which context can influence the child's performance. It is also important that providers give the family complete attention when they respond to questions or express concerns or priorities related to their child's goals and outcomes.

Making Recommendations After evaluation results are reviewed and clarified, the facilitator can explain service options and make recommendations. The professionals on the team need to be sensitive yet honest in the feedback they provide to the family. It can be difficult for a family to contend with the unknowns related to their child's disability. Although professionals are often understandably reluctant to make predictions, they need to be straightforward and avoid being evasive (Rothbaum, Raia, Amorapanth, Picone, & Ziskin, 1994). It is possible to be honest without destroying hope. Highlighting strengths as well as areas of concern can help, as can allowing families to talk about both their fears and their expectations for the child. Such discussions can help families adapt to their child's disability and still have aspirations and goals. It is important not to communicate discomfort if a family member cries or becomes angry at meetings — these are often normal reactions to unwelcome information. At the same time, it is helpful to avoid clichés such as "I know how you feel" or "Things always work out for the best." It is also critical that professionals not elicit guilt by using statements such as "I know you want what's best for your child, so I think you'll agree with our recommendations."

Additionally, providing opportunities for families to ask questions and clarify information is important. Professionals need to be sensitive to any verbal or nonverbal cues indicating that the parent is unclear or confused about information that has been presented. In such circumstances, the facilitator can interrupt and specifically ask if the parent has questions. For example, the facilitator might say, "Mrs. Smith, you look puzzled . . . do you have concerns about that?" Remember that, at times, families may ask the same question more than once. It can be difficult for anyone to remember all information, particularly if the issues that are discussed are emotional, if there is a lot of information presented, or if there are several different options available. It is important that professionals empathize with the difficulty of processing a lot of information, avoid getting irritated, and not convey the message that the family is using up too much time.

All family members need the opportunity to respond to areas of concern. When one parent does all of the talking, it cannot be assumed that the other parent has nothing to add. The facilitator can make an effort to elicit comments from a family member who has been quiet by asking open questions intended to draw the family member out. (See Chapter 3 for a discussion of open questions.) If the family member chooses to remain quiet, however, it is important to respect this preference.

Service providers need to be honest about their knowledge and limitations. If a professional does not know an answer or have a solution for a concern, it is acceptable to say "I don't know" and explain the steps that will be taken to address the issue. A commitment to team efforts, goals, and creative solutions should be evident. Professionals also should avoid raising a new area or subject near the end of the meeting if there is not time to fully address the issue. Instead, another meeting date and time can be set to address additional areas of concern.

Limiting Professional Jargon   Language that is clear and easily understood by all team members should be used by professionals in the meeting. If a language difference exists, an interpreter needs to be present before, during, and after the meeting to assist with any questions or concerns. Although it is important to limit the use of professional jargon and acronyms, one way to empower family members is to provide a list of common terms and abbreviations. Such information can help families participate more actively during the current meeting as well as throughout the time their child receives services. Professionals also can learn terms unique to a particular family (e.g., nicknames for special objects or people, how the child communicates in the family setting). Although personal preferences vary across families, it is respectful to use "people-first" language when speaking to or about a child with a disabling condition and his or her family members (e.g., child with cerebral palsy rather than CP child).

Avoiding Communication Barriers   Service providers need to be aware of potential barriers to communicating effectively with families during this process. Many of these barriers are described more extensively in Chapter 3. Behaviors such as frequently checking the time, avoiding eye contact, or speaking in a derogatory or impatient manner can create barriers to partnership because family members sense that they are not really appreciated as equal members of their child's educational team. The use of many of the skills described in Chapter 3, such as active listening, effective questions, and reflection, helps to communicate respect. If a professional does not understand what a family member has said, he or she can ask for clarification. This communicates that the speaker's input is valued as central to the decision-making process. It also sends the message that the family member's decisions, even when different from those of the service providers, are respected.

Concluding the Meeting As the end of the meeting draws near, the facilitator should review the points covered in the meeting and ask the family if all of their concerns have been addressed. It may also be informative to ask the family if they have any specific concerns about the goals or plans developed at the meeting. The facilitator can then explain what will happen next, who they should contact if questions arise, and how to contact the other team members. All team members need to know what the plan is and who is responsible for each component. The facilitator can then thank everyone for attending and for their time and input. It is also helpful to ask the family members how they thought the meeting went and to solicit suggestions for future meetings. If there is disagreement on how to proceed, the facilitator can ask what the family has tried before and what has and has not worked. Professionals should model collaborative problem solving (see Chapter 7), and, if a conclusion cannot be reached at the meeting, another date and time can be set to further address the issue after more information or strategies are available.

As written documents are prepared, any implicit messages need to be considered. Complex, lengthy documents frequently are overwhelming and time-consuming for families to process. Moreover, when outcomes are established for families (as in the IFSP), it is critical that they not become lists of performance objectives for families (Beckman & Bristol, 1991; McGonigel & Garland, 1988). Instead, they need to be viewed in terms of the services that will be provided for children and families.

Following the Meeting

One important way of establishing trust and building the relationship with the family is to ensure that follow-up is provided for any commitments made during the meeting (e.g., to provide further information, to initiate services, to investigate a placement alternative). It can be quite frustrating for parents to wait for long periods for appropriate follow-up. Even if the service provider is awaiting further information, he or she can call the parents to let them know that their request has not been forgotten and to update them on its status.

Follow-up calls may be useful under other circumstances as well. For example, if a family member was visibly upset or appeared confused at the meeting, a call to ask how he or she feels or if there are additional questions can communicate sensitivity and contribute to the development of a positive relationship. Thus, service providers can communicate respect for the family member's feelings and for their relationship with the family.

CONCLUSIONS

Planning meetings and conferences are important parts of the overall relationship that is established between professionals and a family. This chapter describes some basic strategies for working with families during these meetings. These strategies are intended to facilitate a sense of true collaboration and partnership. Of course, they must be used consistently with the policies of the program or agency in which services are being provided. At the same time, creating truly collaborative and positive exchanges means that professionals often need to extend themselves beyond the requirements of the law. Although this may require additional time and effort, the good will that is created is likely to have long-term positive implications for the relationship between the family and the service providers with whom they work.

ACTIVITIES AND DISCUSSION

1. Divide into small groups of four to six participants. Each group should select one of the family case studies at the end of this book (Case Studies I–V) and assume appropriate roles based on the case study (e.g., parent, service coordinator, teacher, therapist, nurse). Enact an IEP or IFSP meeting based on the issues described in the case study. After the role-playing experience, discuss the following:
    a. Describe the dynamics of the meeting. For example, did one person dominate the discussion? Was one participant especially quiet?
    b. What feelings did the behavior of other participants elicit?
    c. What efforts were made to influence the behavior of other participants? (For example, did one member try to elicit more participation from a quiet member? Did someone try

to soften the behavior of another participant who was abrasive or dominating?) What feelings did these efforts elicit?

d. Were all participants satisfied with the outcome of the meeting? Why or why not?

e. What strategies were used that were especially effective? Which were less effective? What could have been done differently?

2. For this cooperative problem-solving activity, you need one set of materials for every four participants.

a. Materials include
- a 12-piece child's puzzle
- a box large enough to cover the puzzle with two hand-holes cut out on each side of the box
- a towel or sheet to cover the box

Put the disassembled puzzle inside the box and ask participants to insert their hands in the holes to complete the task. Do not provide any strategies for solving the problem, just ask participants to complete the task and explain that it should take about 10 minutes. Drape a towel or cloth over the sides so that participants cannot peek into the holes to solve the problem. Participants must put the puzzle together by working cooperatively as a team. Because no one member has enough information to accomplish the task alone, participants need to communicate desired information about the pieces they are finding and come up with a joint plan for solving the puzzle.

After the groups complete the puzzle, discuss the process and address the following questions:

b. What strategies enabled the group to work cooperatively?

c. What factors interfered?

d. What lessons does this experience offer about working together on a team?

3. Think of two times when you were part of a team or committee, one that worked together well and one that did not work well. Discuss the following:

a. Describe the team briefly.

b. Did the team have a specific function or task?

c. Did team members have clearly defined roles?

d. What was the power structure, and how were decisions made?

e. Were there conflicts, and how were they resolved?

f. What do you think the barriers were to team functioning? What worked well?

REFERENCES

Bailey, D.B. (1987). Collaborative goal-setting with families: Resolving differences in values and priorities for services. *Topics in Early Childhood Special Education, 7*(2), 59–71.

Beckman, P.J. (in press). The service system and its effects on families: An ecological perspective. In M. Brambring, H. Rauh, & A. Beelman (Eds.), *Early childhood intervention: Theory, evaluation and practice.* Berlin: de Gruyter.

Beckman, P.J., Boyes, G.B., & Herres, A. (1993). The IEP and IFSP meetings. In P.J. Beckman & G.B. Boyes (Eds.), *Deciphering the system: A guide for families of young children with disabilities* (pp. 81–100). Cambridge, MA: Brookline Books.

Beckman, P.J., & Bristol, M.M. (1991). Issues in developing the IFSP: A framework for establishing family outcomes. *Topics in Early Childhood Special Education, 11*(3), 19–31.

Beckman, P.J., Newcomb, S., Frank, N., Brown, L., Stepanek, J.S., & Barnwell, D. (1996). Preparing personnel to work with families. In D. Bricker & A. Widerstrom (Eds.), *Preparing personnel to work with infants and young children and their families: A team approach* (pp. 273–293). Baltimore: Paul H. Brookes Publishing Co.

Beckman, P.J., Robinson, C.C., Rosenberg, S., & Filer, J. (1994). Family involvement in early intervention: The evolution of family-centered services. In L.J. Johnson, R.J. Gallagher, M.J. LaMontagne, J.B. Jordan, J.J. Gallagher, P.L. Hutinger, & M.B. Karnes (Eds.), *Meeting early intervention challenges: Issues from birth to three* (pp. 13–31). Baltimore: Paul H. Brookes Publishing Co.

Brinkerhoff, J.L., & Vincent, L.J. (1986). Increasing parental decision-making at the individualized educational program meeting. *Journal of the Division for Early Childhood, 11*(1), 46–58.

Dinnebeil, L.A., & Rule, S. (1994). Variables that influence collaboration between parents and service coordinators. *Journal of Early Intervention, 18*(4), 349–361.

Dunst, C.J., Johanson, C., Trivette, C.M., & Hamby, D. (1991). Family-oriented early intervention policies and practices: Family-centered or not. *Exceptional Children, 58*(2), 115–126.

Fish, M.S. (1990). Family-school conflict: Implications for the family. *Reading, Writing, and Learning Disabilities, 6,* 71–79.

Gill, K.M. (1993). Health professionals' attitudes toward parent participation in hospitalized children's care. *Children's Health Care, 22*(4), 257–271.

Gliedman, J., & Roth, W. (1980). *The unexpected minority: Handicapped children in America.* San Diego, CA: Harcourt Brace Jovanovich.

Harry, B. (1992a). *Cultural diversity, families, and the special education system: Communication and empowerment.* New York: Teachers College Press.

Harry, B. (1992b). Developing cultural self-awareness: The first step in values clarification for early interventionists. *Topics in Early Intervention, 12*(3), 333–350.

Harry, B., Allen, N., & McLaughlin, M. (1995). Communication versus compliance: African-American parents' involvement in special education. *Exceptional Children, 61*(4), 364–377.

Harry, B., & Kalyanpur, M. (1994). Cultural underpinnings of special education: Implications for professional interactions with culturally diverse families. *Disability and Society, 9*(2), 145–165.

Individuals with Disabilities Education Act Amendments of 1991, PL 102–119. (October 7, 1991). Title 20, U.S.C. §§ 1400 et seq.: *U.S. Statutes at Large, 105,* 587–608.

Lash, M., & Wertlieb, D. (1993). A model for family-centered service coordination for children who are disabled by traumatic injuries. *ACCH Advocate, 1*(1), 19–41.

Leviton, A., Mueller, M., & Kauffmann, C. (1992). The family-centered consultation model: Practical applications for professionals. *Infants and Young Children, 4*(3), 1–8.

Lynch, E.W., & Hanson, M.J. (Eds.). (1992). *Developing cross-cultural competence: A guide for working with young children and their families.* Baltimore: Paul H. Brookes Publishing Co.

Lynch, E.W., & Stein, R. (1982). Perspectives on parent participation in special education. *Exceptional Education Quarterly, 3*(2), 56–63.

McGonigel, M.J., & Garland, C.W. (1988). The individualized family service plan and the early intervention team: Team and family issues and recommended practices. *Infants and Young Children, 1*(1), 10–21.

McGonigel, M.J., Kaufmann, R.K., & Johnson, B.H. (1991). *Guidelines and recommendations for the individualized service plan.* Bethesda, MD: Association for the Care of Children's Health.

Mehan, H., Hartwick, A., & Meihls, J.L. (1986). *Handicapping the handicapped: Decision-making in students' education careers.* Stanford, CA: Stanford University Press.

Minke, K.M., & Scott, M.M. (1993). The development of individualized family service plans: Roles for parents and staff. *Journal of Special Education, 27*(1), 82–106.

Petr, C.G., & Barney, D.D. (1993). Reasonable efforts for children with disabilities: The parents' perspective. *Social Work, 38*(3), 247–254.

Rothbaum, P.A., Raia, O., Amorapanth, V., Picone, D., & Ziskin, L.Z. (1994). Parents of young children with developmental delays speak to health care professionals. *ACCH Advocate, 1*(2), 47–52.

Salett, S., & Henderson, A. (1980). *A report on the Education for All Handicapped Children Act: Are parents involved?* Columbia, MD: National Committee for Citizens in Education.

Seligman, M., & Darling, R.B. (1989). *Ordinary families, special children: A systems approach to childhood disability.* New York: Guilford Press.

Shelton, T.L., & Stepanek, J.S. (1994). *Family-centered care for children needing specialized health and developmental services* (3rd ed.). Bethesda, MD: Association for the Care of Children's Health.

Souffer, R.M. (1982). IEP decisions in which parents desire greater participation. *Education and Training of the Mentally Retarded, 17*(2), 67–70.

Strickland, B. (1983). Legal issues that affect parents. In M. Seligman (Ed.), *The family with a handicapped child: Understanding and treatment* (pp. 27–39). New York: Grune & Stratton.

Turnbull, A.P., & Strickland, B. (1981). Parents and the educational system. In J.L. Paul (Ed.), *Understanding and working with parents of children with special needs* (pp. 261–263). New York: Holt, Rinehart & Winston.

Turnbull, A.P., & Turnbull, H.R. (1990). *Families, professionals, and exceptionality: A special partnership.* New York: Macmillan.

Vaughn, S., Bos, C.S., Harrell, J.E., & Lasky, B.A. (1988). Parent participation in the initial placement/IEP conference. *Journal of Learning Disabilities, 21*(2), 82–89.

Walker, B., & Singer, G.H.S. (1993). Improving collaborative communication between professionals and parents. In G.H.S. Singer & L.E. Powers (Eds.), *Families, disability, and empowerment: Active coping skills and strategies for family interventions* (pp. 285–316). Baltimore: Paul H. Brookes Publishing Co.

Witt, J.C., Miller, C.D., McIntyre, R.M., & Smith, D. (1984). Effects of variables on parental perceptions of staffings. *Exceptional Children, 51*(1), 27–32.

Chapter 7

Resolving Conflicts with Families

**Paula J. Beckman,
Nancy Frank,
and Jennifer Smith Stepanek**

The prospect of becoming engaged in a prolonged dispute with a family can raise anxiety and elicit insecurity about professional competence for many service providers. Few individuals who have chosen careers in the service professions relish the idea of conflict with those they serve. Understanding the barriers to effective communication and practicing the skills identified in Chapter 3 can help professionals avoid conflicts with families. In the event that conflicts arise, however, an understanding of strategies for resolving them can be extremely useful.

The ability to handle disagreements successfully contributes to maintaining positive working relationships with families and generates confidence in one's own professional skills. It is the responsibility of the service provider to make every reasonable effort to work collaboratively with families and to attempt to resolve any disagreements positively. The provider sets the tone for this process through actions, words, and overall demeanor. The provider needs to keep in mind that the parents' goal usually is to help their child achieve his or her maximum potential. Disagreements often arise when parents feel that a particular policy or recommendation is at odds with this goal. The chapter briefly describes the causes of conflict between parents and service providers, the impact of such conflict, and strategies for resolving conflicts. It also briefly describes strategies that can be used in the event that a disagreement escalates to the point of a due process hearing.

CAUSES OF CONFLICTS BETWEEN
FAMILIES AND SERVICE PROVIDERS

There has been increased emphasis since the mid-1980s on the importance of collaboration both among professionals (Friend & Cook, 1996; Idol, Nevin, & Paolucci-Whitcomb, 1994) and between professionals and families (Shelton & Stepanek, 1994; Stepanek, 1995; Turnbull & Turnbull, 1990). Collaboration can result in more effective service delivery and more creative solutions to problems. It also creates the need for individuals to work closely together who may differ in their goals, concerns, values, experiences, priorities, beliefs, and worldviews, however (see Chapter 4; see also Friend & Cook, 1996; Walker & Singer, 1993). Such conditions increase the potential for conflict.

Conflict can arise for a variety of reasons. Administrative policies can often prevent service providers from responding to parents' concerns as they would like, can set parameters on services to be offered, or can interfere with communication. Examples of such circumstances abound. Parents may want their child fully included in a program with children who are developing typically, but the program may not serve this population and may not work with local child care settings. Alternatively, a working parent may want home visits in the evening, but administrative policies may require that services be provided during the day.

Conflict also can result from differences that occur between individuals on issues such as what is best for the child or from differences in interpersonal communication styles. (See Chapter 3 for in-depth discussion.) For instance, a service provider who is most comfortable when decisions are made quickly may find him- or herself frustrated with a parent who takes more time to make decisions.

In addition, the often personal and potentially sensitive nature of work with children and families can trigger conflict. When parents are receiving information or making decisions that have implications for their children's future, emotional overtones (e.g., hope, fear, pride, disappointment) are likely. Although this is true for all families, it is particularly true when discussions involve the survival, health, or long-term development of the child. Professionals may be uncomfortable delivering unwelcome information or making difficult recommendations. Thus, the need to discuss topics that are sensitive (e.g., problem behaviors, test results, lack of progress) can sometimes trigger difficult exchanges between families and professionals (Walker & Singer, 1993).

Several authors have noted that parents' experiences with other professionals also may make it difficult to establish a collaborative relationship (Gerry, 1987; Seligman & Darling, 1989; Turnbull & Turnbull, 1990). For example, if parents have had difficulty obtaining needed services or have been treated insensitively by professionals in the past, they may have developed a distrust of professionals or a belief that they must fight to get services for their child.

In addition, it can be difficult for practitioners when parents are critical, angry, or disagree with their recommendations (Walker & Singer, 1993). If such exchanges seem to challenge the professional's competence, the professional also can find the conflict to be emotional. Service providers who interpret parents' anger or disappointment as criticism of their program or services may find it difficult to negotiate with the family.

Another source of disagreement can occur when parents feel that decisions have been made without their participation (Gerry, 1987). In many instances, service providers engage in such actions unintentionally. For example, during an informal discussion in the staff lounge, the teacher and therapist may think of a new recommendation. It can create difficulties, however, if the parents feel excluded from participation. In other circumstances, one or more participants may not really view the parents as an integral part of the decision-making process. Service providers need to be aware that excluding parents can produce distrust, disagreement, and conflict.

It is also possible that parents and professionals who have established a partnership that works well under most circumstances may disagree about a specific decision. For example, the parent may believe that the child needs more individual physical therapy and a service provider may believe that therapy goals can be implemented by the teacher in the classroom. Conflict resolution strategies can be used to achieve a satisfactory solution that builds on the strengths of the ongoing relationship and which does not weaken the relationship between the service provider and the family.

IMPACT OF CONFLICT

Conflict can be difficult and time-consuming for everyone concerned. This section identifies the potential impact of conflicts.

Negative Impact

Based on interviews with families involved in adversarial relationships with professionals, interviews with family therapists and advocates, and interviews with professionals, Fish (1990) described a number of stressful effects that were attributable to conflict. One was the expenditure of time and energy. Some mothers reported that the time required to deal with conflict resulted in less time for siblings; several parents felt as if they were neglecting the needs of their other children. In some instances, conflicts with professionals influenced the relationship between spouses. For example, much of the conversation that occurred between parents revolved around the conflict. Fish (1990) reported that when one spouse had to play a more active role in the conflict, it sometimes elicited feelings of resentment toward the less active spouse. Furthermore, in some cases, conflict with professionals interfered with parents' responsibilities at work. For example, some parents had to spend time on the telephone to deal with professionals and had to take time off. Time away from work may be necessary for many reasons: to obtain second opinions, obtain additional assessment information, and/or attend meetings. Some parents reported being more distracted and less effective at work because of their involvement in the conflict.

Fish (1990) also found that parents often were caught in a bind; they were afraid that their efforts on behalf of their child could result in negative backlash for the child, but they were also determined to advocate for their child's needs. For example, parents may fear that professionals will behave differently toward their child, that their child will be singled out in some way, or that the long-term relationship with the program will be affected.

Finally, conflicts that cannot be resolved and are carried to the point of due process can result in considerable financial costs. Strickland (1983) found that the costs associated with obtaining expert witnesses, hiring attorneys, and the other expenses involved in preparation were often high. She noted that it could cost families up to $4,000 to exercise their due process rights. That cost is likely to be even higher in the mid-1990s than it was during Strickland's study.

Conflict as Opportunity

Although conflict is almost never enjoyable and frequently can be a source of stress, it is important to recognize that, when managed effectively, the lessons learned sometimes strengthen relationships. Friend and Cook (1996) identified several potentially positive outcomes that can emerge when a conflict has been well managed. First, they believe that the decisions that result from a conflict being resolved are often good because there has been an effort to incorporate varying perspectives and to generate alternatives. Second, participants often become committed to carrying out decisions because they have a sense of ownership as a result of their participation in resolving the conflict. Third, in the process of communicating their position to others, participants must sharpen their own thinking, resulting in better discussion and generating more options. Fourth, when participants handle conflict well, it can result in more open, trusting relationships. Finally, experience managing conflict can teach valuable lessons that may be used in future situations. For instance, service providers may learn the importance of communication skills or about their own strategies for resolving conflict.

Other literature concerning conflict also suggests potential opportunities. For example, effective management of controversy can result in better perspective taking, better problem solving, more creative solutions, and higher levels of satisfaction (Idol et al., 1994). Of course, the key to finding opportunities in conflict lies to a great extent in learning to manage it effectively. The next section describes different styles of managing conflict.

CONFLICT MANAGEMENT STYLES

Just as individuals differ in their personal styles (see also Chapter 3), they also have different styles of responding to conflict. Learning about differences in styles of managing conflict can be an important initial step in learning how to achieve resolution. Friend and Cook (1996) described five conflict management styles that are common among individuals, based on the work of Thomas and Kilmann (1974). These styles vary along two dimensions: 1) cooperativeness and 2) assertiveness. Although most individuals have a preferred style, it is possible for different styles to be used in different contexts.

The *avoidance style* is the least cooperative, as well as the least assertive, style. Friend and Cook (1996) suggested that individuals who use this style tend to ignore the differences between their goals and the goals of others. One disadvantage of this style is that the conflict often remains unresolved, because the other participants' goals are not recognized. The conflict may become exacerbated because it has not been addressed effectively.

However, Friend and Cook (1996) believed avoidance that can be appropriate under certain circumstances. For instance, avoidance may be a good strategy if there is inadequate opportunity to address a conflict constructively or if an issue is relatively unimportant. It also may be an effective temporary measure if a participant has become angry or upset and needs time to regain composure.

In contrast, the *competitive style* of resolving conflicts is generally high on the assertiveness dimension and low on the cooperativeness dimension. It is characterized by attempts to overpower others without regard for potential negative repercussions. In this style, the emphasis is on winning or having the individual's solution or recommendation accepted. The disadvantage of this style is that it can damage the evolution of collaborative relationships and meaningful exchanges with others. Friend and Cook (1996) suggested, however, that a competitive style may be appropriate in certain circumstances (e.g., serious questions of ethics, when a decision is required in a situation where one person bears the bulk of the responsibility).

The *accommodating style* is low on the assertiveness dimension and high on the cooperative dimension. Individuals who use this style tend to give in when conflicts arise. As a result, accommodating typically brings conflict to an end quickly. The emphasis is on ending the conflict rather than on negotiating a shared solution. Friend and Cook (1996) see this style as useful when the issue is unimportant or when an assessment of the situation leads an individual to believe that he or she cannot alter it. A disadvantage, however, is that one participant may feel taken advantage of or that his or her ideas have been devalued.

A *compromising style* falls in the middle of the assertiveness and cooperativeness dimensions. Those who use a compromising style typically are willing to give up on some things while expecting others to do the same. This style is expedient, and both parties in the conflict get some of their goals met. As a result, Friend and Cook (1996) wrote that it is useful when time is important, when the issue is not too problematic, and when two competitive individuals are in conflict. Each side wins some and loses some. The disadvantage can be that neither side feels completely satisfied, and thus the conflict may reemerge later.

Finally, a *collaborative style* is characterized by high levels of cooperativeness and assertiveness. This style sometimes can result in solutions different from those originally generated by either party individually. Collaborative solutions are forged when each side examines all points of view and mutually develops solutions that incorporate these views. Friend and Cook pointed out that collaboration can be time-consuming, however, and requires a certain amount of mutual trust. As a result, it may not be effective or possible in all instances.

Although individuals may have a preferred style of managing conflict, they may learn and practice other styles as well. Using other styles requires an awareness of one's preferred style and a sensitivity to the style of others. For professionals who work with families, developing a collaborative style allows professionals to respect the family's decision-making role and allows families to make an important contribution to the decision-making process.

CONFLICT MANAGEMENT STRATEGIES

Strategies for communicating effectively with families are described extensively in Chapter 3. Despite the best efforts of even the most seasoned professionals, however, it is possible to become involved in difficult exchanges with families. This section describes strategies that service providers can use if a conflict with a family occurs.

Recognize Indirect Signals

It is important for service providers to be sensitive to and recognize signals of a breakdown in communication. Sensitivity to such signals, in some circumstances, can help avert more serious conflicts later. Several authors have identified cues that indicate that communication with another party is ineffective (Hepworth & Larsen, 1986; Shulman, 1992; Turnbull & Turnbull, 1990). When another party changes the subject, verbally or nonverbally rejects the message, ignores suggestions, appears detached, becomes defensive, appears confused, argues, expresses anger, or misses appointments, there may be an indirect message that something is not working. These cues need to be placed in the context of other events, however. For example, a parent may miss appointments because of transportation difficulties or child care problems for siblings. Someone who seems defensive may be experiencing other personal problems not directly related to services for the child.

Because there may be many explanations for the signals a family member sends, it is important that the professional carefully assess each individual situation. The professional can ask him- or herself the following questions:

- Are there unresolved issues pending?
- Has the family member mentioned other issues that may be producing stress (e.g., an impending layoff from work, the illness of another family member)?
- Has the family shared expectations or hopes about the child that are not being realized?

It is also important for service providers to check their perceptions with the family member to see if they are interpreting the situation accurately. For example, if the family frequently misses appointments, the providers could ask if another time would work better.

Depersonalize the Exchange

When exchanges with families become negative, it is easy for professionals to feel personally attacked and to become defensive. Walker and Singer (1993) believed that when this occurs, participants often engage in negative self-talk about themselves and the other parties in the exchange. For instance, a service provider who is frustrated with a family's push for a particular type of service may find him- or herself thinking that the family is being unrealistic. Rather than personalizing the exchange, Walker and Singer suggest framing the upsetting behavior as a logical response to stress or frustration. Although the service provider may feel that the family is being critical of him or her, the provider needs to remember that underlying the family's concerns is their sense of responsibility for their child.

Use Collaborative Problem-Solving Techniques

One way to approach conflict resolution is for the professional to acknowledge the common goal of appropriate service for the child and to think about it from a collaborative decision-making or problem-solving perspective (Friend & Cook, 1996; Hepworth & Larsen, 1986; Idol et al., 1994; Raver, 1991; Spencer & Coye, 1988; Wasik, Bryant, & Lyons, 1990). Although the specific steps vary slightly from author to author, several steps commonly specified are identified in this section.

Identify the Problem This step is critical because subsequent steps in the problem-solving process depend on how well the problem has been defined (Friend & Cook, 1996; Idol et al., 1994; Nezu & D'Zurilla, 1981). Different participants may perceive the problem differently. Friend and Cook (1996) suggested stating the problem in ways that identify the discrepancy between the current situation and the desired situation. It also is important that the problem statement be free of potential solutions so that the solutions that are generated are not limited.

There are a number of strategies that can facilitate the problem-solving process. One strategy is to describe the problem in concrete and specific language and to ensure that participants understand the terms used (Friend & Cook, 1996). Terms such as *aggressive* or *disruptive* frequently mean different things to different participants. Identifying differences in individual perceptions can help participants understand the basis of a conflict. Therefore, if one participant describes a child as "so active," the specific behaviors that the child exhibits that are active should be clarified. It is also helpful in understanding the conflict to assess the relevant dimensions of the problem. For example, who is affected by the conflict? What are the specific requests? What needs do various participants have that should be considered as part of the solution?

Another problem-solving strategy is to challenge underlying assumptions that are fundamental to the conflict (Friend & Cook, 1996). For example, parents may want their child with complex medical needs who uses supplemental oxygen to be included in a general classroom setting. School officials may resist because they have concerns about liability or simply because it has never happened before. Identifying and challenging underlying assumptions can help produce a more precise definition of the problem and the source of the conflict. In this example, school officials may be assuming that the child is not mobile and would need special assistance to move around. Alternatively, they may assume that if the oxygen is inadvertently disconnected, there will be risks to the child's life or health. Once these assumptions are identified, they can be examined. It may turn out that, for this particular child, a disruption in oxygen for a brief period would not be problematic. Moreover, they may learn that the child has a way of carrying the oxygen himself and is as mobile as other children. Thus, examining the assumptions underlying the source of the conflict can help resolve the issue.

Finally, it is helpful for professionals to use language that promotes joint problem solving. In their work on collaborative consultation, Idol et al. (1994) suggested that some conflicts take the form of turf building (e.g., the service provider asserts, "That's a motor problem."). These authors believe that using language that assumes joint ownership of a problem can promote joint problem solving.

Generate Alternative Solutions After the problem is identified, the next step is to find potential solutions. One way is by using brainstorming to generate alternatives without evaluating them (Friend & Cook, 1996; Raver, 1991; Spencer & Coye, 1988). Remaining open during this process avoids prematurely eliminating solutions that may have considerable potential. At this point in the process, service providers may want to encourage more participants as potential sources of new directions or ideas.

Evaluate Solutions Both positive and negative aspects of potential alternatives need to be systematically evaluated. This provides an initial basis for eliminating some alternatives. Participants then can evaluate remaining solutions in terms of the tasks and resources involved in each solution.

Select a Solution   Friend and Cook (1996) suggested that the solutions that remain on the list after the evaluation process can then be reviewed and one (or more) selected. They recommend that criteria such as potential intrusiveness, feasibility, and individual preferences be used to make this selection.

Implement and Monitor the Solution   Once a solution is identified, it is important to follow the agreed-upon plan exactly (Raver, 1991). Raver suggested that failure to do so can create new conflicts. In addition, participants need to monitor the solution's effectiveness on an ongoing basis. It is also important that potential criteria are identified for determining whether the solution is useful, effective, or successful in resolving the original problem. Participants can monitor the implementation of the solution based on these criteria. They also need to remain alert to any unintended outcomes (both positive and negative) and to include these unintended outcomes in their evaluation of the solution. Suggesting a follow-up meeting focused on monitoring the agreed-upon plan conveys that all parties are still working together and are jointly responsible for the implementation of the resolution to the conflict.

General Tips for Conflict Resolution

In addition to systematically applying the steps in problem solving, many general strategies have been identified in the literature that can help maximize the effectiveness of the problem-solving process (Friend & Cook, 1996; Turnbull & Turnbull, 1990; Walker & Singer, 1993).

Conflicts can be emotionally laden, both for parents and for professionals. For parents, these feelings frequently are centered on their concerns about their child's life, health, and development. In contrast, the feelings of service providers often are centered on issues of professional expertise and competence. Conflicts between service providers and families place these fundamental issues in disagreement. As a result, both parties need to be aware of the emotional level and take steps to control it.

Several strategies can help reduce emotional tension. First, focusing on issues on which there is some potential for agreement can emphasize the common ground between participants (Friend & Cook, 1996). Second, demonstrating respect for the concerns and feelings of the family is essential. Many strategies for communicating respect are discussed in Chapter 3 and are applicable here. In addition, Turnbull and Turnbull (1990) suggested that strategies such as writing down what is said, asking for clarification when something is not clearly understood, and asking for and writing down suggestions are positive ways to communicate respect during a difficult encounter. Respect also can be demonstrated by acknowledging the importance of the issue that the family has raised, acknowledging personal mistakes, and acknowledging any negative consequences that personal actions or behavior may have caused (Walker & Singer, 1993).

Third, professionals should note their own emotional reactions as well as those of the family (e.g., Are these feelings defensive, anxious, or argumentative? Has there been an increase in volume of your voice?). Valuable clues to these reactions include both verbal (e.g., substance of message) and nonverbal (e.g., body posture, gestures) aspects of the conversation. It is important for professionals to bring intense feelings under control and, as much as possible, reduce the emotional component of the exchange (Friend & Cook, 1996; Walker & Singer, 1993). Friend and Cook suggested that rather than responding with anger when being questioned or criticized, professionals can respond positively and acknowledge the feelings expressed by other participants. For example, when a father questions his child's speech program because he does not see any progress, the therapist can respond by acknowledging the father's frustration and disappointment. The professional can also share his or her own sense of disappointment and ideas for possible changes. This strategy helps parents feel that their concerns are heard and shared. From this common point, other solutions can be considered.

Another helpful strategy is to focus on the issues rather than on the individuals in the exchange. Focusing on individuals can make the exchange more adversarial and suggests that the problem is personal (Friend & Cook, 1996). Walker and Singer (1993) suggested that focusing on the substantive content of the other party's message can help participants remain neutral during a potentially upsetting exchange. These authors also suggest that when discussing a particular concern, concrete examples are helpful. Thus, rather than saying, "Tony has been very aggressive," it may be more informative to say, "Tony seems to hit when he cannot communicate his needs."

Finally, professionals should not engage in negative behaviors, including arguing, judging, being defensive, generalizing, personalizing, belittling, criticizing, blaming, raising one's voice, or minimizing a concern (Turnbull & Turnbull, 1990; Walker & Singer, 1993). Such behavior is sure to make parents feel that the service provider views them as the problem and does not understand the real concerns about their child that are being expressed.

THIRD-PARTY SOLUTIONS

Despite everyone's best efforts, there may be occasions when it is impossible to resolve a conflict with a family without help. Under these circumstances, a third party may be the only solution. This can be done informally by bringing a neutral party into a conference with the family. There are also more formal mechanisms that can be used when necessary, including mediation and due process.

Mediation

Mediation is a collaborative process that is an alternative to more adversarial measures, such as due process hearings, in states in which it is offered. Although the way in which mediation is implemented varies from jurisdiction to jurisdiction, it is typically a voluntary way to resolve disputes. The intention generally is to help parents and service providers reach a decision that is mutually acceptable and to protect the interests of the child.

General Guidelines When mediation is available, the procedures and guidelines may differ from system to system. One example is provided by the system of mediation in special education used in the state of Maryland (Hebeler, 1990). This system illustrates several key components of the mediation process. First, both parents and service providers must agree to comply with established guidelines for participating in the process and with the resulting agreement. Second, because mediation is a collaborative process, participation is voluntary. Either the parent or the provider can request mediation, and either can decline.

Third, a request for mediation cannot interfere with the right to a timely due process hearing. As a result, in Maryland, mediation should occur as soon as possible after a request has been made and within 30 days of a written request. If all participants agree, time lines can be extended. Mediation is conducted in one session that typically lasts 3–4 hours. If all participants agree, however, one or more subsequent sessions can be scheduled. Sessions are held at times and in locations that are convenient for all participants.

The Maryland guidelines require that participants include the parents and someone from the school system with the authority to make a decision. To make the meeting manageable, it is advised that no more than two persons accompany each participant. Professional advocates or attorneys cannot be present.

Because the purpose of mediation is to facilitate discussion and true collaboration, these guidelines specify that there are no notes kept, no record of the discussions, and no recordings of the session.

Details and information presented during the mediation session cannot be used as evidence at any subsequent legal proceedings. Similarly, participants waive the right to compel the participation of the mediator(s) in subsequent legal proceedings, and the mediator(s) agrees not to serve as a witness in such proceedings.

Finally, the guidelines state that mediators cannot compel any action by either participant. Agreements are developed if the participants are in accord on at least some of the issues. The agreements are signed at the end of the session, and, when applicable, the parties agree to incorporate the terms of the agreement in the individualized education program. If not implemented as agreed, the parties may reenter mediation or can proceed to due process.

Steps in Mediation   Hebeler (1990) provided an overview of the general steps in the mediation process. Although the steps described here are again specific to Maryland's mediation process, they provide a general overview of the kind of process that can be expected.

After all participants are introduced, the ground rules for conducting the mediation are explained. The next step typically involves fact finding. During this step, each participant describes the child, any concerns, and anything that may resolve the conflict. Participants then discuss the issues that have been raised. In the collaboration phase, there is an effort to summarize comments that have been made and focus on areas of agreement. Participants then collaborate on ideas for solving remaining issues. At resolution, an agreement is developed, agreed on, and signed. Participants work out as many details as possible, including specific steps that will be taken and the precise wording of the agreement. Under the Maryland guidelines, participants have 3 days until the agreement becomes binding.

Throughout the process, mediators continually clarify points made, summarize what has been said, and focus on areas of agreement. There is also an effort to keep the focus on the child. This includes discussion of the participants' hopes and fears for the child as well as their perception of the child's strengths and needs.

Advantages of Mediation   The previous description illustrates several important advantages of mediation. The process is less formal than a due process hearing. Limitations on the use of information provided during the mediation session, the absence of attorneys, and other similar precautions promote honest discussion and collaborative problem solving. This can help to build trust and promote better parent–professional relationships. Mediation is less time-consuming and less expensive than a due process hearing. Mediation also provides a framework for further conversations and collaboration.

Due Process

If previous efforts to resolve a dispute with a family are unsuccessful, participants may find themselves in due process hearings. Due process hearings are formal mechanisms that protect the rights of the child and the family. Because they are formal, they can be costly, time-consuming, and emotionally draining for everyone involved. Edmister (1993) noted that many disputes that lead to due process hearings involve disagreements over evaluations and assessments, eligibility for services, placement, and what the child's program should include. For example, because eligibility requirements are somewhat different under Part H of the Individuals with Disabilities Education Act (IDEA) (PL 101-476) than they are under Part B of IDEA, children's eligibility for services may change as they move into preschool. Parents who wish to maintain a certain type or level of service may decide to push to retain services for their children when they enter preschool.

The procedures for conducting due process hearings vary from state to state and from jurisdiction to jurisdiction. In some states, there are different requirements under Part H than there are under Part B. Professionals who become involved in such a process need to become familiar with the specific procedures that apply to their state. Some general strategies may be useful in preparing for the hearing, however. The service provider also needs to maintain a working relationship with the family before, during, and after the hearing. This rest of this section identifies some potential issues and suggests guidelines for preparation and personal conduct.

Involvement in a due process hearing can elicit numerous feelings from service providers. Edmister, Robbins, and Ekstrand (1986) identified feelings such as fear, anxiety, resentment, anger, and defensiveness. For example, Edmister et al. (1986) suggested that professionals may be afraid because they have to defend their qualifications, feel unprepared, or may let their colleagues or the parents down. In some circumstances, the service provider may fear that their own offhand or confidential remarks about the administration, the school, or the parent will become public during this hearing. Edmister et al. (1986) also suggested that service providers sometimes experience a conflict between their loyalty to the program and their loyalty to the family or their belief that the parents are right in their challenge.

Such a challenge is also tremendously difficult for the family. Fish (1990) cited a relatively large body of evidence that suggested such conflicts can take a tremendous emotional toll on families and are reflected in family relationships and family functioning. Strickland (1983) reported that due process hearings require tremendous personal and financial resources from families. Furthermore, parents have their own fears about the process. For example, they often fear that taking a challenge to the level of a hearing will have a negative impact on the way their child is perceived and treated in the program (Fish, 1990). They also may be concerned that during the course of a hearing a service provider will betray a confidence or that providers with whom they have positive relationships will be put in a difficult position (Edmister et al., 1986).

Edmister et al. (1986) suggested several strategies for working effectively with families under such circumstances. First, they recommend that service providers continue to behave in a friendly manner, giving appropriate responses to the family regarding the child and the child's progress. They caution, however, that it is important not to be drawn into conversations on issues that are being challenged. If questions arise, they suggest checking with supervisors before answering. They also recommend referring attorneys, advocates, and other representatives of the family to appropriate supervisors on appeal issues. Edmister et al. (1986) also urged service providers to understand the importance of maintaining confidential information. Because service providers often have developed a personal relationship with the family, it can be tempting to confide personal concerns about the program. Edmister et al. (1986) urged service providers to avoid such situations because further problems can be created if conflict escalates to the level of due process.

CONCLUSIONS

The ability to manage conflicts is an important skill for professionals who work with families of children with disabilities. Many of the skills for successfully managing conflicts are the same as those involved in other aspects of working with families. These skills include self-reflection and self-awareness as well as strategies for communication and collaboration. If these have not been effective and disagreements escalate, service providers need to be aware of steps in the conflict resolution process as well as alternatives to due process such as mediation. Although sometimes difficult, it is critical that service providers remember that the family's motivations most often come from their beliefs about what is best for their child and their attempts to achieve this goal. If professionals can join in this goal and communicate this to parents, it is often possible to achieve common ground.

ACTIVITIES AND DISCUSSION

1. Read Case Study II, the Martínez Family. Set up a role-playing exercise based on the concerns that Rosa expressed about the services planned for Ana. This exercise should include the following characters: Rosa Martínez, the service coordinator, a representative from the infant and toddler program, the doctor, and the vision specialist.

   After role playing, discuss the following questions:

   a. What concerns did Rosa Martínez have about the services that were recommended for Ana?

   b. What is the source of Rosa's concern about each type of service?

   c. How did each participant feel during the role-playing exercise?

   d. Were the differences of opinion resolved during the role-playing exercise? How?

2. As an exercise in self-reflection, think of a conflict you have experienced in which you had to deal with a large company or agency and you were the consumer. This can include a variety of conflicts (e.g., a dispute with a bank or credit card agency, a traffic ticket). Discuss the following questions:

   a. What was the source of the conflict? What feelings did the conflict elicit?

   b. What did the person who served you do or say that was helpful? What did you find frustrating?

   c. How was the conflict finally resolved?

3. Assume that several individuals are planning a wedding. The point of this role-playing exercise is to see how conflict arises and to simulate a process in which many individuals are trying to make decisions for another. Follow these steps:

   a. First, have participants in your group assume different roles. One group of two or three individuals should assume the roles of expert wedding planners. These individuals will be responsible for developing a comprehensive plan for the wedding to which they must get other participants to agree. These individuals have a lot of training and experience in planning weddings and should be of considerable help to the participants. Remaining members of the group should assume the roles of family and friends who will be participants. At a minimum, you should have a bride, parents of the bride, a groom, and parents of the groom. You also may have additional participants (e.g., a stepparent, a best friend, a grandparent).

b. With all participants in the same room, have the expert team ask the bride and groom a series of questions about basic preferences. These questions should *not* be specific about the wedding; rather, they should include basic questions on favorite colors, favorite subjects in school, favorite sports, employment, income, income of both families, type of car they drive, how they get news, where they are from, the number of siblings, music preferences, and so on—generally anything that can be used to make assumptions about what the bride and groom might want.

c. Form several small groups to separately discuss their preferences and make plans for the wedding. At least three separate groups should form, including the bride and groom, the families (in whatever configuration), and the group of wedding experts. The professional wedding planners should have a concrete plan to propose (e.g., where the wedding will be held, how many guests, colors, reception plans). This plan should be based on their knowledge of the bride and groom (as acquired in Step b).

d. Bring the groups back together, and have the expert team present their plan. Anyone who disagrees must explain his or her reasons and convince the expert team to change the plan.

e. After playing out this scenario, discuss the following:
   • How did each participant feel during the process?
   • Did conflict arise? If so, how did it occur?
   • What perpetuates the conflict?
   • What causes differences in opinion to turn into conflict?
   • Whose opinion should have taken priority? Did it?

4. Watch a television program in which individuals are having a conflict. What are they doing that creates or perpetuates the conflict? Are they able to resolve it? How? What might help them resolve the conflict?

REFERENCES

Edmister, P.A. (1993). Due process. In P.J. Beckman & G.B. Boyes (Eds.), *Deciphering the system: A guide for families of young children with disabilities* (pp. 117–127). Cambridge, MA: Brookline Books.

Edmister, P., Robbins, M.J., & Ekstrand, R.E. (1986, April). *Due process hearing: Preparation and participation.* Paper presented at the annual convention of the Council for Exceptional Children, New Orleans, LA.

Fish, M.C. (1990). Family-school conflict: Implications for the family. *Reading, Writing, and Learning Disabilities, 6,* 71–79.

Friend, M., & Cook, L. (1996). *Interactions: Collaboration skills for professionals.* New York: Longman Publishing Group.

Gerry, M. (1987). Procedural safeguards: Insuring that handicapped children receive a free appropriate public education. *News Digest* (National Information Center for Handicapped Children and Youth), No. 7, 1–7.

Hebeler, J. (1990). *Maryland special education mediation: Procedures and guidelines.* Unpublished manuscript, Maryland State Department of Education, Annapolis.

Hepworth, D.H., & Larsen, J.A. (1986). *Direct social work practice: Theory and skills.* Chicago: Dorsey Press.

Idol, L., Nevin, A., & Paolucci-Whitcomb, P. (1994). *Collaborative consultation.* Austin, TX: PRO-ED.

Individuals with Disabilities Education Act (IDEA) of 1990, PL 101-476. (October 30, 1990). Title 20, U.S.C. §§1400 et seq.: *U.S. Statutes at Large, 104,* 1103–1151.

Nezu, A., & D'Zurilla, T.J. (1981). Effects of problem definition and formulation on the generation of alternatives in the social problem-solving process. *Cognitive Therapy and Research, 5,* 265–271.

Raver, S.A. (1991). *Strategies for teaching at-risk and handicapped infants and toddlers: A transdisciplinary approach.* New York: Macmillan.

Seligman, M., & Darling, R.B. (1989). Professional-family interaction: Working toward partnership. *Ordinary families, special children: A systems approach to childhood disability* (pp. 214–240). New York: Guilford Press.

Shelton, T.L., & Stepanek, J.S. (1994). *Family-centered care for children needing specialized health and developmental services* (3rd ed.). Bethesda, MD: Association for the Care of Children's Health.

Shulman, L. (1992). *The skills of helping: Individuals, families, and groups.* Itasca, IL: F.E. Peacock Publishers.

Spencer, P., & Coye, R. (1988). Project BRIDGE: A team approach to decision making for early services. *Infants and Young Children, 1*(1), 82–92.

Stepanek, J.S. (1995). *Moving beyond the medical/technical: Analysis and discussion of psychosocial practices in pediatric hospitals.* Bethesda, MD: Association for the Care of Children's Health.

Strickland, B. (1983). Legal issues that affect parents. In M. Seligman (Ed.), *The family with a handicapped child: Understanding and treatment* (pp. 27–59). New York: Grune & Stratton.

Thomas, K.W., & Kilmann, R.H. (1974). *The Thomas–Kilmann Conflict Mode Instrument.* Tuxedo, NY: X. Comm.

Turnbull, A.P., & Turnbull, H.R. (1990). *Families, professionals, and exceptionality: A special partnership.* New York: Macmillan.

Walker, B., & Singer, G.H.S. (1993). Improving collaborative communication between professionals and parents. In G.H.S. Singer & L.E. Powers (Eds.), *Families, disability, and empowerment: Active coping skills and strategies for family interventions* (pp. 285–315). Baltimore: Paul H. Brookes Publishing Co.

Wasik, B.H., Bryant, D.M., & Lyons, C.M. (1990). *Home visiting: Procedures for helping families.* Beverly Hills, CA: Sage Publications.

Chapter 8

Developing and Implementing Support Groups for Families

Nancy Frank,
Sandra Newcomb,
and Paula J. Beckman

During the 1980s and early 1990s, researchers and interventionists recognized that one of the most important forms of support available to families of young children with disabilities is the support they receive from other families (Santelli, Turnbull, Lerner, & Marquis, 1993). Various ways have evolved to ensure that support from other families is available, such as the emergence of family-to-family support programs and the evolution of information and training networks for families (Santelli et al., 1993; Smith, 1993). A common way to provide families with access to other families is through the development and implementation of support groups. These groups often can meet a variety of family needs, including the need for emotional support, the need for information, and the need for a connection to a network of families (Seligman & Darling, 1989). Support groups also can give families a place where their problems and concerns are understood; where they can safely express feelings that they perceive as negative or unacceptable; and where they can receive respect, guidance, and support (Dreier & Lewis, 1991). Furthermore, groups are an effective use of resources to address the needs of the families.

Although groups can be a meaningful source of support for families, to be maximally effective, they should be based on an understanding of how groups function. Factors such as membership and length can have a potential impact on the success of a group. It is helpful to understand how groups evolve and what dynamics may be expected at various points in their evolution. Understanding such issues can make the difference between a group that is effective in supporting families and one that is fraught with difficulties. Without carefully considering such issues, group organizers may be confused and frustrated when attendance is low or when a group develops a negative or destructive dynamic. Thus, the process of establishing and implementing support groups takes careful thought, an understanding of their evolution, and an understanding of group dynamics.

This chapter provides basic information and guidelines for individuals who are developing and implementing support groups for families. A brief overview of the value of groups is followed by a description of the types of groups and a review of factors to consider when planning groups. The chapter also describes ways that groups typically evolve, and common issues that arise during this evolution. Issues for individuals who lead or facilitate groups are discussed as well.

VALUE OF GROUPS

Support groups have been seen as a way to meet the emotional and practical needs of individuals who share a common issue, problem, or concern (Atwood & Williams, 1978). Moreover, groups provide the opportunity to create a mutual aid system for their members (Seligman, 1990; Shulman, 1992). Mutual aid systems are created when members are empathetic and help each other by sharing similar experiences. Such aid also is provided by an exchange of information and coping strategies (Atwood & Williams, 1978; Shulman, 1992). These attributes characterize many different types of support groups that have been formed around a range of common issues and concerns.

All groups have their own character that makes them unique and enables them to be beneficial. These features do not depend solely on the content or format of the group, but rather are inherent to the group modality. One inherent feature is that support is derived from others who truly know and understand the individual's situation (Dreier & Lewis, 1991; Seligman & Darling, 1989). This shared experience provides a sense of belonging for group members and consequently a reduction in the feelings of being alone or isolated (Beckman, Newcomb, Frank, Brown, & Filer, 1993; Shulman, 1992).

Groups provide opportunities for members to both give and receive help, creating an atmosphere of shared problem solving. This can restore a feeling of competence and empowerment to the members (Shulman, 1992). The sense of having shared experiences also creates an atmosphere in which members feel free to express their concerns and feelings, even on taboo subjects, without worrying about how others may react (Dreier & Lewis, 1991). Being understood and having a give-and-take of ideas and opinions often restores a sense of direction and hope to the members (Shulman, 1992). Shapiro and Simonsen (1994) noted that groups facilitate networking, help to normalize the family's experience, enlarge perceived options, enhance empowerment and responsibility, develop problem-solving skills, and provide multiple models (e.g., other parents, the facilitator, speakers).

Yalom (1975) identified several beneficial elements that support groups share. These elements include the opportunity to express emotions, share information, instill hope, establish a sense of universality and altruism, develop socializing techniques, and imitate behavior of other members. Similarly, Shulman (1992) suggested that groups provide mutual aid by sharing information, discussing formerly taboo topics, discovering that members are not alone, developing a universal perspective, providing mutual support, establishing expectations, problem solving, providing a place where members can test ideas and skills, and providing a sense of strength in numbers.

There has been relatively little research examining the effectiveness of support groups for families of children with disabilities. The existing literature on support groups in general does suggest that many of these beneficial elements are also relevant to families of children with disabilities. Several studies have found multiple benefits from support groups with this population. These benefits include evidence of decreased depression (Shapiro, 1989; Vadasy, Fewell, Greenberg, Dermond, & Meyer, 1986), decreased isolation (Beckman et al., 1993; Newcomb, Stepanek, Beckman, Frank, & Brown, 1994), increased satisfaction with social supports (Vadasy et al., 1986), improved access to information (Beckman et al., 1993; Hornby & Murray, 1983; Newcomb et al., 1994), a sense of acceptance and identification (Hornby & Murray, 1983; Newcomb et al., 1994), and a sense of self-esteem (Beckman et al., 1993; Newcomb et al., 1994; Shapiro, 1989).

TYPES OF GROUPS

There are several different types of groups. Although each has its own particular focus and direction, all types generally share the potential benefits previously described. Three major types of groups have been identified consistently in the literature (Friedlander & Watkins, 1985; Seligman, 1990; Shulman, 1992): 1) psychotherapy, 2) support, and 3) growth and education.

Psychotherapy groups are concerned with the individual members' emotional and social growth and the resolution of issues that impede their growth. Friedlander and Watkins (1985) noted that this type of group for families of children with disabilities was common in the 1950s and 1960s because it was based on prevailing views of pathology in the reactions of families to the birth of a child with a disability. During the 1980s and 1990s, professionals have become increasingly aware that family members are likely to be quite healthy individuals who are simply adjusting to potentially difficult circumstances (Seligman & Darling, 1989). As a result, the approach to such groups for families of children with disabilities has changed to an emphasis on family strengths (Seligman, 1990).

The second type, support groups, are aimed at helping individuals faced with a life crisis to stabilize and begin coping with these life events. These groups emphasize common concerns or issues (Atwood & Williams, 1978). Support groups operate on the premise that emotional support and shared problem solving can facilitate adaptation to a crisis or a difficult life event.

The final types of group are the growth and education groups, which focus on imparting specific competencies and life skills. This model assumes that providing specific information and skills will facilitate family adaptation and the family's ability to meet their own needs as well as the needs of their child.

Groups for families of children with disabilities most frequently fall into one of the latter two categories. Many groups are organized to provide specific training for parents. Examples include groups that teach behavior management techniques and groups that inform parents about their legal rights. Other groups are specifically intended to provide emotional support or to facilitate networking among families or may blend elements of both types. The type of group planned in any given program should be based on the needs of the participants. For example, a group designed to give parents information might function best as an education-based group. In contrast, if the impetus for forming the group comes because parents express an interest in meeting other parents, a support group may be the appropriate type of group to implement.

FACTORS IN PLANNING GROUPS

Individuals who are organizing groups need to think carefully about major elements that can fundamentally affect how the group functions. This section describes some factors that should be examined when planning a group, including membership, culture, duration, frequency, leadership, and size.

Membership

Considerations about group membership can be very important in the ultimate functioning of the group. These considerations include determining who participants will be as well as when new members will be included (Seligman, 1982; Shulman, 1992).

Who Participants Will Be Organizers need to determine if potential participants have some similar needs and can join in a mutual support network. Although the presence of common needs may appear somewhat obvious (e.g., a support group for families of children with disabilities), there are additional considerations that may have implications for the way the group functions.

The first consideration for determining membership is establishing the purpose of the group. If the group is intended to provide information to families about their rights, it may be most useful for parents who are relatively new to the system or for parents who have encountered difficulties with the system. When targeting potential participants, however, it is important not to make assumptions about what will interest families. For instance, if the purpose of a group is to facilitate coping and adaptation, it is important not to assume that certain families are having difficulty coping and invite only those families to participate. A better strategy is to be clear about the purpose of the group when it is publicized and let families decide for themselves if the group is likely to meet their needs.

The planners may also want to consider the needs of a particular subgroup. For example, some groups can include mothers, fathers, extended family members (e.g., a grandparent who is the primary caregiver), foster parents, and so on. Group organizers, however, may want to ensure that the needs of a certain subgroup are being met. For example, organizers may want to have a group that is specifically designed for fathers or a group that is specifically designed for adolescent mothers.

Another basis for establishing membership may be the age of the children. For example, support groups in school-based settings may include families whose children range considerably in age. The advantage is that parents who have been in the system for a long time can offer valuable information to parents who are new to the system. In an evaluation of the group component of Project Assist (see Preface; see also Beckman et al., 1993; Newcomb et al., 1994), however, parents indicated that they liked having a group that was limited to parents of infants and toddlers. The relatively restricted age range meant that parents were more often concerned with common issues (e.g., getting a diagnosis, making the transition to preschool services). Furthermore, several parents felt that because they were still adjusting to their child's disability, they were not yet ready to face the longer-term issues that might be raised by families of older children. These parents felt that having children of similar ages was a more important factor for them than issues pertaining to a specific type of disability. Some parents even reported that they had dropped out of groups with a broader age range. Thus, before attempting to form a group, it is useful for organizers to think through such issues and to talk about such considerations with potential participants.

When New Members Will Be Included An equally important issue involves when to include new members. Organizers need to decide between an open-membership policy and a closed-membership policy (Atwood & Williams, 1978; Seligman, 1990; Shulman, 1992). Groups can offer open membership, where individuals can come and go and membership varies from meeting to meeting. Open membership offers an opportunity for a continual influx of new members and new ideas and concerns. But it presents a challenge to maintaining a group identity and creating an intimate environment. It also can be difficult for new parents to enter an established group. Some parents have reported that they were reluctant to attend existing groups, because they felt that other participants already knew each other and they feared that they would feel isolated within the group (Beckman et al., 1993; Newcomb et al., 1994).

In contrast, closed membership means that the individuals attending the group are constant, and new members join only at specified times. Closed membership can provide opportunities for greater closeness and cohesion and a strong sense of group identity (Atwood & Williams, 1978). The group can sometimes stagnate or dissolve, however, if members are unable to bond or evolve as the needs of the group change.

Culture

Issues of culture and diversity can influence the way groups function. The literature suggests that it can be difficult to attract some members of cultural minorities to support groups (Shapiro & Simonsen, 1994). Shapiro and Simonsen (1994) identified some barriers to the inclusion of Latino families in groups that also may pertain to members of other cultural minorities. These barriers include language, a predominance of individuals from the majority culture, discomfort with a group discussion format, and differences in worldviews and values. For instance, these authors point out that self-disclosure is not a strong value in some cultures. In these cultures, it may be viewed as more appropriate to talk with a religious leader, particularly if the family perceives the concern to be religious or spiritual in nature.

Despite such barriers, Shapiro and Simonsen (1994) argued that supportive and effective groups have been established for members of nonmajority cultures. Henderson, Gutierrez-Mayka, Garcia, and Boyd (1993) suggested that facilitators promote participation by members of diverse groups by developing their ethnic competence and by involving community leaders in the development and implementation of the group. These authors also suggest that facilitators use ethnic media to conduct outreach, have personal contact with members, and get feedback to ensure cultural relevance. It can also be helpful for facilitators to select a culturally significant location for the group meetings.

Duration

The duration of the group also can influence the way the group functions (Seligman, 1982, 1990). Duration refers to the number of times the group will meet. Groups can be open-ended in that they are ongoing and have no set ending date. Open-ended groups offer the chance to meet individual needs over time. Yet sometimes members become concerned about the amount of time required or the level of commitment expected. In contrast, time-limited groups run for a set length of time (e.g., weekly for 10 weeks). Time-limited groups offer specific boundaries to the duration. Members know the required time commitment from the beginning. They are aware of the beginning, middle, and end of the group. This can stimulate group problem solving and reduce dropout rates (Atwood & Williams, 1978; Shulman, 1992). A disadvantage is that some individuals may feel that the time is too short or may be unwilling to invest in a group that lasts only a brief time.

Frequency

The frequency with which the group meets depends on its purpose (Seligman, 1982, 1990). Some groups meet monthly, whereas others meet more frequently (e.g., weekly or every other week). For instance, an education-based group may meet monthly, but groups that provide emotional support may meet weekly. In considering the frequency with which the group should meet, organizers should remember that many factors can interfere with the ability of a family to attend a particular meeting. For example, parents may be unable to attend if their child is ill or if the weather is particularly bad. Although these issues can affect any activity, they are particularly salient for families of children with disabilities or with chronic health problems. If a group meets every other week and a parent is unable to attend a meeting, there will be a month's time between meetings. This much time between meetings may not interfere with the goals of groups that are primarily oriented to providing information. If a group is oriented to providing social support and facilitating relationships among parents, however, the same amount of time between meetings may hinder the group's ability to achieve its goals.

Leadership

Groups vary in their approach to leadership. Groups can be facilitated by parents, by professionals, or by both. Parents who serve as facilitators often have previous experience participating in groups. Professional facilitators may come from a variety of different disciplines such as psychotherapy, social work, and special education. Facilitators also may have specialized training in a specific area, such as a hospice worker. The role of the facilitator differs, depending on the type of group that is established. Facilitators for groups focused on education and training often organize the training and direct group activities and discussion. In contrast, when a support group facilitator is a staff member, this individual often acts more as a sponsor.

Regardless of who serves in this role, group facilitators have several important tasks. One such task is to accurately identify both individual and group dynamics (Hepworth & Larsen, 1986). Second, facilitators need to help individuals in the group relate effectively to one another (Shulman, 1992). A third task is to intervene when necessary to modify the group process, particularly if destructive behavior patterns emerge (Friedlander & Watkins, 1985; Hepworth & Larsen, 1986). For example, if one member of the group is judgmental about the decisions of another member, the facilitator's role is to intervene to ensure that the group remains a safe environment for all members. Fourth, group facilitators need to attend simultaneously to the behavioral patterns that occur both within individuals and within the group (Hepworth & Larsen, 1986). Thus, it is important to note if a particular member dominates meetings or if another member rarely participates. In such instances, the facilitator may be able to help achieve more balanced participation by saying something such as, "I'm interested in whether anyone else has had experience with this issue."

In addition, groups vary in how the agenda is established. At one end of the continuum are groups that have a preestablished agenda and a set format. At the other end are groups that have an open-ended agenda that is generated by group members. Groups also may have members develop the agenda in conjunction with the facilitator or may permit the agenda to change as the needs of the group change.

An example of a member-led group with a set format can be found in Alcoholics Anonymous (AA). Even with a dictated agenda, there can be considerable variation from group to group, depending on who facilitates the meeting. Parents of children with Down syndrome often run member-led support groups that have topics desired by the entire group membership as the agenda.

The way in which the agenda is developed depends on the purpose of the group. For example, support groups often have member-directed agendas. A leader-generated agenda may be more appropriate when the focus is a specific form of training, such as cardiopulmonary resuscitation (CPR). Parent-training groups may have an agenda that includes both leader-directed material and member-requested information.

In selecting a group facilitator, other considerations can also have an impact on group functioning. For example, if the group facilitator is an employee of a program or agency in which a child is receiving services (e.g., the special education teacher), that child's family may feel somewhat constrained in their ability to share concerns. If a family has a complaint about the way in which services are being delivered to their child, they may feel reluctant to discuss these concerns in front of a representative of the agency. This is particularly true if an adversarial relationship has emerged. As a result, the amount of support that the family receives from the group may be limited.

Leadership style also is an important consideration. If the service provider who is facilitating the group is most comfortable in a teaching role, an information- or training-based group will be easiest for that individual. When two facilitators are involved, they must negotiate the logistics of organizing and maintaining the group, openly discuss each other's unique style, and identify an approach that they can agree on and mutually accomplish. Regardless of what is planned, however, it is important to note that each group is unique in its evolution, and the facilitator must be flexible enough to adapt his or her leadership style so that the group truly addresses the concerns of its members. Some groups are composed of individuals who need little guidance in addressing issues, whereas other groups may require considerable support and structure to effectively meet the members' needs. If the facilitator is not able to adjust to these normal group variations, he or she may expect the parents to conform to his or her style. This is counterproductive to providing support to parents and is inconsistent with a family-centered approach to intervention.

Size

In examining the influence of size on group functioning, several factors need to be considered. Larger groups provide members with access to more problem-solving skills and resources because of the larger number of participants. As the group size increases, however, the willingness of some members to talk may decrease. This can result in gaps in participation and increase the likelihood that a small number of participants will dominate. In contrast, if groups are too small, there may be an insufficient number of participants at a given meeting. Although there is no absolute number that has been consistently identified as ideal, most literature suggests that groups function best with about 6–12 members (Seligman, 1982).

Additionally, when recruiting participants for a family support group, organizers should keep in mind that not everyone who initially indicates an interest is likely to actually attend. Therefore, before actually beginning a group, organizers may want to identify approximately two to three times the number of people who express an interest than is needed to achieve the desired size.

SYSTEMATICALLY PLANNING A GROUP

There are many examples of support groups for parents of children with disabilities. Ultimately, each program needs to identify a model that fits its unique combination of goals, needs, and constraints. Such a model will be a combination of the characteristics described previously in this chapter. This section uses the group model identified as part of Project Assist (see Preface; Beckman et al., 1993; Newcomb et al., 1994) to illustrate how deliberate use of these characteristics can help create a model that matches the needs of participants.

Illustration: Project Assist

The model of parent support groups developed by Project Assist targeted parents of young children with special needs who were primarily receiving home-based educational services. Membership in the group was closed, so that after the second group meeting the same people returned each time. This allowed parents to get to know one another and to develop a stronger sense of group cohesion. The groups were intentionally time-limited, running for eight weekly sessions. A time-limited approach was chosen for several reasons. First, it allowed the project to include more participants than could be accommodated in a single group. By limiting the duration of the group to 8 weeks, several different groups could be held during the course of a year. In addition, 8-week groups fit easily within the school calendar and avoided most major school holidays. Groups were cofacilitated by two professionals (a social worker and a special educator or veteran parent) who were not directly involved in services the children received. Because facilitators were not involved in direct services, members could openly discuss concerns about the services their children were receiving.

The agenda for the 8 weeks was developed by the members through a brainstorming activity in the first meeting of each new group. This strategy allowed each group to reflect the unique concerns of its members. Typical topics identified by members included parents' feelings about their children, their feelings about the reactions of other people to their children and to their decisions, and their feelings about the professionals and organizations serving their children. Parents also frequently wanted to discuss the service needs of their children, behavior management (both typical age-related behavior and atypical disability-related behavior), stress management, and other family concerns (e.g., siblings, marital issues).

The format of the group meetings was primarily open discussion, with occasional speakers on specific topics such as communication or behavior management. Typically, families used the group for obtaining information, for sharing feelings, for coping, for gaining support, and for mutual problem solving. Having a young child with special needs was the common denominator for the group members. Ancillary services of child care and transportation were provided, enabling both parents to attend the group and allowing families of various economic backgrounds to participate.

Follow-up evaluation of the project has indicated several positive benefits. Specifically, families reported a reduced sense of isolation, a sense of support from other parents, a sense of empowerment, an increase in available resources, a sense that they could help others, and a sense of safety and acceptance (Beckman et al., 1993).

Building a Model

Several issues need to be considered when establishing a parent group. It is important that organizers understand the impetus for creating the group and whose needs the group is serving. The answers to these issues can have an impact on the long-term success of the group. For example, an agency may view groups as a cost-effective way to serve parents. If the parents are not interested, however, establishing a group is difficult.

If there is a need for a group and there are interested participants, planners need to evaluate whether an existing group in the community can accommodate the individuals. Are there ways of adapting existing services for these families? It is important to avoid duplication of services, especially when funding for programs is so limited. Furthermore, to be consistent with the general goal for co-ordinated community-based services, the service community needs to work together to support parents rather than compete for their involvement.

The format and structure of a parent group should be based on several factors, including the needs and desires of the parents, the constraints of the setting, and the preferences of group facilitators. Facilitators need to determine what the parents want to gain from participating in a group. To some extent, this influences the type of group established. For example, if parents request an opportunity to meet once in a while to share resources, the best strategy may be to meet every other week or once per month, have open membership, and focus on sharing information as the main goal. If parents are interested in meeting other parents and getting together to talk, however, the group might focus more on developing some cohesion among the members so that they can share their thoughts and feelings more openly. This can be done by establishing a group with a closed membership that meets more frequently, such as once per week.

A relatively common model of support groups is that offered through school-based programs. These groups may run weekly, every other week, or once a month and target parents of children in the program. Strategies for developing agendas vary. In some instances, facilitators plan topics that are the focus of the meeting. In others, agendas are developed from concerns expressed by families. The focus of such groups is often information-based and may include the use of speakers who address specific issues of concern for participants. Membership is usually open and includes all parents of children in the program. As a result, participation often varies from meeting to meeting as different individuals attend each time. The group typically runs for the length of the school program; thus, it has some natural time constraints. Other support groups for parents, such as those offered in hospitals, frequently share many of the features of this model. They usually have open, rotating membership; an information- or training-focused agenda; and time limitations that are based on the constraints of the setting. (For example, the length of participation in the group is based on the child's hospital stay or the amount of material to be conveyed to parents.)

GROUP PROCESS AND DEVELOPMENT

Groups develop fairly predictably and independently of the content or the specific focus of the group (Seligman, 1982). Understanding the phases of the group development process helps the facilitator enhance the supportive aspects of the group and avoid as much as possible the negative or unproductive influences. Many authors have delineated phases of group development (Friedlander & Watkins, 1985; Hepworth & Larsen, 1986; Loeb, 1977; Seligman, 1982, 1990; Seligman & Darling, 1989; Shulman, 1992; Yalom, 1975). Although the precise number of phases and the specific labels attached to them vary, these descriptions share several characteristics. Perhaps most important is that they focus attention on the concept that groups evolve over time and may function somewhat differently at various points in this evolution. All descriptions highlight particularly important issues that frequently arise at the beginning and ending phases of the group. For the purpose of this chapter, these developmental stages are identified as the beginning phase, the cohesion phase, the working phase, and closure or the ending phase (Beckman et al., 1993). Each stage of a group's life has specific tasks and issues associated with it, and each stage can require different types of facilitation.

Beginning Phase

The beginning phase has two primary tasks: 1) the members' identification with the group and 2) the establishment of general group goals or consensus (Shulman, 1992). Individuals need to feel some affiliation with the group. Participants may have questions about how the group is going to help them or meet their needs and whether they really belong in the group. Members often evaluate whether the group's goals and focus are congruent with their needs and concerns. They want to know if other members have similar issues and points of view. An underlying theme may be whether the participants want to identify with the group. Sometimes members may know that they have similar concerns but are not yet ready to identify with other members. For example, parents may know that the issues and concerns of a group of parents who have children with special needs reflect their concerns, but they may not be ready to define their child as one with special needs.

During this phase, members also may be concerned with whether other group participants like them or whether they like the others. Members evaluate where they fit within the group by looking for commonalities between themselves and others. This often occurs as members describe how they learned about their child's disability. These disclosures offer points of shared experience and identification with one another (Friedlander & Watkins, 1985).

Hepworth and Larsen (1986) cautioned that, in the first phase, periods of silence are common. This silence often occurs because participants are preoccupied with their own concerns and may be uncomfortable or apprehensive about the group.

The beginning phase is also the time for the facilitator to provide basic information and establish ground rules. This information defines the concrete boundaries of the group. Boundaries can help the group to establish a sense of identity and cohesion. Issues such as the overall purpose of the group (e.g., "This group is a place where parents of children with special needs can talk about their concerns."), who is sponsoring the group, group time, number of sessions, location of sessions, and expectations for attendance are addressed.

One topic that is important to address is confidentiality. Every group needs some guidelines about keeping information discussed in the group confidential, and these need to be stated explicitly. If the group is sponsored by an agency, it is important to understand the agency's policy about confidentiality and how it applies to the group. Guidelines about what information is private and what can be shared also help develop group boundaries and, consequently, a sense of safety for the group.

Parents also may have concerns about whether the information they share is shared with other service providers. For example, they may worry that if they share feelings of dissatisfaction about the way an assessment was conducted or the way they were treated by the program director, this information will be passed on after the group. Policies and procedures need to be developed for handling these potential conflicts of interest. It is also important that these policies are clear to the participants from the beginning. These issues are particularly critical if an individual who is providing direct services to a child is responsible for the parent group.

Another form of creating boundaries occurs through modeling the norms for group behavior. Such norms may include responding to parents in a nonjudgmental manner, respecting all participants' thoughts and opinions, and providing support for parents as they reveal their children's histories. Commenting on both the facts that the parents are presenting and the feelings they may have experienced conveys that the group is a safe and acceptable place for parents to discuss their experiences.

A specific goal of the group facilitator is to create a common bond among the parents who are attending the group. Specifically, the facilitator can generalize statements made by one parent so that other parents may identify with what was expressed. The facilitator often ties together statements made by various participants by pointing to the common issues presented or the similar feelings experienced. By so doing, the facilitator is consciously attempting to link individuals so that they feel comfortable with one another and have a sense of common purpose. The facilitator also can support members' efforts to interact with one another. The facilitator can attempt to define these interactions in ways that reflect respect for each person's viewpoint, a nonjudgmental attitude, and support for all group participants.

Although all groups are somewhat different, some themes emerge frequently and also have been reported in the literature (Atwood & Williams, 1978; Beckman et al., 1993; Friedlander & Watkins, 1985; Newcomb et al., 1994; Seligman, 1990). For instance, parents often describe the family's story as it pertains to the child's disability. This includes information about the child, the history of diagnosis and placement, and descriptions of interactions with professionals. Initially, these issues may be described in a somewhat objective manner, because parents may not yet be ready to share more personal information, such as their feelings about or reactions to their child's history.

Cohesion Phase
At this point in the development of the group, members often start to feel a bond with one another and gain a sense of mutual identification. Group identity is emerging. Members are now frequently interested in finding out what topics or feelings are going to be discussed in the group (Friedlander & Watkins, 1985). This includes discovering what the group members are comfortable sharing with one another and how safe it is to bring up particular topics or issues. Each group begins to develop a unique direction and focus. Some groups may begin to openly discuss feelings and issues that they fear are unacceptable, such as feelings of anger toward their children or toward other family members. Other groups may operate more

on a cognitive level, with less sharing of feelings or discussion of emotionally difficult content.

As group members try to determine the way in which the group will meet their needs, questions may arise about who is in charge (Friedlander & Watkins, 1985; Hepworth & Larsen, 1986). Some members may speak as if they are talking for the group as a whole, or a dominant member may act as if he or she is the group leader. Groups often develop an emotional leader, or someone whom other members use as a model or a referent for behavior and attitude. Underlying these issues are often questions of group safety and direction. There also may be concerns about whether the group is a place where members can get their needs met and reveal personal information about themselves without being judged or hurt in any way.

Along with these types of questions, members may try out the group by sharing more intimate and personal details. Individuals are not necessarily interested in discussing these concerns or feelings in depth until the aforementioned issues are resolved (Seligman, 1982).

The group facilitator's task is to ensure that each member has the opportunity to participate and that all concerns are acknowledged. The facilitator should model behavior that indicates the group is a place where an individual can discuss feelings without fear of sharing something inappropriate. Another concern for the facilitator is to ensure that everyone feels that they have equal opportunity, and an equal right, to participate. Often during this phase, the facilitator must balance more vocal members with the quieter members so that each feels heard and respected and so that no one person or subgroup dominates the sessions.

The facilitator also must help the group to support each member's style and manner. This is especially important when members give unsolicited advice to one another. As described in Chapter 3, giving advice can often be detrimental because other parents may interpret the advice as judgments about them, their style, or their decisions. At this stage in the group's development, it is common for some group members to give unsolicited advice. Members may feel that advice is a way to contribute and support each other. Advice can be perceived as patronizing, however. The facilitator can acknowledge the concern and support expressed by the member who is giving advice and simultaneously reframe the advice as one example of how to deal with an issue or as a particular individual's style of coping. This strategy can lead the group to a discussion about other methods of coping. This type of open discussion helps the group move into the working phase.

Working Phase

The working phase in the group's development is when members really benefit from the mutual aid that comes from participating in a group. By the time members reach this phase, sharing typically occurs openly and spontaneously among members (Hepworth & Larsen, 1986). When an individual raises an issue, he or she may also share feelings associated with the topic. For example, if parents have just taken their child for an assessment, they may not only report that the assessment took place but also describe their feelings about the process, the professional conducting the assessment, or their child's progress. If parents have negative feelings on a particular topic, they may be more willing to share these feelings and to describe how they are managing them. Parents may openly ask others for ideas or suggestions.

In addition to sharing how they handled specific situations, individual members may frequently ask others what they might do in certain situations or how they would handle a particular problem (Hepworth & Larsen, 1986). Members may seek more information to help them deal with a concern, having gained a sense of support for their feelings and their ability to manage their situation. If the group has access to speakers, the working phase is often a good time to invite them.

During the working phase, the facilitator often does not need to be as active, because group members are eliciting each other's feelings, opinions, and problem-solving strategies. The facilitator can acknowledge members' unique approaches while expecting participants to respect and support one another. The facilitator's task is to monitor the balance between individual and group needs. The group in this phase can accommodate the tension between individual issues and opinions and group norms and expectations without having to emphasize or choose one or the other.

The facilitator may need to help the group negotiate this phase. For example, it may be necessary to find common ground for a member whose feelings are different from those of the other group participants. The facilitator needs to support the members in finding points of identification with all individuals in the group without criticizing or negating the importance of others. An individual may also feel like an outsider if he or she believes that his or her situation is dramatically different from the others or if his or her style of sharing or coping is not congruent with the expectations of the group. For example, this may happen with a member who persistently gives advice and is unable to switch this to a more personalized form of sharing or with a member who does not wish to share feelings when a majority of the group discusses feelings openly. Usually, though, members feel enough identification with the group by this time that the facilitator can support and highlight those areas in which the individual has a strong sense of connection with the others.

Another function of the facilitator during this phase of group development may be to redirect the group's attention to issues that the members have stated they want to discuss but are finding difficult to pursue. For instance, the participants may need encouragement to begin discussing a difficult topic such as ambivalent or angry feelings toward their children. If the members continue to avoid a topic even with such encouragement, the facilitator may assume that members' needs and concerns have changed and that particular topic is no longer relevant or of interest to them. Whatever the reason, it is important to respect the group's wishes about such topics.

Closure or Ending Phase
The final phase is closure or the ending phase. This is often one of the most difficult and overlooked phases of group development. Bringing a group to an end with a positive sense of what has occurred is difficult because it can raise feelings in everyone present. Most people have some experience with endings and the loss of important relationships. These feelings, both positive and negative, can be evoked when other relationships end. Often individuals wish to avoid saying good-bye and want endings either not to happen or just to be over. This does not mean that the group experience was insignificant or unimportant. Members may act as if everything is the same and go on with business as usual in the group. Members often comment that it cannot possibly be time to end, even if the group was time-limited and they have been aware of the ending date. They may reminisce about the group, remembering times they shared or significant moments. Sometimes group endings get obscured in larger endings; for instance, school-based groups have their ending overshadowed by the end of the school year and the transition to summer.

Much can be gained by directly addressing the ending of the group. By acknowledging its end, the facilitator affirms the importance of each member's participation in the group. This highlights the ways in which each individual contributed to the group and gained from the group experience, and members can use these same skills and strengths in other situations. Parents' ability to share openly, give and get support from others, and have their needs for information and understanding met are skills that all members can take with them, thus helping them feel more prepared to handle new situations.

In some instances, members may express feelings of anger and frustration, as well as sadness, that the group is ending. Although difficult, these feelings demonstrate the importance of the group to the individual. If groups are open-ended, some of these feelings are diminished because members leave when they choose. Therefore, terminations are often marks of success and transitions to other situations. In these cases, the facilitator reviews the terminating member's contribution to the group and the successful management of the group experience by that person. Facilitators also may need to address the remaining group members' feelings that they are not managing as well, because they are not yet ready to leave the group.

In a time-limited group, the facilitator can begin to acknowledge the end two or three sessions before the last meeting. Members may wish to plan some final event, such as eating dessert together, to mark this occasion. At the last meeting, the facilitator might begin a discussion of the ending of the group by offering a personal expression of what the group has meant, how the group has affected him or her, and what the group has accomplished. Such modeling may help other members to offer their own reactions.

Another function of the group facilitator during the closure phase is to provide members with alternatives or other services that they may wish to pursue. Some members may want to continue to be involved in a group or other support service. By discussing such options, the facilitator can help families prepare for other situations and offer ways for families to get the support they desire.

CONCLUSIONS

Support groups offer families of children with special needs the opportunity to explore with others the many facets of their experiences. Groups can address different needs and concerns, such as the need for information, for emotional support, for a reduced sense of isolation, for coping strategies, and for a sense of hope and promise. Members benefit not only from the content of each group—what is said—but also from being a part of a shared experience with other individuals who truly understand each other. Participants' perspectives change and evolve over time, shaping and being shaped by other members as they get to know one another. By being aware of the way groups function, it is possible to create a truly supportive and enriching experience for families.

ACTIVITIES AND DISCUSSION

1. Read Case Study VI, the Parent Group. Discuss the following:
    a. Think about each of the group participants. What issues, concerns, and characteristics does each bring to the group that influences how it worked?
    b. What experiences and feelings do the parents have in common that influence their ability to invest in the group? What seems unique to individual members?
    c. Think about the third group session. Based on your understanding of the phases of group development, what phase do you think the group is in? Why?
    d. Think about the fourth session. Why do you think this starts so slowly? How would you feel as the facilitator if group attendance were poor? What do you imagine the group members think when attendance is low?
    e. What do the facilitators do to manage the various needs of different members? Is there anything they overlook or do not address? What more might they do?
    f. Think about the way the group functions together during the first two meetings and contrast this with the way it functions by the end. What differences do you see?
    g. What is the facilitator's role when there is an outside speaker present?
    h. What are the parents' reactions to the end of the group? How well do you feel the facilitators handle these reactions?
2. Divide into groups of seven or eight people. Assign two persons in each group to be group facilitators and the remaining participants to be parents. Assign each parent in the group a child with a disability. For example, one parent may have an 8-month-old baby with Down syndrome, another a 2-year-old child with seizures and developmental delays, and a third a child who is medically fragile with a tracheotomy and accompanying feeding difficulties. With this set of participants, simulate a parent group. After this experience, discuss the following:
    a. What feelings did you experience in your role?
    b. How did it feel to be in a group that has children with such varying needs? For instance, did you have any sense that you did not want to participate?
    c. What other reactions did you experience during this simulation?

Explore these and any other issues that arise from this experience. Also ask the group facilitators about their feelings.

3. Take turns being the group facilitator and simulate the first meeting. Introduce yourself and the purpose and function of the group. Try different ways to start the group. The objective is to find ways to encourage participants to become involved with one another so that they feel that the group is worth their time and commitment. Discuss your reactions to different experiences.

4. Assume that you are a group facilitator. Discuss ways to handle the following scenarios:
   a. A situation where one participant is giving another unsolicited advice
   b. One participant dominating the conversation
   c. One participant becoming angry or defensive
   d. A speaker who is not addressing issues of concern to group members
   e. A situation in which one participant unintentionally makes a comment that is insensitive, hurtful, or offensive to another
   f. A situation in which members are all quiet and do not talk in depth about their concerns
   g. A group with inconsistent attendance

5. When providing supervision to new group facilitators, ask each to respond to the following after a group meeting. These can serve as a basis for discussion.
   a. Describe two main issues the parents discussed in the group.
   b. How did the parents react to these issues? Describe the various reactions of all members.
   c. Did you notice any roles that particular members took? How did you determine this? How did these roles affect the group as a whole?
   d. What do you think was the main group task this week? (This relates to group process, not to the group content.)
   e. What kinds of interventions did the group facilitators make? What did these interventions achieve? Did they promote group cohesion and development? How?
   f. What interventions did you make in this group? How did you decide what to say? Did this achieve the goal you intended? How did you feel about your interventions?

6. The following are factors to think about after each meeting when facilitating a parent support group. This list is not exhaustive.
   a. Who was present? What did you think about attendance?
   b. What was the initial tone of the group?
   c. What actions did the facilitators take to maintain the group tone or to change the tone?
   d. What was the content of the group?
   e. What was the group process?
   f. How did the group evolve, both in terms of content and group process? Where did it start, and where did it end?
   g. How did the facilitators contribute to these changes? Did they do particular things that helped or hurt?
   h. How did different group members facilitate the group's process and cohesion?
   i. Evaluate different roles played by different members of the group.
   j. What was your role in the group? What were your strengths and weaknesses?
   k. What feelings were expressed by the group?
   l. Did you have any feelings during the group? Were these about the group content (individuals' stories and experiences) or about your performance in the group?
   m. What do you anticipate will be the issues, process, and dynamics of next week's group?
   n. What would you plan for next week's group?

REFERENCES

Atwood, N., & Williams, M.E.D. (1978). Group support for the families of the mentally ill. *Schizophrenia Bulletin, 4*, 415–425.

Beckman, P., Newcomb, S., Frank, N., Brown, L., & Filer, J. (1993). Innovative practices: Providing support to families of infants with disabilities. *Journal of Early Intervention, 17*, 445–454.

Dreier, M.P., & Lewis, M.G. (1991). Support and psychoeducation for parents of hospitalized mentally ill children. *Health and Social Work, 16*, 11–18.

Friedlander, S.R., & Watkins, E.C. (1985). Therapeutic aspects of support groups for parents of the mentally retarded. *International Journal of Group Psychotherapy, 35*, 65–78.

Henderson, J.N., Gutierrez-Mayka, M., Garcia, J., & Boyd, S. (1993). A model for Alzheimer's disease support group development in African-American and Hispanic populations. *Gerontologist, 33*, 409–414.

Hepworth, D.H., & Larsen, J.A. (1986). *Direct social work practice: Theory and skills.* Chicago: Dorsey Press.

Hornby, G., & Murray, R. (1983). Group programmes for parents of children with various handicaps. *Child Care Health and Development, 9*, 185–198.

Loeb, R.C. (1977). Group therapy for parents of mentally retarded children. *Journal of Marriage and Family Counseling, 3*, 77–83.

Newcomb, S., Stepanek, J.S., Beckman, P.J., Frank, N., & Brown, L. (1994). Providing family support services as part of a comprehensive early intervention system. *ACCH Advocate, 1*(2), 21–24.

Santelli, B., Turnbull, A.P., Lerner, E., & Marquis, J. (1993). Parent to parent programs: A unique form of mutual support for families of persons with disabilities. In G.H.S. Singer & L.E. Powers (Eds.), *Families, disability, and empowerment: Active coping skills and strategies for family interventions* (pp. 27–57). Baltimore: Paul H. Brookes Publishing Co.

Seligman, M. (Ed.). (1982). *Group psychotherapy and counseling with special populations*. Baltimore: University Park Press.

Seligman, M. (1990). Group approaches for parents of children with disabilities. In M. Seligman & L.W. Marshal (Eds.), *Group psychotherapy interventions with special populations* (pp. 147–163). Newton, MA: Allyn & Bacon.

Seligman, M., & Darling, R. (1989). *Ordinary families, special children: A systems approach to childhood disability*. New York: Guilford Press.

Shapiro, J. (1989). Stress, depression, and support group participation in mothers of developmentally delayed children. *Family Relations, 38*, 169–173.

Shapiro, J., & Simonsen, D. (1994). Educational/support group for Latino families of children with Down syndrome. *Mental Retardation, 32*(6), 403–415.

Shulman, L. (1992). *The skills of helping: Individuals, families and groups*. Itasca, IL: F.R. Peacock Publishers.

Smith, P.M. (1993). Opening many, many doors: Parent-to-parent support. In P.J. Beckman & G.B. Boyes (Eds.), *Deciphering the system: A guide for families of young children with disabilities*. Cambridge, MA: Brookline Books.

Vadasy, P.F., Fewell, R.R., Greenberg, M.T., Dermond, N.L., & Meyer, D.J. (1986). Follow-up evaluation of the effects of involvement in the fathers program. *Topics in Early Childhood Special Education, 6*(2), 16–31.

Yalom, I.D. (1975). *The theory and practice of group psychotherapy* (2nd ed.). New York: Basic Books.

Chapter 9

Strategies for Supporting Families During Transitions

Sandra Newcomb
and Lynn Brown

Change is a lifelong process and involves a number of transitions during the life span. Although change occurs for all families, there are particular transitions that are unique for families of children with disabilities. Many such transitions are integrally related to the delivery of services to young children with disabilities. The importance of transitions has been acknowledged in the regulations governing Part H of the Education of the Handicapped Act Amendments of 1986 (PL 99-457). These regulations require a transition plan for children moving from infant–toddler services to preschool services. This chapter describes strategies for supporting families during these transitions. It begins with a brief overview of the theoretical basis for understanding the impact of transitions and a description of typical transition points in the lives of families who have young children with disabilities. This is followed by a discussion of common issues that arise for families as they adapt to transitions. Finally, specific strategies for working with families during transitions are identified.

THEORETICAL BASIS FOR UNDERSTANDING TRANSITIONS

Understanding the reaction of families to the transitions that accompany parenting a child with a disability requires that professionals have a general understanding of changes that occur for families during the life span. Turnbull, Summers, and Brotherson (1986) noted that, over time, changes alter the priorities of families. To explain this change process, McCubbin and Figley (1983b) distinguish between the concepts of *normative* and *nonnormative* transitions. Normative transitions are changes that are predictable and expected. They include relatively common events such as marriage, childbearing, and retirement. In short, they are life events that most people anticipate.

In contrast, *nonnormative* transitions are changes that are not typical and are unpredictable. Families that have a child with a disability experience nonnormative transitions as well as normative ones (Rosenkoetter, Hains, & Fowler, 1994; Turnbull et al., 1986; Turnbull & Turnbull, 1990). For example, when a family brings their child who is chronically ill home from the hospital, they must interact with many different medical professionals as well as adjust the household to manage medical equipment and to meet the medical needs of the child. All of this must occur at the same time that the parent is adjusting to the more typical experiences associated with parenting.

Because transitions involve change, they involve adjustment and adaptation on the part of individuals within the family. Turnbull et al. (1986) described transitions as periods characterized by change and discontinuity that take place when families shift from one period of development to the other. Because transitions require so many adjustments, many authors have argued that transitions are potential points of stress for families (Minuchin, 1974; Turnbull et al., 1986).

Some of the transitions experienced by families of children with disabilities are directly related to the service system. Service-related transitions can happen for families of children with disabilities in many ways. Some transitions are formal and predictable, such as the move from infant–toddler services to preschool services. Other changes, such as a change in a teacher or therapist during the school year, may be less predictable. One factor that can affect the amount of stress that occurs around transitions is the predictability of the event. The more predictable the change, the more time the family has to prepare and experience a sense of control (McCubbin & Figley, 1983a). This suggests the importance of planning transitions as carefully as possible.

MAJOR TRANSITIONS

One way for service providers to support families who are experiencing change is to be familiar with typical points of transition and the emotional, logistical, and legal requirements that may accompany them. Such knowledge helps service providers assist families during the planning process. This section describes common transition points that are important to recognize when working with families of young children with disabilities.

Diagnosis

One of the biggest transitions a family makes occurs with the diagnosis of a child's disability (Harris, 1987; Wikler, 1981). Many years later most parents can still describe in great detail the way that they learned of their child's disability. Some received a diagnosis early and precisely, whereas others experienced a longer period of waiting and concern. Still others began with the belief that their child was healthy and typical, only to discover later that there were significant problems. Whatever the scenario, parents remember and are affected by the way that they learned of their child's diagnosis (Seligman & Darling, 1989).

These experiences can have a long-lasting effect on parents' subsequent experiences with service providers. For example, if an early diagnosis was inaccurate, parents may have difficulty trusting subsequent efforts to identify the child's difficulties. Service providers may have to deliver difficult news to a family or work with the family after someone else has made a diagnosis. Either way, this experience can affect the relationship that exists between service providers and families. Because this is such an important transition, professionals need to understand its significance and be prepared to assist parents through it.

Featherstone (1980) described her initial response to the birth of her son with multiple disabilities by saying, "Nine days later (after birth) the world fell in" (p. 4). Seligman and Darling (1989) stated that the crisis of "first information or suspicion" is probably the most difficult for families, and it is at that time that families most need support. In an effort to understand the range of reactions that families experience, some authors have described a model of reacting to disability in stages (Drotar, Baskiewicz, Irvin, Kennell, & Klaus, 1975; Gargiulo, 1985; O'Hara & Levy, 1984). Stage theories usually include stages of shock, denial, sadness, anger, anxiety, guilt, and, finally, adaptation or reorganization. Other authors (Moses, 1992; Wikler, Wasow, & Hatfield, 1983) have argued that the reactions described in stage-based models do not necessarily occur sequentially and may occur more than once cyclically, depending on each family's individual circumstances. In either case, parents experience a range of reactions to the diagnosis, and professionals need to be aware of these reactions to assist parents with this transition.

Hospital to Home

For some families, one of the earliest transitions occurs when they bring their child home from the hospital. When children are discharged from a neonatal intensive care unit or a pediatric intensive care unit, families must adjust the home environment and scheduling to the health needs of the child. For many parents, the biggest issue at this time involves their fears surrounding their child's health status (McCluskey-Fawcett, O'Brien, Robinson, & Asay, 1992). Once the family adapts to the child's medical needs, they must find appropriate developmental services for their child. Services that previously were provided at the hospital (e.g., physical therapy, medical examinations) now involve traveling to service providers, juggling appointments, or having professionals come to their home. Discharge planners from the hospital initially may help the family locate and access appropriate services. As the child's needs change, however, the family must often find other ways to gain access to appropriate services. Families also must begin to adjust to early intervention services. The whole concept of early intervention—how it works, what the services are, the family's rights, and the process of developing an individualized family service plan (IFSP)—is usually new for the family.

Service coordinators can assist families with this transition in several ways. They can help families understand the system and how it works. The service coordinator can use strategies suggested later in this chapter to assist families with the logistical and emotional issues of transition into early intervention services. (For further description of the job of the service coordinator, see Chapter 5.)

Home-Based to Center-Based Services

Another typical transition for families of young children is the change from home-based to center-based services. This change may take place while the child is receiving Part H services or when the child moves from Part H to Part B services. Sometime during the first 5 years of life, children typically begin to attend programs outside of the home and in a group setting with other children. This is a big step for children, involving growing up and going out; confronting new challenges; and adjusting to new people, new places, and new routines (Rosenkoetter et al., 1994). Some of the adjustments for the child may involve coping with transportation (e.g., bus ride), participating in a group setting, separating from a primary caregiver, and negotiating peer interactions.

Families also have their own adjustments when changing to a setting outside of the home for services. They must prepare their child for the changes and cope with changes themselves. Families must now communicate with new professionals in a different setting and often in a different manner. In the home, the parent can see the professionals as they are with the child and talk directly to them. In a center, parents may not always have the same direct contact with the people providing services. They may have to communicate in writing, by telephone, or during scheduled conferences. If they wish to be more involved in the child's program, they may have to make special visits to the school, which can be difficult if both parents are employed. For some families, this is the first time the child has been away from home without the parent. Parents must also adjust to separation from their child. Trusting the professionals and ensuring the child's safety while away from home are common issues, particularly if the child does not talk and cannot tell the parent what happens at the center. Thus, the change from home- to center-based services is usually a major transition for the child and family.

Infant–Toddler to Preschool Services

The transition from infant–toddler to preschool programs is significant because it reflects differences in the legislation governing these programs. Differences include changes in legal requirements for eligibility, in the services being offered, and in the focus of the services. For example, after children move from infant–toddler to preschool services, they no longer receive service coordination. Services shift from an interagency model to an education-based model that includes special education with related services. The eligibility requirements change, and a diagnosed disability may be needed to qualify for services. In some instances, children who qualify for services under Part H no longer qualify under Part B (Harbin, Danaher, & Derrick, 1994). In most instances, the formal plan for services changes from an IFSP to an individualized education program. Services are no longer year-round, but instead follow a school calendar. Sometimes no services are provided in June, July, and August. In addition, although infant–toddler services tend to be more family-oriented, services at the preschool level tend to be more child-oriented. Each of these changes requires adaptation and change by families.

Preschool to School-Age Services

Another major shift involving changes in eligibility and service delivery is the transition from preschool to school-age services. Even
if a diagnosed disability was not required for eligibility at the preschool level, it is required at the school-age level. Decisions must
be made about the extent of the child's participation in general education. Again, there may be new staff and a shift to a new location.
Parents may be faced with questions about whether the child can
go to a neighborhood school or must attend a special center, whether
he or she will be fully included with peers, and whether his or her
education will focus on traditional academics or on more functional
life skills. At school age, the child is sometimes becoming aware
that he or she is different from other children. Parents also may need
to take more initiative to maintain involvement with the child's educational program.

Ongoing Changes Within a Program

Even if a child stays in the same program for several years, there
are often transitions within the program. Children change from
school services to summer services (e.g., camps, extended school
year services). Teachers and therapists change from year to year or
sometimes within a given year. These changes, although not as major as some, also require planning to make the transition smooth
and not interrupt the child's developmental progress.

Family Relocation

Change also occurs when the family relocates. This often requires
deciphering a new school or early intervention system and gaining
access to appropriate services within this new system. Changes in
places, people, sites, and program structure are all required with a
move. In addition to changes in services for the child, the entire
family must adjust to a new home and community. Extra support
and planning are needed to facilitate a smooth transition.

COMMON ISSUES FOR FAMILIES IN TRANSITION

Because families go through a variety of changes during their children's early years, professionals need to be aware of typical issues
that may arise. This section discusses the most common issues for
families.

Emotional Issues

Change can bring feelings and reactions based on an individual's
history with previous changes (Shulman, 1992). When a child

makes a transition across or within programs, his or her family must cope with any feelings or reactions raised by the change. Each family member has made other transitions and may have had a variety of different experiences. Perhaps an earlier transition from hospital to home lacked proper planning. The family may have been on their own to find appropriate services. In such a case, the family's previous feelings of being alone without necessary information may make them more anxious at the transition from infant–toddler to preschool services. Service providers need to be aware that experience can affect the family's need for information and support in the current transition.

Change also means a loss of familiar staff and settings for the family. Mixed reactions are common (Shulman, 1992) and may include denial, anger, sadness, and fear, as well as excitement and anticipation. Families may express a desire not to leave or change. They may experience a sense of loss and sadness as they move from one program to another. Parents may have concerns about the prospect of new staff, settings, and schedules. A new program or new staff member represents a risk, particularly if the family was satisfied with the previous program or with a specific professional. Family members may have questions about whether the new program or professional will be as good for their child and family as the previous one was.

Transitions also represent milestones in the child's development. If a child moves from special education to a general education program, a celebration may be in order. In other cases, not making an expected transition may remind some families that their child has made limited progress or has continuing needs. For instance, if a child was premature and the family expected the child to be caught up by age 3, the move to a preschool special education program may trigger renewed grieving centered around the child's disability. For a family whose child remains in special education while his or her peers are going to kindergarten, failure to make this transition may be difficult (Turnbull & Turnbull, 1990). By being aware of what the transition represents for each family, professionals can provide appropriate supports for that family's needs.

Understanding the New Services

Another common issue for families in transition is understanding a new system or new program options. At each stage of intervention, families must learn to negotiate with health, education, and social services agencies as they arrange for services for their children. To complicate matters, the nature of this interagency collaboration often varies significantly between infant–toddler and preschool services and between geographic regions. Families who are new to early intervention and the tasks of transition may need more assistance in identifying and sorting out available options. Even experienced families, however, confront new and sometimes confusing expectations during transitions. It often takes time for each family to understand their options fully.

Knowing What Questions to Ask

Families in transition frequently face a seemingly endless barrage of new information, assessments, paperwork, terminology, and professionals. Even experienced service providers find it taxing to keep track of changing legislation, regulations, eligibility criteria, program options, and state-of-the-art practices. For many families, simply knowing what questions to ask about a program or new system can be an issue. Families can and do ask about concerns that are relevant to their current situation (e.g., Will my child be safe on the bus? Will my insurance pay for physical therapy?). They may not, however, think to ask about other features of the service system that can have a significant impact on their family (e.g., time lines for the intake process, inclusive program options, availability of parent support groups). Frequent overviews about what a family can expect are helpful. Some parents may appreciate assistance in formulating questions and asking for information. This can minimize misunderstandings or gaps in services.

FACILITATING TRANSITION

The preceding sections have identified predictable logistical and emotional issues for families as they enter each new system of services. This section identifies specific strategies that can facilitate smooth and productive transitions.

Although not every family will need or benefit from all of the following strategies, it is important for service providers to be aware of various ways to support families through transitions. For example, Spiegel-McGill, Reed, Konig, and McGowan (1990) found that a parent education program involving workshops and transition assistance was helpful in easing the transition to preschool. Early transitions often affect later ones, and the skills developed in one transition can be used again in a lifelong process of change (Lazzari & Kilgo, 1989; Rosenkoetter et al., 1994; Turnbull & Turnbull, 1990). Professionals who are aware of transition issues and offer appropriate support help families not only to manage the current transition successfully but also to develop skills that may be used for a lifetime.

Service providers have often developed a positive working relationship with a family by the time a transition occurs (see also Chapter 2). It is within the context of this relationship that service providers can support families through various transitions. The skills needed to develop a positive relationship with families, such as conveying a sense of respect for the family and a nonjudgmental attitude, are vitally important during transitions and are essential at this stressful time. Service providers who join the family in their view of the child and respond empathetically help make the transition proceed smoothly. (For further discussion of skills needed in a working relationship with families, see Chapter 3.) In addition to skills and strategies used to build positive relationships, several additional strategies specifically aimed at facilitating transitions can help service providers support families during these times.

Be Supportive When Explaining Diagnostic Information

Understanding potential reactions to the process of receiving a diagnosis can help professionals support parents as they come to terms with their child's disability and what it means for their family. A consistent finding in the literature is that families need complete and honest information about the child's condition (Gowen, Christy, & Sparling, 1993; Greig, 1993; Turnbull & Turnbull, 1990). If at all possible, the information should be presented to both parents at the same time. For some families, it may be necessary to repeat information in many ways and many times, avoiding the use of medical or educational jargon or defining terms if they are used (Turnbull & Turnbull, 1990). Even families who appear to understand the information the first time it is presented may find that they think of new questions or want the same information repeated.

At the time of diagnosis, families often find it helpful to talk to other families who have had a similar experience. Providers need to have available any information about parent-to-parent or support group resources. Written resources also can be helpful, such as books about specific disabilities or about another parent's experience. Families also may wish to discuss ways to tell siblings or extended family members about the child's disability (Turnbull & Turnbull, 1990).

Parents have a variety of feelings and need time to express and come to terms with these feelings. Some parents may be angry and express their anger at professionals. The professional needs to avoid being defensive, remembering that the anger is often at the diagnosis and not at the professional (Turnbull & Turnbull, 1990). Some parents may be sad and cry. The best support for the family at such a time is simply to be with them in their pain. Often professionals want to do something to make the pain go away, because it is hard to see another person suffer. Regardless of how difficult it is to witness such a painful time, there is little another person can do to alleviate this type of pain. By accepting the feelings of the family, professionals actually help parents move through the grief process and facilitate the reorganization needed to adapt (Moses, 1992).

Some families may want to obtain other opinions because they want more information about the diagnosis. Professionals can encourage families to seek further opinions if they so desire and work constructively with them to understand and integrate the information they receive about the child. Professionals also need to avoid becoming defensive. The job of the service provider is to support the family as they receive difficult information and to help them obtain appropriate services.

Become Informed About Transition Guidelines

The extent to which professionals are accurately informed of issues and regulations can determine how smoothly transitions are made. It has been suggested that personnel preparation targeting transitions is a key priority (Shotts, Rosenkoetter, Streufert, & Rosenkoetter, 1994). Through preservice, in-service, and continuing education programs, professionals can become aware of local, state, and national regulations and time lines regarding transition. Administrators can support staff members by offering opportunities to obtain such training. Professionals need accurate information on local models and descriptions of interagency agreements, agency roles, and funding sources.

Provide Information for the Family

Families need accurate information on which to base their decisions about their child's services (Gowen et al., 1993; Greig, 1993; Rous, Hemmeter, & Schuster, 1994). Greig (1993) found that one of the major determinants of the amount of support parents perceive is the quality of information received from professionals. Assuming that professionals have the necessary facts or have access to them, another key consideration is ensuring that this information is communicated in a parent-friendly manner. At least two factors affect how parents receive information. The first is the parents' emotional state at the time information is shared. For parents who are still adapting to their child's disability or adjusting to the loss of a familiar program, it is difficult to retain new material in one exposure (Rosenkoetter et al., 1994). The second factor is how the material is presented: in writing, by telephone, in person, or in a large meeting. Some parents prefer to receive information in person whereas others prefer written information so that they can refer to it again later. It is important that providers be sensitive to family preferences regarding the way information is provided. Although no one way is better than others, a match between how the family prefers to receive the information and how it is given can facilitate communication.

In general, when sharing information, it is helpful to provide the same information in more than one format in several sessions. Providers also need to be prepared to repeat the same information at different times and in various forms throughout the transition process. This can be helpful as families adjust to many new options (Rosenkoetter et al., 1994). Parent perceptions and questions need to be checked frequently during or shortly after any information-sharing session. To be fully informed, parents need to be as clear as possible about information that has been shared. Questions should be actively encouraged and responses forthcoming. If a staff member does not know the answer to one or more questions, seeking this information in a timely manner can be part of a transition plan (Fowler & Titus, 1993). For parents whose primary language is not English, written material needs to be available in the family's native language, or an interpreter should be available to facilitate discussions between staff and family.

The information needed by families varies with each situation. For a child making the transition from infant–toddler services to preschool services, the service provider might share types of program options, including opportunities for inclusion, time lines, and eligibility requirements. If a child is moving from one classroom to another, the service provider can describe how the two classes are similar and different as well as what skills the child will need in the new class. Families who relocate need information about the new system, contact persons, telephone numbers, program options, and how to gain access to services. It is important that information be specific to the needs of the family and the nature of the transition.

Learn from the Family
Parents have a wealth of information and resources to share with professionals about their child and family as well as questions and needs that they want addressed during a transition. A parent can

share vital information concerning the child's strengths and specific needs in reference to the transition itself. The parents also can share their questions about, and priorities for, the transition.

Parents have many insights into these areas to offer professionals. For example, parents know how their child handles change and what strengths the child brings to this change. Because parents may not always use the same terminology to describe the child that professionals use, service providers need to elicit this information and communicate its value by making it part of the planning process. The parents' knowledge is essential to a complete understanding of a child's abilities and therefore to a smooth transition.

A transition also typically requires many changes and adjustments by the child. For instance, the child must learn to relate to new adults or peers; separate from previous teachers, caregivers, and friends; function in a group outside the family; comply with directions; use safety skills; and ride the bus (Fowler & Titus, 1993). Regarding the changes required, families may have questions and concerns that are particular to their child. It is helpful for the provider to elicit these questions and address them early in the transition process and to meet regularly throughout the transition.

The process for helping parents identify their strengths, questions, and needs involves many of the communication strategies identified in Chapter 3. For instance, active listening combined with the use of probing questions can help the family identify what they know and what they want to know about the transition process. Encouraging parents to think about and organize their questions and concerns before they need to address numerous professionals in a team meeting can be a tremendous source of support. Open-ended questions allow the parents to reveal their own knowledge, resources, and needs. Asking a question such as, "How are you doing with the preparation for this program change?," encourages the family members to share the areas of success or concern that are important to them.

As families discuss the process, the staff person can listen for key transition topics. Professionals need to convey that the parents' views are recognized and understood. It is also appropriate to encourage discussion of new areas with broad questions such as, "Is there anything else you're wondering about this transition?"

Providers can help elicit information about topics the parents have not mentioned. For example, parents may have a lot to say about the kind of program they would like for their child and about their worries regarding whether their child is ready for such a program. Sensitive questions that touch on parents' hopes for their child, as well as their reactions to prior changes, can help elicit discussion of these issues. It is important that providers acknowledge anything the parents have done to prepare for the transition, affirm their feelings about the process, and respect their views about what is most important.

Facilitate Family Involvement

In a study of families whose children were about to make the transition to preschool, Hanline (1988) found that parents had several areas of concern. One major concern was how to remain involved in the decision-making process for their child. They also were concerned about quality of services and family involvement. It is important for service providers to be aware of whether parents have these concerns and ensure that they are addressed as families move from one program to the next. This may be done by providing parents with specific information about resources available in the new program (e.g., parent groups), information about their rights, and information about procedures for effecting a change in the child's new program.

Help Families Prepare Necessary Records

Families have not only a wealth of knowledge concerning their child but also materials such as reports or health records that may be needed during the transition process. Once they are aware of what materials are needed (e.g., reports, assessments, health data, birth certificates), gathering these documents can be another logistical hurdle. It is useful if staff provide parents with a list of documents that they may need with enough notice to gather them. Wherever possible, staff can help by providing copies of relevant materials. To assist in organization, one staff person from an agency can collect all documents from that team. Staff can also assist parents by providing key telephone numbers and sample letters for requesting copies of documents.

For a family who is new to the system or does not yet feel comfortable managing the paperwork related to their child, it may be helpful if guidelines are provided for setting up an information management system. One such system was described by Beckman, Boyes, and Herres (1993). Fowler and Titus (1993) also provided helpful suggestions that parents can use to manage information.

Arrange Program Visits and Placement Meetings

Service providers are responsible for scheduling necessary placement meetings and can facilitate parent visits to prospective program sites. Whenever possible, a staff member familiar with the family's priorities should participate in these meetings or visits to ease transition-related communications with the receiving team. The presence of a trusted staff person also can increase the parents' comfort and sense of belonging in settings with many service providers, some of whom are new to the family.

Transition team meetings ideally include members from both the sending team and the receiving team, along with the family, to ensure that all issues are addressed (Rosenkoetter et al., 1994). For further suggestions on conducting meetings and facilitating family involvement, see Chapter 6.

Support Various Participation Styles

The degree to which parents can and do choose to participate varies from family to family, and it also varies for any given family at different times. Staff members should remain open to a variety of participation styles and options. Some families want to be present at all meetings, visit a variety of programs or classrooms, and take an active role in determining their child's future placement. Other families may want the sending team to make decisions about appropriate future placements. If a family prefers to be less active, it does not imply that the professional is a substitute for the family or that professionals should not attend to the family's input.

More participation can be encouraged by offering information and training with respect to the transition process (Spiegel-McGill et al., 1990). Spiegel-McGill et al. described a program that included the following topics: 1) the effects of transition, 2) knowing your child, 3) program options and services, 4) effective communication, and 5) educational rights. These authors found that in a survey of 91 parents whose children were making the transition to kindergarten, those who had received explanations about the transition and the new placement were more satisfied with the transition.

It is critical that professionals not make assumptions about the level of involvement for any family, but instead ensure that all families know that their involvement is welcomed and that the extent of their involvement is their choice. Whether a family chooses to be minimally involved or to fully guide the transition process, their choice deserves respect and full cooperation from the other team members.

Provide Emotional Support

As the service provider gives and receives information, helps organize reports, and reviews program options, he or she needs to be aware of the family's emotional needs. The provider needs to simultaneously attend to the process as well as the content of what is happening.

Several strategies may be helpful. One such strategy is to listen to and validate the family's feelings about the transition, acknowledge the family's sense of loss or celebration, and examine the affective as well as the factual content of messages. When a family asks questions about the new class or school, they genuinely need facts about the new class. They also may want reassurance, however, that this is a good move for enhancing the child's development.

Providers should not hesitate to use or to ask for information about the family's history of transition—for example, their experience in moving from home- to center-based services or from hospital to home. In the discussion, the professional can listen for strategies that the family has used successfully in the past and identify and affirm those strategies. Professionals can point out what the family is doing well and how well they have handled change in the past. For example, if the family has been persistent in making telephone calls that resulted in desired outcomes, a provider can comment on their skill in getting what their child needs. If the family has been able to communicate their child's needs and strengths especially well in the past, the provider can let them know what a valuable skill this is for relating to the new set of professionals.

Finally, it is important that professionals understand what this particular change means to the family. For example, what is it like for the child to be 5 years old and not going to kindergarten? Families and providers can talk about ways to address any emotional needs individual members may have, such as how to meet other parents who have made a similar transition. Parent mentors are an excellent resource for other families.

Say Good-Bye
Special attention needs to be directed to the skills of ending a relationship, because transition often involves leaving one provider and going to another. Saying good-bye is a difficult task of transition. Both the family and the service provider need to achieve closure. In a transition, this part of the process should not be ignored. One way to achieve closure is to share thoughts and feelings about what has occurred during the time the family and professional have worked together. Service providers can make a specific effort to say good-bye and review the progress of the child during his or her time in the program. A specific activity to say good-bye, such as making a picture album or having a good-bye party, lets the family know how meaningful their participation has been. A healthy ending for

the relationship sets the foundation for the family to build trust and form new attachments in the next program and for the professional to welcome new families. Change is indeed a lifelong process for everyone.

CONCLUSIONS

Transitions are a natural part of a family's experience across the life span. When a family has a child with special needs, it is important to attend to specific tasks of transition. Knowing what these tasks are and what emotional reactions there may be can make the transition one that is positive for all parties concerned.

Service providers can support families in a number of ways during transitions. They can provide clear and honest information in ways that help parents make decisions about their child's services. They can facilitate family understanding of transition through information, training, and discussions. Recognizing that change can be stressful, providers can support families who are preparing for change by listening to their concerns. By understanding the significance of transition for each family, the provider can be sensitive to each family's unique needs during times of transition and respond in ways that support them in meeting the needs of their child.

ACTIVITIES AND DISCUSSION

1. Divide into small groups and assign each group one of the following case studies to read: Case Study I, the Barnes Family; Case Study II, the Martínez Family; and Case Study IV, the Miller Family. Within each group, discuss the following:
    a. What transitions does this family face?
    b. What factors may have influenced their adjustment to the changes? What factors may influence future adaptation?
    c. What emotional issues related to each transition need to be addressed?
    d. What steps should the interventionist take to address the issues that emerge around transition?
    e. What additional supports may facilitate this transition?
    After discussing each case study during small group, go back to the large group. Have a spokesperson from each small group summarize the responses to each question. As a large group, identify any issues that are common to more than one of the case studies.

2. Think about at least one significant transition in your life (e.g., beginning a new job, starting college, moving). What feelings did you experience during this transition? What did you do to cope with the transition? Which strategies were helpful and which interfered with your ability to adapt? Did anyone support you during these changes? In what ways were they helpful?

3. Form small groups of four to six participants each. Assign each group a particular type of transition that is typical in early childhood programs (e.g., hospital to home; home-based to center-based services). Have each group identify suggested guidelines for supporting families during this particular transition. In a large group, go over these guidelines. Which guidelines are similar? Which are specific to the transition?

REFERENCES

Beckman, P.J., Boyes, G.B., & Herres, A. (1993). Managing the information. In P.J. Beckman & G. Boyes (Eds.), *Deciphering the system: A guide for families of young children with disabilities* (pp. 39–48). Cambridge, MA: Brookline Books.

Drotar, D., Baskiewicz, A., Irvin, A., Kennell, J., & Klaus, M. (1975). The adaptation of parents to the birth of an infant with congenital malformation: A hypothetical model. *Pediatrics, 56,* 710–717.

Education of the Handicapped Act Amendments of 1986, PL 99-457. (October 8, 1986). Title 20, U.S.C. §§ 1400 et seq.: *U.S. Statutes at Large, 100,* 1145–117.

Featherstone, H. (1980). *A difference in the family.* New York: Viking Press.

Fowler, S.A., & Titus, P.F. (1993). Handling transitions. In P.J. Beckman & G. Boyes (Eds.), *Deciphering the system: A guide for families of young children with disabilities* (pp. 101–116). Cambridge, MA: Brookline Books.

Gargiulo, R.M. (1985). *Working with parents of exceptional children: A guide for professionals.* Boston: Houghton Mifflin.

Gowen, J.W., Christy, D.S., & Sparling, J. (1993). Informational needs of parents of young children with special needs. *Journal of Early Intervention, 17*(2), 194–210.

Greig, D. (1993). *Extremely low birth weight infants (800 grams or less): Medical and developmental outcome at one to five years and social support needs of their mothers.* Unpublished doctoral dissertation, University of Maryland, College Park.

Hanline, M.F. (1988). Making the transition to preschool: Identification of parents' needs. *Journal of the Division for Early Childhood, 12*(2), 98–104.

Harbin, G., Danaher, J., & Derrick, T. (1994). Comparison of eligibility policies for infant/toddler programs and preschool special education programs. *Topics in Early Childhood Special Education, 14*(4), 455–471.

Harris, S.L. (1987). The family crisis: Diagnosis of a severely disabled child. In M. Ferrari & M.B. Sussman (Eds.), *Childhood disability and family systems,* (pp. 107–118). New York: Haworth.

Lazzari, A.M., & Kilgo, J.L. (1989). Practical methods for supporting parents in early transitions. *Teaching Exceptional Children, 22*, 40–43.

McCluskey-Fawcett, K.M., O'Brien, M., Robinson, P., & Asay, J.H. (1992). Early transition for the parents of premature infants: Implications for intervention. *Infant Mental Health Journal, 13*(2), 147–156.

McCubbin, H.I., & Figley, C.R. (1983a). Bridging normative and catastrophic family stress. In H.I. McCubbin & C.R. Figley (Eds.), *Stress and the family: Vol. I. Coping with normative transitions* (pp. 218–228). New York: Brunner/Mazel.

McCubbin, H.I., & Figley, C.R. (1983b). Introduction. In H.I. McCubbin & C.R. Figley (Eds.), *Stress and the family: Vol. I. Coping with normative transitions* (pp. xxi–xxxi). New York: Brunner/Mazel.

Minuchin, S. (1974). *Families and family therapy.* Cambridge, MA: Harvard University Press.

Moses, K. (1992). *Not me, not my child: Dealing with parental denial and anxiety.* Evanston, IL: Resource Networks.

O'Hara, D.M., & Levy, S.M. (1984). Family adaptation to learning disability: A framework for understanding and treatment. *Learning Disabilities, 3*(6), 63–77.

Rosenkoetter, S.E., Hains, A.H., & Fowler, S.A. (1994). The rationale for transition planning: Why do we need a bridge? In *Bridging early services for children with special needs and their families: A practical guide for transition planning* (pp. 1–11). Baltimore: Paul H. Brookes Publishing Co.

Rous, B., Hemmeter, M.L., & Schuster, J. (1994). Sequenced transition to education in the public schools: A systems approach to transition planning. *Topics in Early Childhood Special Education, 14*(3), 374–393.

Seligman, M., & Darling, R.B. (1989). *Ordinary families, special children: A systems approach to childhood disability.* New York: Guilford Press.

Shotts, C.K., Rosenkoetter, S.E., Streufert, C.A., & Rosenkoetter, L.I. (1994). Transition policy and issues: A view from the states. *Topics in Early Childhood Special Education, 14*(3), 395–411.

Shulman, L. (1992). *The skills of helping: Individuals, families, and groups.* Itasca, IL: F.E. Peacock Publishers.

Spiegel-McGill, P., Reed, D.J., Konig, C.S., & McGowan, P.A. (1990). Parent education: Easing the transition to preschool. *Topics in Early Childhood Special Education, 9*(4), 66–77.

Turnbull, A.P., Summers, J.A., & Brotherson, M.J. (1986). Family life cycle: Theoretical and empirical implications for families with mentally retarded members. In J.J. Gallagher & P.M. Vietze (Eds.), *Families of handicapped persons: Research, programs, and policy issues* (pp. 45–65). Baltimore: Paul H. Brookes Publishing Co.

Turnbull, A.P., & Turnbull, H.R. (1990). *Families, professionals, and exceptionality: A special partnership.* New York: Macmillan.

Wikler, L. (1981). Chronic stress of families of mentally retarded children. *Family Relations, 30*, 281–288.

Wikler, L., Wasow, N., & Hatfield, E. (1983). Seeking strengths in families of disabled children. *Social Work, 28*(4), 313–315.

Chapter 10

Helping Families Support Siblings

Nancy Frank

Raising a child with special needs can place considerable demands on the entire family. Parents must address the specific needs of the child with a disability as well as those of other children in the family.

Parents of children with special needs who also have children who are developing typically may frequently express concern about whether the needs of all family members are being addressed adequately. Professionals can support parents by understanding some generic aspects of sibling relationships as well as some unique issues that are often raised by having a sibling with a disability. Individual families also are influenced by factors such as the health and development of the child with the disability, the number of siblings in the family, the characteristics of these siblings, general stressors affecting the family, the parents' child-rearing style, and the amount of social support available to the family. This chapter focuses on the needs of siblings and on issues that families may encounter as they address those needs.

FACTORS THAT INFLUENCE SIBLING RELATIONSHIPS

The effects of a child's disability on his or her sibling are perhaps best understood from a family systems perspective (Bronfenbrenner, 1979; Minuchin, 1974). A systems perspective is described in Chapter 1. As applied here, the larger family consists of several smaller subsystems (e.g., mother–child, child–child dyads). Interactions occur within and across subsystems. Each subsystem, in turn, can affect other family subsystems, causing adaptation and change within the family. For example, the interactions that occur between parents can influence the internal dynamics between two siblings. Similarly, the dynamics between or among siblings affect the other parts of the family system.

Because of these multiple influences, it can be difficult to separate the unique contribution of a particular family member from the dynamics of the entire family (Stoneman & Brody, 1993). In addition to the difficulty of separating such influences, little research has focused exclusively on the sibling relationship and its influence on each of the children and his or her own development (Stoneman & Brody, 1993). Researchers and interventionists, however, have recognized the importance of sibling relationships and some factors that influence these relationships.

Age
One of the longest lasting and most enduring relationships that an individual may have is with a sibling. The nature of sibling relationships varies over time, based on both the ages and the personal characteristics of the individuals involved (e.g., gender, temperament, birth order, spacing, number of children in the family, cultural expectations, family norms). Sibling relationships are frequently a source of companionship, support, and social learning. The roles of each sibling vary over time, and, consequently, the benefits and influences of the relationship change over time as well (Goetling, 1986; Seligman & Darling, 1989; Stoneman & Brody, 1993). In the early years, sibling relationships often involve companionship, power struggles, and ongoing negotiations. The older child also participates in socializing the younger sibling. This relationship is affected by the gender of the siblings because older brothers and sisters often assume different responsibilities with respect to their younger siblings and therefore exert different influences (Brody & Stoneman, 1993).

As children grow older, sibling relationships provide considerable companionship as siblings spend a lot of time together. Sibling relationships continue to offer opportunities for learning many important social skills, such as negotiation, compromise, and conflict resolution (Powell & Gallagher, 1993). Ambivalence may characterize this relationship during adolescence as each child attempts to form a sense of identity that is congruent internally and consistent with the family value system and with the external peer network (Bryant, 1982; Powell & Gallagher, 1993; Seligman & Darling, 1989). As adults, siblings have a more equal relationship that can provide support and acceptance. The importance of this relationship continues into old age. Often the sibling bond strengthens as parents die and children leave home and establish their own lives (Goetling, 1986; Seligman & Darling, 1989; Seltzer & Krauss, 1993).

Family Characteristics

In addition to the influences of age and developmental stages, several family characteristics, such as gender of children and birth order, shape sibling relationships (Brody & Stoneman, 1993). In their review of the literature, Brody and Stoneman (1993) identified several interesting effects of these characteristics. For example, the gender of the older sibling can influence types of play (solitary or interactive) and the choice of play material. Younger siblings of older brothers tend to engage in more male-type play and more solitary play. Older sisters tend to assume teaching and managing roles with younger siblings. Levels of conflict or friction also can be influenced by gender, with same-sex siblings having higher conflict levels, possibly because they are similar to one another (Brody & Stoneman, 1993).

Two other important influences include the number and spacing of children in the family (Breslau, 1982; Crnic & Lyons, 1993; Powell & Gallagher, 1993). Larger numbers of siblings offer larger social networks but also can create the need for siblings to rely on one another for more of the child-rearing needs. Spacing may mediate sibling influences, with brothers or sisters who are close in age having less experience to offer to their siblings. Closely spaced siblings, however, may provide more companionship and influence as children grow older but may increase conflict as siblings face similar developmental challenges at the same time.

Factors such as the financial resources of the family to cope with the ongoing needs of the child can greatly affect how much stress parents experience and how much involvement is required of their other children (Powell & Gallagher, 1993). For instance, in families with limited financial resources, more caregiving may be required of older siblings. Furthermore, it may be difficult to provide siblings with as many opportunities when existing resources are needed by the child with disabilities.

An additional factor that can influence sibling relationships is the temperament of each child (Brody & Stoneman, 1993; Brody, Stoneman, & Burke, 1987; Stoneman & Brody, 1993). Temperament can influence the parents and their child-rearing efforts and the relationships that occur between children. For example, Brody et al. (1987) found that high energy and emotional intensity on the part of one child can cause conflict and friction among family members. The relationship between temperament and sibling relationship, however, appears to be complex. Sometimes the temperament of the older sibling can act as a buffer for that of a younger sister or brother. Stoneman and Brody (1993) found that a low activity level on the part of an older sibling served as a buffer for highly active younger siblings. These pairs showed less conflict than pairs in which both siblings were active. This buffer did not occur, however, when the less active sibling was younger.

Parental adjustment and attitude also play a key role in how children with disabilities affect their siblings. Children are likely to use their parents as models as they attempt to understand and cope with having a brother or sister who has a disability. The parents' ability to talk with siblings about the disability, the type of parenting each child receives, and the parents' own emotional reactions can all influence the siblings' responses (Powell & Gallagher, 1993). Parents in turn are influenced by the larger community and the support they have or do not have. Factors such as religious beliefs, cultural acceptance and definition of the disability, and open acceptance or acknowledgment by the extended family all contribute to the family's well-being.

Stoneman and Brody (1993) noted that the parents' child-rearing strategies are potentially important in sibling relationships. Styles of conflict resolution, behavioral expectations, assignment of roles and responsibilities within the family, cultural expectations, children's relationships with one another, preferential or differential treatment of children, and parental styles of communication and negotiation can all have an impact on the sibling relationship and influence the dynamics of this family subsystem. These issues are discussed in more depth later in this chapter.

Type of Disability
Factors related to the disability itself can exert an influence on sibling relationships. These factors include the severity of the disability, the need for specialized care, health needs and concerns, and behavioral issues (Powell & Gallagher, 1993; Seligman & Darling, 1989; Simeonsson & Bailey, 1986; Stoneman & Brody, 1993).

Although distinct differences in adjustment have not been found based on type of disability, some characteristics of the child with special needs are hypothesized to be important to adjustment (Simeonsson & Bailey, 1986). Such characteristics include temperament, functional behaviors, and individual traits. Lobato (1983) suggested that the sex and age of the children in the family, and parents' attitude toward and adjustment to the child with special needs, are more influential for siblings than is the specific disability.

The severity of the disability and the consequent caregiving demands are also factors that appear to affect adjustment (Powell & Gallagher, 1993). These issues can have a direct impact on siblings who may need to help with child care for the child with a disability.

Characteristics of Siblings Without Disabilities
The characteristics and abilities of the siblings without disabilities also play a role in their adjustment to having a brother or sister with special needs. One key feature appears to be the sense of competence that the child without disabilities feels (Simeonsson & Bailey, 1986). Several authors have identified factors that can influence this sense of competence (Powell & Gallagher, 1993; Seligman & Darling, 1989; Simeonsson & Bailey, 1986). One set of factors includes cognitive skills, athletic abilities, creativity, and any other special qualities of the child. Other factors include the age and gender of the child in relation to the sibling with a disability and the support the child receives from his or her parents. Older children appear to have fewer adjustment difficulties, unless these older children, usually an older sister, are required to assume many caregiving responsibilities. Issues of identity, which are most likely linked with a sense of competence, are important to adjustment. Age and gender differences are associated with a positive sense of self in siblings (Powell & Gallagher, 1993; Seligman & Darling, 1989; Simeonsson & Bailey, 1986). The greater the similarities of the sibling to the child with the disability, the more likely that sibling will experience some adjustment difficulties (Powell & Gallagher, 1993).

The issue of what influence a child with special needs has on the adjustment of his or her brothers or sisters is very complex, and it is difficult to specify one key feature. Instead, many factors interact to exert both positive and negative influence on all of the children in the family.

ISSUES EXPERIENCED BY SIBLINGS

Parents can expect that their children may have concerns or issues related to their brother's or sister's disability. The presence of such concerns does not mean that the family is not functioning adequately or that the needs of the children without disabilities are not being met. Furthermore, the presence of concerns does not imply that all effects of having a brother or sister with a disability are negative. Considerable literature has documented many positive effects that result from this relationship (Powell & Gallagher, 1993; Seligman & Darling, 1989; Simeonsson & Bailey, 1986). For parents and service providers to adequately address the needs of siblings, however, it is important that they understand some common issues that may arise. Some of these issues are influenced by the age and developmental level of the child without disabilities. Others may evolve from family functioning style.

Young children who have siblings with special needs have somewhat unique reactions because they have difficulty understanding information about the disability. Lobato (1993) noted that before the age of 5, children are egocentric in their view of the world and often magical in their thinking. Therefore, they can sometimes misunderstand information about a sibling's disability or medical condition. Their sense of cause and effect is greatly influenced by how closely events occur in relation to one another. For example, young children may think that something they did or thought caused the disability, or they may interpret parental absences or anxiety as relating to themselves, rather than understanding that these are consequences of their sibling's disability (Lobato, 1993).

As siblings get older, misunderstandings about a sibling's disability can persist if the siblings are not adequately informed about their brother's or sister's special needs. Older siblings are often very aware of differential treatment by parents (Furman, 1993). Some studies of children without disabilities have found differential treatment can have a negative effect on sibling relationships (Brody, Stoneman, & McCoy, 1992; Daniels & Plomin, 1985; Dunn, Stocker, & Plomin, 1990). This relationship, however, appears to be somewhat complex. For instance, McHale and Pawtelko (1992) found that discrepancies in the way siblings are treated seemed to have more positive implications for older siblings of children with disabilities. These authors speculated that the presence of a disability may legitimize the variations in treatment. This suggests that differential treatment does not necessarily have a negative impact if the "typical" sibling can perceive and understand the reasons behind the difference in parental expectations and attitude. Yet angry and guilty feelings of the sibling are not unusual (Powell & Gallagher, 1993; Seligman, 1983; Seligman & Darling, 1989) and may be related to the time, attention, and accommodations parents make for the child with special needs.

Children without disabilities also may experience jealousy. This can be particularly true for young children who are less able to understand the special needs of their brother or sister. Siblings who are older may resent their brother or sister with special needs, because that child does not have to meet similar expectations. A subtle difficulty sometimes experienced by children without disabilities is a feeling that their accomplishments have been overlooked or taken for granted. At the same time, every achievement of their sibling is treated with great excitement and pleasure (Seligman & Darling, 1989). Therefore, the children without disabilities may not gain positive self-esteem or increased self-confidence from their accomplishments.

The effect that having a brother or sister with special needs has on the sibling's self-esteem and overall self-concept is uncertain (Seligman & Darling, 1989). Self-esteem may be influenced by the unique circumstances of the family, including the special demands created by the child with a disability. These may directly affect siblings by increasing their caregiving responsibilities. The literature suggests that siblings without disabilities, particularly older sisters, frequently are expected to assume caregiving responsibilities for their younger sibling (Powell & Gallagher, 1993; Seligman & Darling, 1989). As with all factors influencing sibling relationships, such demands can have mixed effects. In a positive sense, the sibling may feel that what he or she does makes a difference, which can enhance self-esteem and self-confidence. However, siblings can resent their brother or sister for depriving them of more "normal" activities, such as playing with friends or being part of extracurricular activities (Powell & Gallagher, 1993).

There is also some indication in the literature that siblings sometimes experience a sense of loneliness and isolation from others (Featherstone, 1980; Meyer & Vadasy, 1994). Isolation also can be influenced by factors such as the appearance, behavior, and unique health concerns of the child with a disability. For example, siblings may feel isolated from their parents if parents must spend extended periods at the hospital with a child who is chronically ill (Lobato, 1993). The reactions of extended family members, peers, and others in the community to the child with disabilities can influence the typical sibling's sense of connection to others or feelings of isolation (Seligman & Darling, 1989). The typical child's own perceptions of the nature and meaning of the disability may influence his or her behavior. For example, the child may feel embarrassed, may withdraw, or may develop behavior problems of his or her own (Meyer & Vadasy, 1994; Powell & Gallagher, 1993).

Seligman and Darling (1989) noted that another factor that influences the relationship is the behavior that the child with special needs exhibits toward his or her sibling. The more aggressive or atypical the behavior, the more likely that it will affect the feelings of his or her sibling. Children without disabilities may believe that they are not allowed to defend themselves because of their brother's or sister's disability (Seligman & Darling, 1989). Children also may feel that they have to defend the child with special needs from outside teasing or attack (Powell & Gallagher, 1993; Seligman & Darling, 1989). The more unusual, either because of the visibility of the disability or the deviance of the behavior from ordinary social standards, the more complex the sibling's feelings may be (Powell & Gallagher, 1993). These include feelings generated by sibling interactions and those provoked by community responses to the child with special needs.

The effect of having a sibling with special needs may be counterbalanced by other circumstances in the typical child's life. Parental support and awareness of the needs of other children in the family can mediate stresses caused by the circumstances related to one child's specific situation. Other important influences include the typical child's ability to succeed and gain a sense of competence and mastery in the various areas of his or her life, such as in school, through sports and other extracurricular activities, and with friends. The child's sense of entitlement to time, attention, and emotional support from parents also can affect his or her overall sense of well-being, even if the actual time and attention are less than that given to the child with the disability (Seligman & Darling, 1989). It is important for all the children in the family to gain a sense of support and acceptance from extended family and the support network of the family.

ISSUES EXPERIENCED BY PARENTS

Meyer and Vadasy (1994) argued that "siblings' experiences parallel parents' experiences" (p. 22). Consequently, the parents' reaction and adaptation to having a child with special needs can have an important impact on the siblings' reactions. One of the most significant issues is the parents' adjustment to having and raising a child with a disability (Powell & Gallagher, 1993). For all family members, the process of adaptation to a child with special needs is complex and changes over time. One intense period occurs when the family finds out about the child's disability. During this period, parents must adjust their expectations and dreams to accommodate the knowledge that their child has some unique challenges with which to cope. Siblings may be uncertain of how to respond to the news. All family members feel a sense of normlessness as they face these new circumstances (Seligman & Darling, 1989). Unfortunately, when parents feel overwhelmed, they may have difficulty communicating with other family members. Children may react protectively, not wishing to cause additional pain, and therefore may not ask for information that would help them adjust.

Some research has documented the effects of depression on parenting styles of mothers (Stoneman & Brody, 1993). This literature suggests that feelings of depression, chronic sorrow, and hurt can influence parenting in several ways. These states of mind may drain parents of internal resources necessary to be available to support the siblings. It can also lead to parenting strategies that are inconsistent, that use punitive methods to control behavior, and that induce guilt and anxiety. Parents may be less likely to use intentional discipline strategies, such as rational guidance, and instead may choose less cognitively demanding types of discipline (Kuczynski, 1984). These parenting styles, in turn, can lead to conflicted sibling relationships (Brody, Stoneman, & MacKinnon, 1986). Therefore, parental reactions influence sibling adjustment because they may compromise the parents' ability to effectively manage the sibling relationship (Stoneman & Brody, 1993).

Another factor that can influence sibling reactions is the parents' marital satisfaction. There are mixed research findings about whether having a child with a disability affects the marital unit (Stoneman & Brody, 1993). Increased spousal conflict and decreased marital satisfaction, however, can negatively influence positive or prosocial behavior characterizing sibling relationships (Brody et al., 1987). Also, decreased marital satisfaction influences feelings of support and a sense of isolation experienced by each parent. Thus, to the extent that decreased marital satisfaction occurs, it can affect the quality of sibling relationships.

Other parental influences on sibling relationships include personal characteristics and child-rearing styles that parents bring to the family from their own experiences. Parental styles of communication and negotiation model how information is given and questions are handled in the family. Discussions about the nature of the child's disability and family members' feelings about it are often intense and stressful. If open communication is difficult in other areas within the family, it is likely to be even more challenging around the topic of the child's disability. How parents negotiate disappointment and frustration; resolve conflicts; and manage uncomfortable feelings of sorrow, anger, guilt, and hurt are likely to influence siblings' responses to similar issues.

Parents also may have specific expectations about how children should behave. These expectations influence what behavior parents are willing to tolerate and what kinds of roles and responsibilities they envision each family member fulfilling. Such expectations often vary by gender and age.

STRATEGIES TO HELP PARENTS SUPPORT SIBLINGS

There are several specific ways in which service providers can help parents support the typical siblings of their child with special needs. These include providing information and working toward open and honest communication, supporting the feelings of siblings, balancing responsibilities in the family, providing opportunities to enhance the competence and self-esteem of the typical child, and accepting themselves as parents.

Providing Information and Communication

One of the most fundamental ways in which adults can support siblings is by providing clear information to them about their brother's or sister's special needs. Misinformation, lack of knowledge, and misunderstanding of information all contribute to siblings' feelings of guilt, fear, anger, responsibility, and confusion (Powell & Gallagher, 1993; Seligman & Darling, 1989). Even when parents have made every effort to provide their children with accurate and developmentally appropriate information, children can still misunderstand or interpret the information in idiosyncratic ways. Seligman and Darling (1989) discussed the importance of learning the child's private view or personal understanding of his or her sibling's condition and its causes. This view often represents an integration of both facts and imagination at the child's particular level of cognitive development. It includes the child's synthesis of concrete pieces of information; physical characteristics that the child has noticed are different; and the imagined effects of the child's own actions, feelings, and thoughts (Lobato, 1990). It is important for parents to be aware that children are sometimes able to repeat correct factual information about their sibling while holding an idiosyncratic personal understanding of these facts.

Information must be presented in a way that is consistent with the children's cognitive understanding (Lobato, 1990). Siblings also may need to hear information many times and in different ways to integrate realistic and factual information (Seligman & Darling, 1989). Including children in regular family talks about issues relating to the child with the disability and to the needs of the family can be a natural way to provide factual information. Typical siblings also can be invited to doctors' visits and included in any programs that special education centers, developmental clinics, or hospitals offer for siblings.

Powell and Gallagher (1993) identified several communication guidelines that can help parents facilitate open and honest exchange. These guidelines include using active listening (see Chapter 3), taking time to explain and answer questions, having the necessary information and knowledge, being sincere and honest, responding comprehensively, having an open attitude, presenting balanced information, being aware of nonverbal messages, commenting on nonverbal expressions of feelings, and facilitating and anticipating questions. It is also helpful to follow up on earlier conversations to ensure that the siblings understand key points. Parents also need to be aware of the language they use to describe the child with special needs and avoid words that invite comparison, such as *better* or *worse* (Seligman & Darling, 1989).

One dilemma that typical siblings face is the need to understand their feelings and those that they perceive are experienced by others in the family. The information provided about their sibling's disability becomes part of their internal context, which helps explain the feelings associated with their brother or sister. Children are likely to fill in missing or needed pieces to help manage their feelings. Consequently, parents can support siblings both by providing factual information and by showing an understanding of their feelings. For example, a parent can explain the need for individual home-based physical therapy services to a sibling based on the facts of the child's disability—that his or her brother has trouble sitting and needs help to learn to sit. Then the parent can talk with the sibling about what this is like for him or her (e.g., it may seem unfair that his or her brother gets to bounce on a ball and he or she does not; it may make him or her angry or jealous that the other child gets all that attention from Mommy and the physical therapist).

As the typical child gets older and interacts with the larger community, other dilemmas emerge, such as how to talk to others about the sibling with special needs or what other people might think (Meyer & Vadasy, 1994; Powell & Gallagher, 1993). Parents may have difficulty talking about this with their children, because this is often a difficult area for the parents as well. It may also be challenging because parents try to balance their role of advocate and protector of the child with the disability with their role of encouraging and supporting their other children to move out into the world. Parents and professionals supporting parents can offer children without disabilities and their peers explanations that convey concrete and direct information and a sensitive attitude toward the disability. For example, parents can explain to their son's friend that his sister drools because the muscles in her mouth do not get the message to stay closed and swallow. Such information can diffuse the potential for teasing about an unacceptable or undesirable behavior and promote more sensitivity toward the child with the disability.

Parents also may need to offer concrete suggestions about how and when to include the child with special needs in the play of other children. For instance, parents can suggest games in which all children participate. After a reasonable time, the parent can give the typical children permission to play games that require more sophisticated skills. By structuring ways that both the sibling and his or her friends can interact with his or her brother or sister, the parent helps all the children find ways to connect and to feel successful and important. Typical children often enjoy feeling that they helped or taught someone something. Therefore, rather than viewing the child with the disability as someone to be avoided, peers can begin to find pleasure and satisfaction in their relationship with the child who has a disability, and they may begin to be supportive of him or her.

Supportive Feelings
In addition to information, siblings of children with special needs often require additional support to deal with their feelings. Typical children not only face the usual issues of sibling rivalry, jealousy, and competition but also have some very unique concerns that are directly related to having a brother or sister who has a disability (Meyer & Vadasy, 1994; Powell & Gallagher, 1993). One such concern is that their brother or sister is not "normal" and cannot do the things that the sibling might like him or her to do. Children may be sad that they do not have someone to play with them or to share their thoughts or activities. They may resent the attention that the other child receives or the way he or she interferes with their activities. They may be embarrassed by the way their brother or sister looks, talks, or has tantrums. They may be afraid when their brother or sister is sick, in the hospital, or seeing special doctors. They also may be angry because they feel that their sibling can get away with things they cannot do, does not have to work hard, can always get their parents to take his or her side, or keeps the siblings from doing some of the things they want to do. Compounding all of these feelings may be the sense that no one understands and that they are the only ones who feel this way or have to manage situations like these.

Parents can help by openly talking about feelings that might occur from having a brother or sister with a disability, using the guidelines for communication previously outlined. It may be counterproductive for parents to respond by pointing out all the positive aspects without first listening to the reactions the typical child might have. Such an approach can send a subtle message that negative feelings are unacceptable or that grown-ups do not want to hear them. It is important for children to maintain a balanced view of both the rewards and difficulties of having a brother or sister with special needs. For that balance to occur, however, negative or uncomfortable feelings need to be explored and accepted. This process can be difficult because everyone in the family may have strong emotions about the child with the disability. Furthermore, children may not bring up their feelings, partly because they want to protect their parents from experiencing (or reexperiencing) painful issues (Seligman & Darling, 1989).

Parents can use community resources to help siblings deal with their feelings. These resources do not replace the need to talk within the family, but can offer additional support for children. Sibling support groups or workshops provide opportunities to meet other children who have similar feelings, questions, and experiences (Meyer & Vadasy, 1994; Powell & Gallagher, 1993). This kind of group can lessen the sense of isolation and loneliness that siblings may feel, much the same way that support groups offer parents a sense of connection with others who understand. Sibling groups also can help children fill in missing or confused information. Children often find that other children had similar ideas and feelings. Being able to talk without the worry that this might upset a parent can sometimes meet important needs for children.

Another positive aspect of sibling support groups is that the attention is truly focused on the siblings, and they do not have to compete with or take away time from their brother or sister. Although siblings may feel jealous of the time and attention given to the child with special needs, they may also feel guilty about wanting this attention. A group focused exclusively on siblings implicitly acknowledges their right to special time and attention, and it can be offered without taking away from anyone else. The groups validate the importance of the siblings' concerns and recognize their role and contributions to the family (Meyer & Vadasy, 1994).

There may be times when typical children need additional support through individual counseling. For some children, group situations may be more threatening than helpful. Older siblings may be embarrassed to admit their feelings or concerns to others and consequently may benefit more from a private, individual approach. Individual support can be provided through community health or mental health centers and also through the typical child's school guidance or counseling services. Unfortunately, counseling is still viewed by some people as stigmatizing. Reframing such services as supportive or educational may make them more attractive to parents and siblings. Service providers may want to encourage some parents to seek additional help, especially if their typical child is having significant behavioral, educational, or social difficulties.

Balancing Responsibilities

The impact of a child with special needs is experienced by the entire family. Parents face a difficult task in distributing the responsibilities among the family members in such a way as to prevent anyone from being overwhelmed. Often siblings have to assume some tasks associated with caregiving. This is particularly true if the disability is severe, if the child requires more extensive caregiving, if the resources of the family preclude using outside supports, or if extended family or community supports are limited.

If the family's circumstances require the children without disabilities to assume additional responsibilities, parents have to decide how much to ask or expect of them. In a way, this is a no-win situation: If the parent assumes the bulk of the responsibilities, then he or she is neither emotionally nor physically available to the other children. If the parent assigns responsibilities to the typical sibling, however, it affects the sibling's time and needs. Although there may be no alternative to shared caregiving, it helps if the parents are honest and acknowledge the children's feelings about these family needs. Parents also can make accommodations for each family member. They can ensure that the sacrifices are as evenly shared as possible and that there are times when each child's needs become primary.

Another way to support parents who are trying to balance the needs of multiple family members is for professionals to be sensitive to the needs of the whole family when planning intervention. Service providers should guard against inadvertently encouraging the energy and resources of the family to be focused primarily on one member. They also can help families obtain outside help in the form of respite or child care services. Such support can ensure that the siblings' needs are not overlooked in the multiple demands placed on parents.

Enhancing Competence

A positive self-concept and sense of competence can counterbalance issues or concerns that a sibling may have about a brother or sister with a disability. One way for parents to support the development of competence and positive self-esteem is to encourage the child to participate as fully as possible in the activities of same-age peers. Sometimes this is difficult, given the multiple demands on the family. Parents may need to help the child choose one activity or hobby to pursue. Communicating frankly about family resources and encouraging the child to be part of the decisions about how these resources can be allocated equitably can help alleviate anger and resentment.

Parents also may wish to enlist the help of other community resources available to the child. For instance, communicating to the school about the pressures that the child may be experiencing at home enables personnel to provide extra support and resources for the child's benefit. Schools may have lunch clubs where children get a little extra positive attention from a special teacher or guidance counselor, and they may invite a child who has a sibling with special needs to participate. Church groups may sponsor certain children for special events or activities. Parents and service providers can advocate for their child without disabilities to receive these benefits rather than have all the community resources focused on the child with the disability. Even services primarily aimed at the child with the disability can ensure that typical siblings receive recognition and praise for either a skill or an attribute or for the sensitivity they have for their sibling. For instance, nurses might comment that the sibling is the one most likely to notice when his or her brother or sister is getting hungry. In this way, service providers offer models and reminders of the importance of recognizing and validating the strengths and capabilities of siblings.

Being a "Good Enough" Parent
It is critical that parents are not made to feel guilty or inadequate in the care of any of their children. Parents need support for the effort they exert on behalf of their families. Parents often have misgivings, doubts, and guilty feelings about whether they are doing enough and doing the right things for all their children. Service providers can support parents by listening to and understanding their thoughts and feelings. Two reactions of service providers are common when parents communicate their concerns. One is to offer advice on how to fix the problem, and the other is to reassure the parents that they are doing a fine job. (The difficulty with either of these responses is described in Chapter 3.) Such reactions often do not allow time or space for parents to gain a personal understanding and resolution of their situation.

Unfortunately, given the complexity of raising children, there are times when parents feel that they are not rearing their children as they envisioned themselves doing. Helping parents to examine their feelings associated with this and to reassess their expectations for themselves allows them to identify reachable goals. Parents can gain a broader understanding of both what they have to offer their children and what they cannot provide for them. They arrive at standards of a "good enough" parent, standards that allow them to feel positive about their efforts and not be overwhelmed by feelings of guilt or inadequacy for what they are unable to offer.

Service providers can offer support by listening to parents' concerns and by not offering advice until parents ask them for suggestions. Service providers also may be aware of children's feelings and complaints about their parents. Providers must not take sides or criticize parents for their efforts based on the children's information. Just as it is important for parents and children to work through difficulties in allocating time and resources, it is also critical that service providers adopt a neutral problem-solving stance with parents, supporting them in coping with various demands on their time and resources. Just as parents need to come to their own personal definition of being a good enough parent, service providers need to view parents positively and respect their efforts to manage their families.

CONCLUSIONS

Issues related to siblings of children with special needs are complex and multidimensional. The same factors that influence families in general can influence the sibling subsystem. In addition, factors such as the age of the siblings, their temperaments and characteristics, and the severity of the disability play a role. Yet children's reactions to having a sibling with a disability also are affected by their developmental stage, the parents' response to the child with the disability, the parents' child-rearing practices in general, and the innate abilities of the typical children.

Siblings need parents and service providers to communicate openly and honestly about their brother's or sister's special needs. They also need to express both their positive and negative feelings about their sibling, without feeling guilty or concerned that they are upsetting people. Parents and service providers can find ways to balance the needs of the child with a disability with those of the other children and to talk directly about the demands the family must meet for the child with special needs. Support for the typical child's competence and efforts to promote positive self-esteem and self-confidence are very important and help to counterbalance possible negative effects of having a sibling with a disability.

ACTIVITIES AND DISCUSSION

1. Read Case Study I, the Barnes Family, paying attention to the sibling issues. Discuss the following questions:
    a. What sibling issues are represented by Jonathan's behaviors? Do you agree or disagree with the approach taken by the visiting nurse? Why or why not? What would you have done?
    b. Given Jonathan's age, what concerns or issues do you think he might have about his brother? What do you think he notices about his brother's special needs?
    c. How would you find out Jonathan's understanding of his brother's disability, including his colostomy?
    d. How could you support Beth in explaining David's upcoming surgery to Jonathan? What might be some issues for Jonathan or for a typical 5-year-old in understanding surgery?
    e. Are there any ways Jonathan might feel he is responsible for any of David's problems or for any other difficulties this family is experiencing? How would you find this out?
    f. What has Beth done so far to support Jonathan's development of self-esteem and a sense of competence? Are there any other things you think Jonathan's parents can do?
    g. Are there any potential issues that you might anticipate as Jonathan moves into elementary school?
2. Read Case Study II, the Martínez Family. Discuss the following questions:
    a. Rosa Martínez realizes that her 9-year-old daughter, Carmen, needs information about her sister's health. How might Rosa tell Carmen about Ana's ongoing health concerns?
    b. What may be Carmen's reaction to having a nurse present in the home? If you were part of the nurse's orientation, what would you tell her about Carmen and potential sibling issues?
    c. How do you think other family members are influencing or affecting Carmen?
    d. How would you explain Carmen's withdrawal from her social group at school? Do you think this influences her overall functioning? Do you have any suggestions for changing her pattern?

    e. What do you think some of Carmen's feelings are about the events of the past 8 months and about Ana? How would you support Carmen in talking about her feelings? How might this be influenced by the family's cultural background?

    f. How might Carmen react to a potential medical emergency with Ana? What are your thoughts on how to handle this possibility?

3. Enact the following scenarios for several minutes:

    a. *A home visit.* Include the following characters: a mother, a 3-year-old with cerebral palsy, a 5-year-old sibling without disabilities, and a home-based interventionist. The interventionist brings several interesting toys and physical therapy equipment, such as theraballs, scooter boards, and various items to manipulate. As the interventionist begins to work with the 3-year-old, the 5-year-old starts investigating the equipment and playing with the toys. His mother tries to remove him from the area, but, unless she stays with him, he returns. Role-play this scene for several minutes.

    b. *A family eating dinner at a local restaurant.* The family includes a mother and a father, a 15-year-old, a 12-year-old, and a 9-year-old with autism. The 9-year-old has some stereotypic behaviors, including making a repetitive clicking noise with his tongue, sniffing all the food before eating, and flicking a straw in front of his eyes. He is also quite impatient about getting his food and starts to become upset while waiting for the order to arrive. The restaurant has several other patrons eating there. Enact this scene for about 3–5 minutes.

After each role-playing activity, discuss what feelings the situation evokes for each participant. Then brainstorm ideas for managing similar situations.

REFERENCES

Breslau, N. (1982). Siblings of disabled children. *Journal of Abnormal Child Psychology, 10,* 85–96.

Brody, G.H., & Stoneman, Z. (1993). Parameters for inclusion in studies on sibling relationships: Some heuristic suggestions. In Z. Stoneman & P.W. Berman (Eds.), *The effects of mental retardation, disability, and illness on sibling relationships: Research issues and challenges* (pp. 275–286). Baltimore: Paul H. Brookes Publishing Co.

Brody, G.H., Stoneman, Z., & Burke, M. (1987). Child temperaments, maternal differential behavior, and sibling relations. *Developmental Psychology, 23,* 354–362.

Brody, G.H., Stoneman, Z., & MacKinnon, C.E. (1986). Contributions of maternal child-rearing practices and play contexts to sibling interactions. *Journal of Applied Developmental Psychology, 7,* 225–236.

Brody, G.H., Stoneman, Z., & McCoy, J.K. (1992). Associations of maternal and paternal direct and differential behavior with sibling relationships: Contemporaneous and longitudinal analyses. *Child Development, 63,* 391–400.

Bronfenbrenner, U. (1979). *The ecology of human development: Experiments by nature and design.* Cambridge, MA: Harvard University Press.

Bryant, B.K. (1982). Sibling relationships in middle childhood. In M.E. Lamb & B. Sutton-Smith (Eds.), *Sibling relationships* (pp. 87–122). Hillsdale, NJ: Lawrence Erlbaum Associates.

Crnic, K.A., & Lyons, J. (1993). Siblings of children with dual diagnosis. In Z. Stoneman & P.W. Berman (Eds.), *The effects of mental retardation, disability, and illness on sibling relationships: Research issues and challenges* (pp. 253–271). Baltimore: Paul H. Brookes Publishing Co.

Daniels, D., & Plomin, R. (1985). *Separate lives: Why siblings are so different.* New York: Basic Books.

Dunn, J., Stocker, C., & Plomin, R. (1990). Nonshared experiences within the family: Correlates of behavioral problems in middle childhood. *Development and Psychopathology, 2,* 113–126.

Featherstone, H. (1980). *A difference in the family: Living with a disabled child.* New York: Basic Books.

Furman, W.C. (1993). Contemporary themes in research on sibling relationships of nondisabled children. In Z. Stoneman & P.W. Berman (Eds.), *The effects of mental retardation, disability, and illness on sibling relationships: Research issues and challenges* (pp. 31–50). Baltimore: Paul H. Brookes Publishing Co.

Goetling, A. (1986). The developmental tasks of siblingship over the life cycle. *Journal of Marriage and the Family, 48,* 703–714.

Kuczynski, L. (1984). Socialization goals and mother-child interactions: Strategies for long-term and short-term compliance. *Developmental Psychology, 20,* 1061–1073.

Lobato, D.J. (1983). Siblings of handicapped children: A review. *Journal of Autism and Developmental Disorders, 13*(4), 347–364.

Lobato, D.J. (1990). *Brothers, sisters, and special needs: Information and activities for helping young siblings of children with chronic illnesses and developmental disabilities.* Baltimore: Paul H. Brookes Publishing Co.

Lobato, D.J. (1993). Issues and interventions for young siblings of children with medical and developmental problems. In Z. Stoneman & P.W. Berman (Eds.), *The effects of mental retardation, disability, and illness on sibling relationships: Research issues and challenges* (pp. 85–98). Baltimore: Paul H. Brookes Publishing Co.

McHale, S.M., & Pawtelko, T.M. (1992). Differential treatment of siblings in two family contexts. *Child Development, 63,* 68–81.

Meyer, D.J., & Vadasy, P.F. (1994). *Sibshops: Workshops for siblings of children with special needs.* Baltimore: Paul H. Brookes Publishing Co.

Minuchin, S. (1974). *Families and family therapy.* Cambridge, MA: Harvard University Press.

Powell, T.H., & Gallagher, P.A. (1993). *Brothers and sisters—A special part of exceptional families.* Baltimore: Paul H. Brookes Publishing Co.

Seligman, M. (1983). Siblings of handicapped persons. In M. Seligman (Ed.), *The family with a handicapped child* (pp. 147–174). New York: Grune & Stratton.

Seligman, M., & Darling, R.B. (1989). *Ordinary families, special children: A systems approach to childhood disability.* New York: Guilford Press.

Seltzer, M.M., & Krauss, M.W. (1993). Adult sibling relationships of persons with mental retardation. In Z. Stoneman & P.W. Berman (Eds.), *The effects of mental retardation, disability, and illness on sibling relationships: Research issues and challenges* (pp. 99–116). Baltimore: Paul H. Brookes Publishing Co.

Simeonsson, R.J., & Bailey, D.B. (1986). Siblings of handicapped children. In J.J. Gallagher & P.M. Vietze (Eds.), *Families of handicapped persons: Research, programs and policy issues* (pp. 67–80). Baltimore: Paul H. Brookes Publishing Co.

Stoneman, Z., & Brody, G.H. (1993). Sibling relations in the family context. In Z. Stoneman & P.W. Berman (Eds.), *The effects of mental retardation, disability, and illness on sibling relationships: Research issues and challenges* (pp. 3–30). Baltimore: Paul H. Brookes Publishing Co.

Appendix

Organizations that Specifically Address Sibling Issues

Sibling Support Project
Children's Hospital and Medical Center
P.O. Box 5371, CL-09
Seattle, WA 98105-0371
(206) 368-4911

Siblings for Significant Change
United Charities Building
105 East 22nd Street
Room 710
New York, NY 10010
(212) 420-0776

Siblings of Disabled Children
Parents Helping Parents, Inc.
3041 Olcott Street
Santa Clara, CA 95054-3222
(408) 727-5775

Chapter 11

Strategies for Working with Families When a Child Dies

Jennifer Smith Stepanek
and Sandra Newcomb

Remarkable advancements in lifesaving technology since the 1970s have led to increased survival rates for premature infants, survivors of traumatic events, and individuals with disabling or life-threatening conditions. As neonatal and pediatric care continues to improve, more children are living longer and fuller lives. However, this progress has led to a concurrent increase in long-term morbidity, including chronic health conditions and early death (National Commission to Prevent Infant Mortality, 1988; Newacheck, 1993).

Professionals who provide services to young children with disabilities are subsequently encountering a growing number of young children who are technology users or considered medically fragile (McGonigel, Kaufman, & Johnson, 1991; Taylor & Gortler, 1993). When working with children who have life-threatening conditions, the possibility of death becomes a reality, although it is undeniably difficult and challenging to comprehend. The death of a child is an unnatural loss and an experience that can lead survivors—both family members and professionals—to question their roles in the child's life, their choices, their work, their personal lives, and their spirituality.

Because the death of a child can be challenging in so many ways, preparing professionals to be aware of issues related to loss and to be ready for the potential of a child's death is essential. Clinical, social, and emotional issues related to loss are highly relevant to family and professional decision making, attitudes, and abilities (Jellinek, Catlin, Todres, & Cassem, 1992). Furthermore, competent professional support can facilitate coping as families anticipate and deal with the finality of loss (Harmon, Glicken, & Siegel, 1984).

With the emerging shift toward family-centered services and the broad notion of what constitutes family-centered care and support, many competent professionals often develop close ties with young children and their families (Dunst, Trivette, & Deal, 1994; Shelton & Stepanek, 1994). Caring professionals working with children who have life-threatening conditions and their families must then also work through the pain of loss themselves. Thus, both professional and personal development related to understanding grief, mourning, and bereavement are important for early intervention and special education service providers (Taylor & Gortler, 1993).

This chapter discusses strategies to help professionals 1) understand grief and loss from both professional and personal perspectives, 2) develop policies and practices that promote comprehensive and quality services for families facing loss, 3) work with families after the death of a child, and 4) manage professional and personal loss in ways that foster individual growth.

UNDERSTANDING LOSS:
FAMILY AND PROFESSIONAL PERSPECTIVES

The knowledge and skills of practitioners can be enhanced or diminished by the quality of the relationships they establish with young children and their families (Eggbeer, Fenichel, Pawl, Shanok, & Williamson, 1994; see also Chapter 2 of this book). To be prepared for a relationship that may involve the death of a child, service providers need to understand the basic terminology and processes associated with loss, both for the family and for themselves personally. This can help professionals build a stronger framework for working with families (Gortler, 1992). This section contains information about loss in general, unique features surrounding the loss of a child, gender-related differences in coping styles, and the importance of self-reflection about personal experience related to loss.

Literature concerned with loss has distinguished three major terms: 1) *grief*, 2) *mourning*, and 3) *bereavement* (Access to Respite Care and Help [ARCH], 1993; Taylor & Gortler, 1993). *Grief* refers to an individual's personal experience of loss. It represents the internal feelings associated with loss, which subsequently affect external behaviors. *Mourning* is the outward sharing and expression of pain and grief in a supportive environment. It incorporates the cultural and religious rituals associated with grief. *Bereavement* encompasses the entire process of grief and mourning, as well as the process of moving on and subsequent personal growth. These distinctions are especially important because many people in society feel permission to grieve, but they cannot mourn. This can interfere with a successful bereavement process (ARCH, 1993).

Grief and mourning are universal yet complex and painful processes (Jackson, 1992). However, the way that individuals experience and deal with issues of loss can be quite personal. One substantial body of literature suggests that individuals progress through a series of stages after the death of a loved one. These stages typically include shock, denial, anger, bargaining, depression, submission, and reinvestment (see, e.g., Compassionate Friends, 1990; Jackson, 1992; Kübler-Ross, 1975; Weber & Fournier, 1985). In contrast, other literature indicates that not everyone progresses through these stages in a linear fashion, in the same order, or at the same speed (ARCH, 1993). For instance, Moses (1992) suggested that rather than a linear progression through stages, the movement is cyclical. The stages and associated feelings may come in any order, and individuals may experience some or all of the stages at once.

There are also a number of feelings that are typically identified with the various stages of grief and mourning, including denial, sadness, anger, guilt, anxiety, loneliness, fatigue, helplessness, shock, numbness, and confusion (Kübler-Ross, 1975; Moses, 1992). Behavioral manifestations may include sleeplessness, lack of appetite, social withdrawal, and crying (ARCH, 1993). In some cases, when these typical responses to grief are repressed, adverse effects have been identified such as outbursts of anger, substance abuse, or personal illness (Schiff, 1988).

With all the responses generally associated with loss, it is important not to overlook feelings of hope. Hope can help sustain energy in stressful and difficult times and can help individuals "define positive outcomes toward which they can reach" (Powers, 1993, p. 126). For example, when forced by the loss of a child to examine very basic beliefs related to life and death, some parents and professionals have reached new levels of spirituality (Kelley & Kelley, 1993; Stepanek, 1995a).

The Loss of a Child
For most parents, the worst trial they can face is the death of their child. Fortunately, most parents do not have to face this pain. However, many individuals do experience such a loss or know someone who has. Because such a loss is unique, general conceptualizations about grief are less applicable (Guntzelman, 1992; Rando, 1986; Schiff, 1988).

One potential difference in the bereavement process for parents is the length of the grieving period. Although broadly defined time frames have been identified for typical stages of grief and mourning (Compassionate Friends, 1990; Kübler-Ross, 1975), the grieving process is often lengthened when a child dies. For example, in one study of 34 adults who had experienced 55 instances of perinatal loss, frequent or intense feelings related to the loss lasted for 44 years (Rosenblatt & Burns, 1986).

Guilt, particularly questions relating to what could have been done differently to prevent the death, is common when a child dies (Guntzelman, 1992; Schiff, 1988). The unique way in which children are dependent on their parents can increase this sense of guilt (Rando, 1986). Other features of the parent–child relationship that make the loss of a child unique and grieving more complicated include the amount of caregiving required, the complete dependence of the child, the unnatural timing of the child's death, and the unexpected sequence of events (child dying before parent).

Certain parental responses are common but may make others uncomfortable. Preoccupation with death, looking for similarities to the deceased child in other children, carrying objects that are reminders of the child, and avoiding places that are reminders of the loss are examples of such responses. Other parents have reported responses such as the following:

- Feeling like one is going "crazy"—crying one minute and laughing the next
- Watching for the child to take a breath during the wake period, days after he or she has died
- Taking pictures of the child at the wake or funeral service
- Missing the child's smell and touch, and missing the professionals and even the equipment that may have supported the child's life
- Feelings of not wanting to live without the child and yet not wanting to die
- Wanting to hold and rock the child after death
- Choosing to have the child's wake service in the home, rather than at a funeral parlor
- Wanting to participate in the child's wake and funeral service, such as by writing or singing passages or songs, by choosing readings, or by being one of the child's pallbearers. (Stepanek & Newcomb, 1994)

Each of these reactions can be healthy to some point, because they help facilitate the bereavement process through expressions of grief and mourning.

In addition to parents, other family members also are affected by the death of a child, including surviving siblings, grandparents, and other extended family members. Even siblings yet unborn to the bereaved parents can be affected by the loss of a child, because such an intense loss can affect emotions and parenting styles for a prolonged period (Sahler & Friedman, 1981). Furthermore, the younger the deceased child, the younger the parents, or the fewer number of years the family has been together as a unit have all been found to adversely affect adaptation to loss (Powers, 1993; B.D. Schatz, 1986). Family adaptation can also be affected by specific circumstances surrounding the child's death. By recognizing and appropriately responding to such potentially far-reaching effects, professionals can help facilitate a supportive environment for the bereavement process.

Gender-Related Differences in Coping

A growing body of literature suggests that styles of grieving tend to be gender related (Damrosch & Perry, 1989; Guntzelman, 1992; Powers, 1993; Rando, 1986). For example, in their study of responses to loss, Damrosch and Perry (1989) found that fathers exhibited steady, time-bound adjustment, whereas most of the mothers reported more chronic distress interspersed with crises. Both fathers and mothers reported feeling deep sorrow, although mothers were more likely to express negative affect related to the sorrow than fathers. Additionally, fathers reported that they preferred not to dwell on feelings, whereas mothers preferred being allowed to express their sadness.

The grieving process for mothers is often intense and lengthy (ARCH, 1993; Compassionate Friends, 1990; Rando, 1986). Because mothers are often their children's primary caregivers, they face coping with the loss not only of their children's future but of their own role. The result can be sensory deprivation because the mother is no longer able to love, care for, or nurture the child and because there is no feedback (e.g., touch, smile, words, activities) from the child. Although both parents must deal with memories of the child that are triggered by environmental cues directly related to a personal sensory experience with the child, this tends to happen more often with the mother (B.D. Schatz, 1986).

For fathers, the grief process is more often internal and may become apparent in indirect ways (see, e.g., ARCH, 1993; Compassionate Friends, 1990; W.H. Schatz, 1986). W.H. Schatz (1986) noted that traditional social roles and attitudes can impede paternal expressions of grief. These include the following stereotypes: 1) males are strong and always in control of emotions; 2) males should win when competing; 3) males protect their families and possessions;

4) males are the providers, problem solvers, and fixers for their families; 5) males control things, including their environment; and 6) males are self-sufficient.

Although it is important to avoid stereotyping, awareness of the potential for different styles of grieving can keep communication open and foster mutual respect for individual coping styles within families (Guntzelman, 1992; Powers, 1993). Both mothers and fathers move forward in life and recover from the loss, but neither forget their children, and their lives will never be quite the same (B.D. Schatz, 1986).

Sudden and Unexpected Loss

For some families there is time to process and prepare for the death of a child. For others, a child's death may occur suddenly and unexpectedly. Many of the supports for families who have children with life-threatening illnesses, such as information about resources or anticipatory planning, are not in place when a child dies suddenly. A major factor that distinguishes between reactions to death from illness and sudden death is shock (Sanders, 1986). For parents who must deal with sudden death, the shock component may create grief reactions that are more intense and longer lasting (Parks & Weiss, 1983). In such cases, the shock phase can last for months or even years (Sanders, 1986). Although most parents feel a loss of control with the death of a child, this is intensified when their child dies suddenly and unexpectedly. A world that was orderly and predictable becomes chaotic and unpredictable. Parents do not know what to trust. With no time to even imagine a world without the child, new shocks are often forthcoming. A sudden reminder, such as a special toy or song, can recreate the sense of shock (Sanders, 1986). This feeling of helplessness can then lead to feelings of extreme frustration and anger. Service providers need to remember that any parental grief reaction may be intensified if the child's death was unexpected.

Professionals' Reactions to Loss:
The Importance of Self-Reflection

When working with children and families who are facing loss, a professional needs to consider his or her own reactions to loss. Many adults have unresolved issues related to grief they experienced as a child or young adult (ARCH, 1993; Fitzgerald, 1992). To better support families facing loss, it is helpful if service providers are aware of their own personal issues about grief and can work toward resolving these issues. Self-reflection (Beckman et al., 1996; Jellinek et al., 1992; see also Chapter 2 of this book) is a critical part of preparing personnel to address loss.

For professionals who react strongly to funerals or to the very concept of death, Fitzgerald (1992) offered some suggestions for dealing with long-standing grief issues. She recommends that service providers seek help through an in-depth examination of reactions to loss guided by a skilled professional. This process can help providers identify and deal with their own grief issues. Understanding personal issues, experiences, attitudes, and feelings related to loss prepares professionals to offer support to families facing loss.

Each time a service provider works with a child who has a life-threatening illness, reflective examination of related issues can help the provider become more aware of personal and professional abilities or limitations that may affect his or her work. Once these past issues have been addressed, there are a number of ways to prepare for current and future issues (Jellinek et al., 1992). Table 1 identifies questions that can serve as catalysts for ongoing self-reflection and preparation for meeting the needs of the child and family.

In addition to self-reflection on personal and professional loss, practitioners must also establish personal and professional work-related goals (Stepanek & Newcomb, 1994). During such a process, it may be necessary to redefine professional roles and responsibilities. For instance, Stepanek and Newcomb (1994) suggested that objectives include more than typical intervention tasks. First, actions such as taking the time to find creative activities that meet both the educational and emotional needs of the child and not being afraid to touch or hold the dying child communicate that someone cares. Second, professionals can convey the message that the family is not alone by such actions as sitting with a parent at the hospital or visiting the family at home. Finally, providers can communicate that

Table 1. Self-reflection questions for professionals

- How much do I understand about the situation, including the child's diagnosis and prognosis?
- Have I ever been in a situation such as this before?
- What can I contribute to support this family?
- What more can be done, what should change, and what should be avoided to better help this child and family?
- Am I getting enough support from my supervisor?
- How do I feel about my relationship with the child and with the family?
- How do my personal spiritual convictions affect how I deal with this child and family?
- How do I feel about holding, touching, and working with a dying child and his or her family?
- What type of contact with the family will I feel comfortable with and be able to maintain after the death of the child?

the child is important and meaningful by creating memories for the family that will live beyond the child.

To effectively help children and families cope with loss, professionals need to have knowledge of grief and coping processes, to recognize their own grief reactions, and understand the effects of grief on themselves and on children and families (Moses, 1992). When professionals take care of themselves, mentally and physically, and have peer and professional support, it becomes easier for them to see the child as a child first and an individual with a life-threatening disability second. Professionals can then work toward providing as typical an experience as possible for the child while communicating the value of the child to the family.

CREATING A SYSTEM OF SUPPORTS
FOR FAMILIES AND PROFESSIONALS

Working with children who have life-threatening conditions can be a challenging yet rewarding experience (Harper, 1993). It is important for providers to establish collaborative relationships with the children, families, and other caregivers (Healy & Lewis-Becket, 1987; Shelton & Stepanek, 1994). It is also important that service agencies establish policies and practices that support professionals in their work. This section examines ways to facilitate quality care and support services at the system level. An organized approach to service delivery at the system level can help both professionals and families cope with the complex issues surrounding the loss of a child. This preparation can lead to a better understanding of the dynamics of grief by administrators, supervisors, and other personnel.

Developing Crisis or Bereavement Plans

A comprehensive crisis plan or bereavement program for professionals and families is helpful because it is not unusual for an entire staff to grieve and mourn for a dying child (Harper, 1993). The usefulness of developing a protocol for handling the death of a child has been described by a number of authors (Hodge & Graham, 1985; Rose & Stewart, 1993; White, Reynolds, & Evans, 1984). Bereavement plans can offer guidelines to help professionals at all levels better understand their roles in supporting families before and after the death of a child (Stepanek & Newcomb, 1994). Such programs can also help professionals respond to the unique and varied needs of bereaved families for anticipatory and follow-up support. Formal bereavement plans provide valuable information and examples to professionals, such as sensitive ways to acknowledge the child's birthday or 1-year death anniversary, information about additional supports available for family members, and ways to determine when ongoing professional support should be phased out. Specific components that can be included in a support plan are identified in Table 2.

Supervision for Professionals

For service providers, another useful source of support can come from a well-established supervision process (Beckman et al., 1996; Eggbeer et al., 1994; Stepanek, 1995b; see also Chapter 2 of this book). Particularly before and after the death of a child, supervisors must be able to support the professionals with whom they work so that they are best able to support the children and families they serve (Harper, 1993). In addition to providing support, understanding, and acceptance, supervisors can also help service providers balance their need to "fix" things for children and families.

Peer Support and Collaboration

Establishing a network of peer support and collaboration is another important way to ensure quality services (Johnson, Jeppson, & Redburn, 1992; McGonigel et al., 1991; Shelton & Stepanek, 1994). According to Harper (1993), caring for a dying child needs to be a shared experience, because the burden can be too great for any one person. Furthermore, Healy and Lewis-Becket (1987) reported that collaborative peer partnerships can create an atmosphere of respect for the dignity of a dying child and preserve the family's right to take part in decisions about appropriate treatment.

Table 2. Components of a support plan

- Information sheets that describe the program, the roles of different service providers, and potential resources
- Checklists that can be used to record information about the child and about family preferences and priorities
- Guidelines for normalizing a child's and family's routine and environment
- Guidelines for capturing mementos and creating memories that will exist beyond the child
- Information about emotional, spiritual, financial, and other supports available throughout the experience
- Guidelines for professionals who are establishing follow-up programs, including routine support letters, newsletters, and dissemination of educational materials for families after the death of a child
- Information about memorial services and anniversary events for families and professionals

SUPPORT FOR FAMILIES BEFORE A CHILD DIES

Professionals can show respect for a family and for their child by providing support in various ways. This section identifies some of the ways professionals can help families prepare for the death of their child.

Maintain a Family-Centered Approach

To be consistent with a family-centered philosophy, professionals need to respect family-identified priorities for their child, including preferences for medical goals, developmental activities, educational intervention, and daily routines (Stepanek, 1995b). It is also helpful to offer family members opportunities for privacy and special time with their child as they prepare for death and separation (Healy & Lewis-Becket, 1987; Stepanek & Newcomb, 1994, 1995). This is especially important when circumstances (e.g., hospitalization, on-going presence of home health care providers) require the frequent presence of service providers in the family's daily life.

Encourage Family Involvement

Families can be encouraged to remain involved in their child's development, care, and services. Professionals can help family members identify specific ways to comfort, entertain, and support their child. It is also important to support regular living patterns and to help families maintain ongoing routines and activities (Healy & Lewis-Becket, 1987; Powers, 1993), thus helping the child's life remain as typical as possible. Moreover, family members can build on the memories they will have after the death of their child.

Encouraging families to be involved in their children's care and decision-making processes can also foster a needed sense of control. This is especially important because most family members feel helpless in caring for their children. The amount of control and involvement varies, however, depending on a child's needs and on the abilities and desires of each family member. Some family members may want only to choose their child's clothes each day. Other family members want to be involved in all aspects of medical and developmental care and intervention, from bathing to administering medications and monitoring life-support equipment. Professionals can provide opportunities for family involvement at different levels of care. However, the amount and type of involvement must be the choice of each family member, thus ensuring that services remain individualized.

Support Family Preparations

Professionals can support the family's preparations for the loss of their child, such as decisions regarding personal involvement in intervention plans or decisions about the child's place of death and burial.

In a study of maternal bereavement, LaRoche (1984) found that mothers who experienced physical contact with their baby just before or after death and mothers who were involved in making burial arrangements for their infants were less likely to experience prolonged depression. Families can hold, rock, wash, dress, and carry their child's body to the car that will take the child home or to a mortuary for wake or burial services (Kübler-Ross, 1985). According to New England SERVE (1989), families should always have the opportunity to practice cultural or religious ceremonies or rituals around the death of their child.

Often, however, families do not know what is right or helpful related to their child's care before and after death. Professionals can provide information about what other families have found helpful and can be available to participate in discussions about family wishes and options for the child's death and funeral (Healy & Lewis-Becket, 1987; Stepanek & Newcomb, 1994). Professionals can wait for family cues that they wish to discuss arrangements and can respond in a way that does not cut off or make the topic taboo. Asking directly, "Would it be helpful to talk about the arrangements?" or "Would it be helpful to know what other families have done?," may open the door for such a conversation. Healy and Lewis-Becket (1987) suggested that service providers listen carefully as children and families express their concerns and that they consider emotional as well as educational needs. Providing opportunities to discuss concerns and fears about the care of a dying child and the death process are essential to comprehensive support.

Address Feelings

Although it is important to guard against stereotyping, service providers can also help families prepare for loss by addressing unspoken but typical feelings. Families can be allowed to display anticipatory grief and to express a range of emotions without being judged. Wild (1986) shared portions of a letter from a bereaved parent, who asked that professionals not judge family members by their response to anticipatory or actual grief. It takes time to come to a place where a child's death can be accepted and dealt with appropriately. It is important neither to demean parents' concerns nor to dash their hopes.

Provide Information

Empowering families involves providing them with information about the child's disability, available resources, and how to actively participate in their child's care (Sciarillo, Wachtel, & Gilbert, 1993).

Service providers can help families understand their child's condition. Providing information about the typical stages of grief and coping, or about changes in family and child functioning that may create particular stress (Healy & Lewis-Becket, 1987; New England SERVE, 1989; Powers, 1993), also will help family members better understand their reactions to the loss of their child.

Create Memories

Another way that professionals can support the family is to do activities with the child that create memories for those who will eventually grieve the loss of the child. Some activities that can generate treasured keepsakes include playing with stickers and painting. These are often enjoyable activities for young children, and the resulting projects can be given to family members to remember the child or collected and given as mementos at a later date. Examples of such projects include making place mats, bookmarks, wall hangings, and pencil holders.

Depending on the child's age and developmental skills, professionals may need to be more involved in a young child's creative activities. Hand-, finger-, and footprints of a young child are an infinite source of keepsake projects such as tee-shirts, neckties, wall hangings, and holiday ornaments.

Taking pictures of a child with a life-threatening condition is a sensitive and important way to create memories for the family. Pictures can be taken of both typical and therapeutic activities, creating a lasting impression of all the things that were done for the child. Additionally, a videotape capturing the events of a typical day can be a compassionate gift to a family facing the loss of a child.

SUPPORT FOR FAMILIES AFTER A CHILD DIES

Parents may need unique and specific support after the death of their child, because they experience the emotions that occur during the grieving, mourning, and bereavement processes (Guntzelman, 1992). It is not uncommon for family members to seek the support and company of the service providers who helped care for their children (Stepanek & Newcomb, 1994). When parents lose a child who had been ill or who had a disability, they may also feel the loss of many individuals who supported them during their child's life. Parents may seek information about the child's life and death from the practitioners who knew their child, and they may need to have this information repeated often (Stepanek & Newcomb, 1994). In a study of 165 families experiencing stillbirth, Kellner, Donnelly, and Gould (1984) found that parents desired contact with their baby, attention to their feelings, counseling, and information about the cause of their baby's death. Such support, along with assistance in gaining access to peer and professional support, is an important follow-up service (Healy & Lewis-Becket, 1987; New England SERVE, 1989). This section examines strategies for providing support to family members after the child's death through professional presence, support, and respect. It also briefly examines the support needs of siblings and barriers to the bereavement process.

Be Present
Professionals can remain sensitive to the magnitude and permanence of a family's loss while offering strategies that can relieve the emptiness of grief constructively (Sahler & Friedman, 1981). Understanding and respecting that family members must travel through all of their grief-related emotions, rather than go around them, can help facilitate the bereavement process (Stepanek, 1995a). It is important to be open to various emotional responses and to reassure the family that these feelings, activities, preferences, or preoccupations are typical responses to an unnatural event.

Two of the greatest gifts a professional can give a parent are time and presence. When parents lose a child who has an illness or disabling condition,

> . . . they need the support of people who actually knew the child . . . since people who only knew of the child are more likely to treat the death as the death of a "handicapped child," rather than focusing on the fact that a parent has lost a child. (Harry, 1992, p. 15)

Being available to listen and to share stories and information about the deceased child is perhaps one of the best ways to help a grieving family (Compassionate Friends, 1990; Gortler, 1992). Professionals can be present at many different points. If imminent death is possible or anticipated (e.g., the child may not survive a necessary surgical procedure, the child's condition becomes critical), it may help for a familiar service provider to offer to be with the family. This may be especially important if the family does not have a natural support network. Even if the family declines, letting them know that they are not alone and that their child truly matters can be a source of support. In making such an offer, however, it is important not to interfere in any way with the family's existing support network.

It can also help to listen as the family tells stories about the child. These memories are part of the healing process for families (Stepanek & Newcomb, 1994). Professionals can also share their own stories and memories about the child with the family. This helps build the family's memories of the child and reaffirms the child's importance to others.

It is important that service providers attend any religious rituals around the child's death and maintain some type of contact with the family just after the death (ARCH, 1993; Compassionate Friends, 1990; Stepanek & Newcomb, 1994). Although it may be a difficult and emotional experience, such participation demonstrates that the child was important to the professional and provides a powerful message of caring and support.

The first few days after a child's death are typically busy, and then life returns to the usual routine for those supporting the family. However, life may not proceed so easily for the family. In the weeks and months following the child's death, parents can feel isolated and very much alone. Professionals who made regular home visits on a certain day of the week may want to avoid putting another child into the now-available time slot during the first 2 or 3 weeks after the child's death. Although caseloads and system demands may make it difficult, it can sometimes help both the family and the professional to visit the family on the usual day and time during the week after the funeral. This conveys a message that the child is not so easily replaceable. It can also help the family become accustomed to the loss of what had become a way of life for them. A service provider can offer such support by saying something like, "I know this Tuesday I'll be thinking of Marcela. Would it be okay if I came by to visit you at that time?" Direct questions that make offers and leave room for the family to decline are a sensitive and acceptable way to offer such support.

If an autopsy has been completed, professionals who have worked with the child may find that the family wants to discuss the results with them. Even though the medical information contained in such reports is not within the expertise of many service providers, parents may appreciate the perspective that trusted professionals can offer. This may be particularly true when service providers have been working with a child for a long time or when they have developed a strong collaborative bond with the family. If a family member brings up the topic, the provider can ask a direct question such as, "Would you like to talk about that?" or "What was that (getting the report) like for you?" Direct, open-ended questions communicate a willingness to listen but also that the family is in control of the discussion.

For many organizations that regularly deal with the death of a child, follow-up for families extends at least 1 full year (Rose & Stewart, 1993). A formal bereavement plan, as discussed previously in this chapter, may be useful. In the absence of a formal plan, service providers can support families by remembering birthdays and anniversaries. A call, a card, or a visit at this time can be extremely meaningful (Compassionate Friends, 1990; Gortler, 1992).

Finally, another way to be present for the family is with remembrances. This not only helps families but also can simultaneously provide an outlet for professionals who grieve the loss of the child (Guntzelman, 1992; Rose & Stewart, 1993; Stepanek & Newcomb, 1994). Examples of such remembrances include the following:

- Helping the family create a memory book
- Framing and presenting craft or art projects done by the child or pictures of the child
- Creating a needlepoint or quilting project that incorporates the child's birth and death anniversaries, or some of the child's and family's clothing
- Planting a tree or establishing a memorial to the child
- Writing an original poem about the child who died or framing a poem written by a parent
- Making a donation to a memorial fund

Be Supportive
In addition to being present, there are other ways to support families who have lost a child (Compassionate Friends, 1990). Although there are no real right or wrong ways to share sympathy, family members have reported that some ways are more helpful than others. Professionals can point out that intense feelings of grief are typical and that different people have different responses to grief and coping. It is also helpful to emphasize that the form of such feelings is highly individual and that feelings are likely to vary from moment-to-moment and day-to-day. This support can "both validate the presence of feelings as normal grief reactions and facilitate an important step in breaking a chain of responses that may not be useful or constructive" (Powers, 1993, p. 126).

It is important for providers to be aware that some families find certain well-intended statements unsupportive and even hurtful. Examples of such statements include "You can have more children"; "He or she is in a better place"; "Your child is happy now"; "You must be so relieved that it is over"; "You need to go on with your life"; "Don't let your other children see you cry"; "I know how you feel"; or "It was God's will." Expressions of sympathy that imply a child is replaceable or somehow "better off" can disallow the grieving person's feelings. Furthermore, these statements can indirectly encourage denial of the person's pain by minimizing the loss

(Guntzelman, 1992; Stepanek & Newcomb, 1994). Professionals need to acknowledge and accept the family's grief and pain without diminishing the importance of the child or the parent.

There are many ways to acknowledge the parents' loss. When talking to parents, talk about the child. Use the child's name. Share that you, too, are sorry for the loss. Share your memories or comment on the child's special, positive qualities.

Professionals often want to be supportive but do not know how. One useful strategy is to suggest specific times and places to stay in touch. Instead of saying, "Call me if you want to talk," say, "Can I come over to visit during the child's home visit slot?" Instead of saying, "Call me if I can do anything," offer specific concrete support such as, "I'd like to bring a meal next week" or "Can I make any calls for you?" Being specific offers the family a chance to say "yes" or "no" without putting the burden on them to organize tasks or making them ask for help. In times of extreme stress, it can be difficult for families to know or to express what would be supportive to them (Guntzelman, 1992; Stepanek & Newcomb, 1994).

In addition to listening and providing emotional support, it is often appropriate to touch or to hug the grieving person and to share tears. The tears of a professional may even give the family permission to cry (Fitzgerald, 1992; Guntzelman, 1992; Kübler-Ross, 1985) and can communicate deep caring and commitment. Tears send a powerful message about the importance of the child and the family to the provider.

Service providers can help prevent isolation for the family by identifying supports available locally and nationally. Such professional and peer supports can range from informal gatherings within a community to federally funded organizations providing information to families and professionals. Professionals can encourage family participation in local and national self-help groups (ARCH, 1993). Such supports may exist through extended family, community, churches, schools, or national organizations. It is important that professionals not pressure families to participate in a group or convey personal values, needs, or concerns. Peer support groups can help families realize that their grief is normal and that they are not alone.

Be Respectful and Nonjudgmental
In conversations with other professionals about the child, the family, the death, and so forth, it is important for providers to maintain a tone of respect and empathy. For example, when one professional asks another professional how a parent is coping with the loss of a

child and indicates that a parent is "not doing well," because he or she is crying a lot or is angry about the child's death, it often implies that the parent "should" be coping differently. Instead, concrete answers such as "She is very sad" or "He is spending a lot of time alone" describe the actual coping process without being judgmental and convey that the parent is doing what is needed to cope with the loss (Stepanek & Newcomb, 1994). If a professional is concerned that additional counseling or support may be necessary for a family member, such information can be discussed with respect for the parent and with an understanding of the myriad normal and typical responses to the death of a child.

Be Supportive to Siblings and Other Children

Children, too, grieve the loss of siblings, friends, classmates, and hospital roommates. It is important for professionals to find creative ways to help children understand and mourn the death of another child (ARCH, 1993; Fitzgerald, 1992; Kübler-Ross, 1985; Stepanek & Newcomb, 1995). According to Sahler and Friedman (1981), bereaved children need consistency, involvement, information, and support, just as parents do. Because of their own bereavement, parents may be less available for emotional support and less tolerant of their children's responses to grief. Brothers and sisters particularly may need outside support, such as some continued contact with professionals who cared for their dying sibling.

Siblings often struggle with the cause of the child's death, with guilt related to the death, or with fears that their parents—or even they themselves—will die (Guntzelman, 1992). Professionals and family members should be honest about their own feelings of loss. Modeling appropriate grief responses can give children permission to have a range of feelings as well and can help them work through their own grief.

BARRIERS TO RECOVERY

Often parents' greatest fear is that their child will be forgotten (Stepanek & Newcomb, 1994). For some parents, moving beyond the grief related to the death of the child may seem like a betrayal. Other potential barriers to recovery and bereavement include 1) social isolation, 2) lack of opportunities to talk about the child, 3) avoiding issues and places that are reminders of the child, 4) living completely in the past or memorializing a child or his or her bedroom too long, 5) idolizing the child beyond human capacity, and 6) having to deal with previous unresolved issues related to loss or separation (Schiff, 1988). Parents may resist comfort because a sense of sadness somehow links them to the child or because they feel guilty if they are not sad. Other times parents may even resent others who have not lost a child and who have a complete family.

Although it is important to respect various responses to grief, styles of coping, and time frames for moving through the bereavement process, some responses should signal concern to professionals. The following are some signs that the grief experience may be overwhelming and the family member may need additional counseling and support: 1) a lack of basic self-care or self-respect, 2) unusual and alarming behavior patterns, 3) suicidal threats or attempts, 4) multiple losses that are overwhelming, 5) severe withdrawal and/or depression, 6) substance abuse, and 7) radical lifestyle changes (ARCH, 1993). In such instances, professionals may want to encourage the family member to seek counseling. However, it is crucial not to judge individuals for their responses to grief or for their personal coping styles.

According to Gortler (1992), when a family loses a child with a disability, they may be dealing simultaneously with different grieving processes. Often they have not fully processed their feelings about the child's disability. Although this aspect of parental grieving is not well researched, multiple losses can complicate the grieving process (Rando, 1986). Thus, parents who are grieving the disability and subsequently grieving death may be at additional risk of a more complicated bereavement. Society does not easily acknowledge the grief of a parent whose child is born with a disability or who is diagnosed with a life-threatening illness (ARCH, 1993). Professionals and caregivers can help such families by labeling their experiences as part of a typical grief process and by being present, supportive, and respectful of their needs and responses to the death of their child.

MANAGING PROFESSIONAL LOSS AND PERSONAL REACTIONS

Recognizing and understanding personal grief after the death of a child with whom there was professional involvement is important, both professionally and personally. The death of a child marks the break of a special connection and a loss of the professional role as it relates to the family (Guntzelman, 1992). Feelings related to grief and loss are real, and death, particularly that of a child, often leads to an intense focus on professional and personal values and beliefs. This section explores strategies for service providers who are coping with the loss of a child.

In accepting personal grief, professionals can achieve personal and professional growth. Loss exposes vulnerability. Loss can be viewed as an opportunity for positive change (Jackson, 1992; Moses, 1992). Coping with the loss can lead to more constructive strategies for working with dying children and their families. Professionals can gain understanding, knowledge, and strength as they work through internal and external conflicts related to a child's death. In so doing, they can add a new human, caring dimension to an already existing capacity to be helpful (Harper, 1993).

Service providers need to allow themselves time, space, and opportunities for grief. This can be facilitated by sharing grief with others who understand the loss, including other professionals who remember the child, other individuals who have been through a similar loss, or even the child's family. However, it is important to use caution when sharing with the family. Although sharing feelings and memories with the family may be beneficial for both parties, it is important that the family not feel they have to take care of or support the professional. It is also helpful to allow oneself to cry, to laugh, and to experience a range of grief-related emotions.

There are a number of supports that can help professionals avoid burnout: 1) a stable and caring work environment, 2) an established bereavement or crisis program, and 3) empathic support from supervisors and other staff members (Harper, 1993). Additionally, the use of creative outlets (e.g., keeping a journal, writing poetry, drawing) can facilitate expressions of grief (Fitzgerald, 1992; Stepanek, 1995a). Taking time to relax can also help establish a sense of renewal and coping.

It can also help to engage in a process of self-reflection, as described earlier in this chapter. Self-reflection can include an assessment of the desire and ability to continue working with children who have life-threatening conditions. It is important for professionals to get both the job satisfaction and the personal rewards they seek while working with children who are seriously ill or dying. Asking oneself *how* to cope and to continue such work, rather than asking *why* to continue or even why such work exists, can also help professionals as they struggle to renew their professional and personal goals (Stepanek, 1995a).

When working with children and families who are in physical or emotional pain, it is essential that professionals take good care of themselves, physically and emotionally. Nurturing oneself by being available to children and families, yet setting limits; by occasionally treating oneself in special ways; and by taking moments each day to renew, relax, and appreciate life are all important in coping with loss and avoiding professional burnout (Stepanek & Newcomb, 1994). Although the death of a child can challenge feelings related to competency and justness, it need not be an end to career, family, relationships, or hope for family members or for professionals (Stepanek, 1995a). Facing the death of a child can also bring into focus personal values (Stepanek & Newcomb, 1994). Examining beliefs about life, death, spirituality, relationships, and work process can ultimately lead to both professional and personal growth.

CONCLUSIONS

The comprehensive educational needs of infants, toddlers, and young children with life-threatening conditions cannot be adequately addressed without recognizing their medical, health, and family support needs (Sciarillo et al., 1993). However, Gortler (1992) stated:

> No one likes to think about death. In fact, ours has been a death-denying culture. . . . And the death of a child? The very thought runs counter to one of humanity's core principles: children are our future, they're not supposed to die. However, as professionals who work with special populations of children, it is our responsibility to prepare for the possibility—and for some, the eventuality—that a child in our care might die. We owe it to these children, their families, and ourselves to be prepared. (p. 11)

Knowledge of the grief process, of available resources, and of one's personal experiences and reactions to loss can enhance the effectiveness of support for children with life-threatening illnesses and their families. The death of a child is an unnatural yet real event. Professionals can help make the grief, mourning, and bereavement processes easier for families by supporting them in ways that convey respect and compassion for each child and family.

ACTIVITIES AND DISCUSSION

1. Read Case Study IV, the Miller family. Discuss the following questions:
    a. What is your reaction to this story? How might this reaction affect your decisions about what you would do to support this family?
    b. During P.J.'s life, what things did the staff do to support his family? Are there other things they could have done?
    c. Sheila and Linda stayed involved with P.J. and his family even after he made the transition to home-based interven-

tion with a new teacher and therapist. Why do you think they did this? What would you do in a situation such as this?

d. In what ways would you suggest the professionals support P.J.'s family during the services?

e. Imagine that Jackie comes to Sheila and asks, "You knew P.J. so well. Could you or someone from the school say something at the service?" What do you think Sheila would say? If you were in this situation, what would you say?

f. How might professionals support P.J.'s family after his death?

g. What are some of the ways that Sheila and the school staff might deal with their own feelings of loss?

2. Describe any experiences you have had working with a child who has died or who was medically fragile or terminally ill. How did that experience affect you and your work?

3. Think back on your earliest memory of loss. (This may or may not involve a death.) What was the loss (e.g., death, move, divorce)? How did you understand the loss at the time? What impact do you think that experience has on your present reactions to loss? Write about that experience. Share your writing with a friend or discuss in a small group setting with peers.

4. In writing or in a discussion with a friend, describe your most significant loss to date. What makes the loss so significant? How did this loss affect you? How did you understand the loss at the time? What significance do you think that experience has on present losses?

5. Read a book about the death of a child. Describe the experience of the child's family. How is this reaction similar to and different from any reactions you have had to a loss? Based on the suggestions in this chapter, what might you have done for the family if you had known them?

REFERENCES

Access to Respite Care and Help (ARCH). (1993). Families and the grief process. *ARCH Factsheet, 21,* 1–2.

Beckman, P.J., Newcomb, S., Frank, N., Brown, L., Stepanek, J., & Barnwell, D. (1996). Preparing personnel to work with families. In D. Bricker & A. Widerstrom (Eds.), *Preparing personnel to work with infants and young children and their families: A team approach* (pp. 273–293). Baltimore: Paul H. Brookes Publishing Co.

Compassionate Friends. (1990). Talking about death. *Parent Currents,* 4(3), 1.

Damrosch, S.P., & Perry, I.A. (1989). Self-reported adjustment, chronic sorrow, and coping of parents of children with Down syndrome. *Nursing Research, 38*(1), 30.

Dunst, C., Trivette, C., & Deal, A. (1994). *Supporting and strengthening families* (Vol. I). Cambridge, MA: Brookline Books.

Eggbeer, L., Fenichel, E., Pawl, J., Shanok, R.S., & Williamson, G.G. (1994). Training the trainers: Innovative strategies for teaching relationship concepts and skills to infant/family professionals. *Trends in Professional Education, 7*(2), 63–61.

Fitzgerald, H. (1992). *The grieving child.* New York: Simon and Schuster.

Gortler, E. (1992). Support for families. In J.M. Taylor & E. Gortler (Eds.), *Proceedings of When a Child Dies: Third Annual Conference of the Training Consortium for Early Intervention Services* (pp. 11–13). Baltimore: Governor's Office for Children, Youth, and Families, Maryland Infants and Toddlers Program.

Guntzelman, J. (1992, April). *Grief and the early intervention practitioner.* Keynote Address, When a Child Dies: Third Annual Conference of the Training Consortium for Early Intervention Services, Baltimore.

Harmon, R.J., Glicken, A.D., & Siegel, R.E. (1984). Neonatal loss in the intensive care nursery: Effects of maternal grieving and a program for intervention. *Journal of the American Academy of Child Psychiatry, 23*(1), 68–71.

Harper, B.C. (1993). Staff support. In A.A. Armstrong-Dailey & S.Z. Goltzer (Eds.), *Hospice care for children* (pp. 184–197). New York: Oxford University Press.

Harry, B. (1992). Multicultural perspectives. In J.M. Taylor & E. Gortler (Eds.), *Proceedings of When a Child Dies: Third Annual Conference of the Training Consortium for Early Intervention Services* (pp. 15–17). Baltimore: Governor's Office for Children, Youth, and Families, Maryland Infants and Toddlers Program.

Healy, A., & Lewis-Becket, J.A. (1987). *Improving health care for children with chronic conditions: Guidelines for social workers.* Iowa City: Division of Developmental Disabilities, The University of Iowa.

Hodge, D.S., & Graham, P.L. (1985, December). Supporting bereaved parents: A program for the neonatal intensive care unit. *Neonatal Network,* 11–17.

Jackson, T. (1992). *How can I live with my loss?* Grand Rapids, MI: Radio Bible Class.

Jellinek, M.S., Catlin, E.A., Todres, D., & Cassem, E.H. (1992). Facing tragic decisions with parents in the neonatal intensive care unit: Clinical perspectives. *Pediatrics, 89,* 119–122.

Johnson, B.H., Jeppson, E.S., & Redburn, L. (1992). *Caring for children and families: Guidelines for hospitals* (1st ed.). Bethesda, MD: Association for the Care of Children's Health.

Kelley, B., & Kelley, A. (1993). *Stasia's gift.* Wheaton, IL: Crossway Books.

Kellner, K.R., Donnelly, W.H., & Gould, S. (1984). Parental behavior after perinatal death: Lack of predictive demographic and obstetric variables. *Obstetrics and Gynecology, 63*(6), 809.

Kübler-Ross, E. (1975). *On death and dying.* Englewood Cliffs, NJ: Prentice Hall.

Kübler-Ross, E. (1985). *On children and dying.* New York: Macmillan.

LaRoche, C. (1984). Grief reactions to perinatal death: A follow-up study. *Canadian Journal of Psychiatry, 29*, 14–19.

McGonigel, M., Kaufman, R.K., & Johnson, B.H. (1991). *Guidelines and recommended practices for the IFSP* (2nd ed.). Washington, DC: NEC*TAS and The Association for the Care of Children's Health.

Moses, K. (1992). *Not me, not my child: Dealing with parental denial and anxiety.* Evanston, IL: Resource Networks.

National Commission to Prevent Infant Mortality. (1988). *Death before life: The tragedy of infant mortality.* Washington, DC: Author.

Newacheck, P. (1993). Childhood illness and insurability: Families report chronic conditions and barriers. *Children's Health Issues, 2*(1).

New England SERVE. (1989). *Enhancing quality: Standards and indicators of quality care for children with special health care needs.* Boston: Author.

Parks, C.M., & Weiss, R.S. (1983). *Recovery from bereavement.* New York: Basic Books.

Powers, L.E. (1993). Disability and grief: From tragedy to challenge. In G.H.S. Singer & L.E. Powers (Eds.), *Families, disability, and empowerment: Active coping skills and strategies for family interventions* (pp. 119–150). Baltimore: Paul H. Brookes Publishing Co.

Rando, T.A. (Ed.). (1986). *Parental loss of a child.* Champaign, IL: Research Press Co.

Rose, T.V., & Stewart, E.S. (1993). *Whispers of hope: A hospital-based program for bereaved parents and their families.* Durham, NC: Duke Pediatric Brain Tumor Family Support Program.

Rosenblatt, P.G., & Burns, L.H. (1986). Long-term effects of perinatal loss. *Journal of Family Issues, 7*(3), 237–253.

Sahler, O.J.Z., & Friedman, S.B. (1981). The dying child. *Pediatrics in Review, 3*(5), 159–165.

Sanders, C.M. (1986). Accidental death of a child. In T.A. Rando (Ed.), *Parental loss of a child* (pp. 181–190). Champaign, IL: Research Press Co.

Schatz, B.D. (1986). Grief of mothers. In T.A. Rando (Ed.), *Parental loss of a child* (pp. 303–314). Champaign, IL: Research Press Co.

Schatz, W.H. (1986). Grief of fathers. In T.A. Rando (Ed.), *Parental loss of a child* (pp. 293–302). Champaign, IL: Research Press Co.

Schiff, H.S. (1988). *The bereaved parent.* London: Penguin.

Sciarillo, W., Wachtel, R., & Gilbert, M. (1993). Role of the nurse in the early intervention system. In D. Von Rembow & W. Sciarillo (Eds.), *Nurses, physicians, psychologists, and social workers within statewide early intervention systems: Clarifying roles under Part H of the Individuals with Disabilities Education Act* (pp. 13–28). Bethesda, MD: Association for the Care of Children's Health.

Shelton, T.L., & Stepanek, J.S. (1994). *Family-centered care for children needing specialized health and developmental services.* Bethesda, MD: Association for the Care of Children's Health.

Stepanek, J.S. (1995a). The journey towards healing: Grief and the power of poetry. *The ACCH Advocate, 2*(1), 22–28.

Stepanek, J.S. (1995b). *Moving beyond the medical/technical: Analysis and discussion of psychosocial practices in pediatric hospitals.* Bethesda, MD: Association for the Care of Children's Health.

Stepanek, J.S., & Newcomb, S. (1994, May). *Creating memories, celebrating life: Coping with unnatural loss.* Presentation at the 29th Annual ACCH Conference, Toronto, Ontario, Canada.

Stepanek, J.S., & Newcomb, S. (1995, January). *Does Jamie paint rainbows now?: Children mourning children.* Presentation at Hawaii's Annual Early Intervention Conference, Waikiki.

Taylor, J.M., & Gortler, E. (Eds.). (1993). *Proceedings of When a Child Dies: Third Annual Conference of the Training Consortium for Early Intervention Services.* Baltimore: Governor's Office for Children, Youth, and Families, Maryland Infants and Toddlers Program.

Weber, J.A., & Fournier, D.G. (1985, January). Family support and a child's adjustment to death. *Family Relations,* 43–49.

White, M.P., Reynolds, B., & Evans, T.J. (1984). Handling of death in special care nurseries and parental grief. *British Medical Journal, 289,* 167–169.

Wild, E.L. (1986). Advice from a bereaved parent to physicians. In T.A. Rando (Ed.), *Parental loss of a child* (pp. 459–464). Champaign, IL: Research Press Co.

Case Study I
The Barnes Family

Sandra Newcomb

Sitting at her desk, visiting nurse Carrie Mathews reads the referral information again. Beth and Scott Barnes have two children, 4-year-old Jonathan and 6-month-old David. David was born with Down syndrome, an AV canal (a hole between the ventricles of his heart), and Hirschsprung disease (a congenital condition of the colon). David needed open-heart surgery at 2 months of age to repair the AV canal and to perform a colostomy. He was hospitalized for 2 months. He still has a colostomy bag and will need more surgery in the future. Beth stays home to take care of Jonathan and David. Scott had worked for a local furniture store, moving and delivering furniture. Just after David came home from the hospital, Scott hurt his back on the job. He has been out of work and is applying for worker's compensation. He is also facing possible back surgery in the future. Because of the financial difficulties caused by hospital bills and Scott's unemployment, the family has moved in with Scott's parents. In addition to David's medical care, Beth would like some help in dealing with the behavior of Jonathan. During his brother's hospital stay and during the move Jonathan seemed fine; but he has begun to have toileting accidents and refuses to go to bed at night. He gets very upset and throws tantrums if anything is lost or misplaced or if he cannot have something immediately.

Carrie's role as visiting nurse is to visit once a week to monitor David's weight, colostomy care, and medical supply needs, as well as to provide the family with any additional medical information they may want. When Carrie calls Beth, she is pleasant and expresses interest in getting together. They schedule an appointment at a time when the two boys will be asleep so that they can talk freely about Beth's concerns. Carrie arrives at the agreed-upon time, but no one is home, so she leaves a note in the door indicating she is sorry they missed each other and asking Beth to call.

Back at the office, Carrie makes herself a note to call Beth again if she does not call in several days. Experience has taught Carrie that when she does not have an established relationship with a family, especially when they have multiple things happening simultaneously, it can sometimes take more effort on her part to get things going.

Several days later she calls Beth again. Beth apologizes for missing their appointment and explains that her husband needed to see a doctor at the last minute about worker's compensation and it was the only day they could borrow his father's car. Their car had broken down the week before, and they do not have the money to fix it. She remembered their appointment while at the hospital, but did not have Carrie's number with her. Carrie says that it is perfectly understandable, asks Beth if she wants to reschedule, and offers to call ahead next time. Beth seems very relieved and the two reschedule.

Carrie calls Beth the morning of the day of their visit to confirm their meeting. The family lives with Scott's parents in a small three-bedroom house in a quiet, older neighborhood. Beth answers the door, and she greets Carrie cheerfully. Beth is dressed nicely, and the house is clean and tidy. There are toys in the corner of the room and a baby swing with a few rattles in the doorway to the dining area. As they sit in the living room, Carrie explains that the visiting nurse program offers medical monitoring services for families with children awaiting surgery and that the discharge planner from the hospital referred them to her. She invites Beth to share a little about the family's current situation and her concerns. Beth had explained on the telephone that she is having a difficult time with Jonathan, so Carrie refers to this and asks if she is still having difficulties.

Beth seems to have a good understanding of David's health conditions and necessary medical care. She is concerned that it takes so much time to care for David and that Jonathan often acts out when she is unable to attend to him, such as during David's colostomy care. David also takes a very long time to feed. She barely finishes one caregiving task when it is time for another. "I am constantly having to say, 'Not now, Jonathan. Wait, Mommy will be with you as soon as I'm finished with David.' But, you know, that time never seems to come.

"Scott and I are coping with David's problems, although we do have some questions about his upcoming surgery. He is a happy baby, and we like his teacher. We were upset at first about David's condition, but now he's just a member of our family and we treat him like we did Jonathan when he was a baby. It's just that he takes so much time, and I wish I knew how to speed this process up. I guess that all of this has been a lot for Jonathan. He seemed fine when I first had David, even though I was gone a lot when David was in the hospital. David had surgery when he was very little and was hospitalized for a long time. Jonathan seemed fine with me gone. He stayed with Scott's parents and had a ball. He is very close to his grandparents. They adore him!

"I think we were all handling it okay until Scott hurt his back and lost his job. Then everything fell in on us. First, we couldn't pay our bills. Then we lost our phone. With David's health, we cannot be without a phone, so we decided to come here and stay. Scott's parents are great. They let us store some of our stuff in their basement and garage. The rest we sold to try to get money for basic necessities. I wanted to go back to work, but with Scott's back he really cannot look after the boys. We've been here about a month. Most of the time it's okay. His parents both work. It's just hard for me if David is up at night. I worry that they will lose their sleep. And now with Jonathan becoming such a problem, I worry even more that we may be too much for them. They aren't in the best of health either."

Beth continues the discussion about her in-laws and the events of the past 6 months. Carrie asks Beth to describe some of Jonathan's behaviors that are of the most concern. As the visit draws to an end, Carrie summarizes their discussion and what she understands Beth's concerns to be. She asks if Beth would be interested in some materials on behavior management that she has at the office. "Sure," Beth laughs. "I'll read them between three and four in the morning. It's usually quiet then!" They also discuss David's medical needs and what supplies are needed. Carrie asks if she can watch one of David's feedings at her next visit. They schedule another visit and say good-bye.

As Carrie drives away, she finds herself thinking about all of the things she wants to do for this family. They seem so nice, and life has been so unfair to them. Often the families that are most difficult for Carrie are those she really likes and identifies with. Carries realizes she could easily be homeless herself if her husband lost his income and she had a sick baby. She has a son the same age as Jonathan. Although Carrie knows what she might do if her son were acting out in the same way, Beth's parenting style might be very different. Carrie reminds herself to back off from her own beliefs about parenting and provide the Barneses with needed information while still respecting them as the decision makers.

At the office, Carrie continues to think about the Barnes family. She looks through some information on oral-motor development, thinking that there might be some strategies they can explore to help make efforts to feed David more efficient. She also looks at books on behavior management and at a number of handouts that have accumulated at the office. Beth had made it clear that she does not have time for a lot of reading. Carrie finds a small booklet that simply discusses choosing a few behaviors to modify and the importance of consistency. She wonders if the family has been able to be consistent with Jonathan in the face of all the upheaval.

Carrie realizes that she knows very little about the specifics of David's feeding patterns or Jonathan's behavior and nothing of what Beth and Scott have already tried for either problem. For her own benefit, she writes her questions so that she can organize her next interview. Although she does not intend to read from the list, organizing and writing questions often helps her to be a more effective interviewer. Even if she were unable to get all the questions answered, preparing the list would give her some direction. Some of the questions include:

1. When and where does David's care occur? Will a simple schedule change help?
2. What preparations has the family made for David's upcoming surgery?
3. What has Beth already tried with respect to David's feeding?
4. What was Jonathan like before David was born—easy, difficult, calm, active and so forth?
5. Does Beth have anyone who can help with David's care? Can the in-laws help with David in the evening so that she does not have to make Jonathan wait?
6. What have Beth and Scott tried in the past to deal with Jonathan's behavior?
7. Which of Jonathan's behaviors are the most important to start modifying?
8. What is Jonathan's interpretation of the changes in their family? Does he understand David's health problems? How does he feel about all of the time his parents were away?
9. How does Jonathan feel about living with Grandma and Grandpa? It may be all right for a visit, but is he upset that he lost his own house?
10. Where did they live before? Has Jonathan also lost his friends? Are there children his age in this new neighborhood?
11. How does this family discipline? Do they use time-outs, removing privileges, spankings?
12. What other social support does this family have?

During the next two visits, Beth and Carrie discuss David's colostomy care, and Carrie observes his feeding skills. He is a very slow feeder whose ability to suck is weak. He needs to be fed small amounts every 2–3 hours, and sometimes it takes 45–60 minutes for him to take several ounces. Beth does David's colostomy care in the morning as it was done in the hospital. What this special care routine means is that she gets up, feeds David, does colostomy care, and puts him down for a nap. All of this takes almost 2 hours, and, by the time he has slept for 30–45 minutes, it is time for him to eat again. During this time, Jonathan usually feeds himself breakfast (something easy that he can get by himself) and watches morning TV (cartoons, "Sesame Street," etc.). This system has worked for a while, but recently Jonathan has been "getting into trouble" in the morning or spilling something and needing help.

The picture of Jonathan became clearer. He had always been easy to get along with. He had liked his previous house and his routine and his "stuff." He started preschool this year, and, although it was a big step, several children from his old neighborhood were in his class, and he really liked his teacher. After David was born, Jonathan had to miss preschool frequently. His mother was at the hospital, and he spent his days with a variety of friends and neighbors and his nights with his grandparents.

After the move to his grandparents' house, he was no longer able to attend his preschool program. It was too far away, and Beth and Scott could not afford it. After David came home from the hospital (after surgery), Jonathan began to become "difficult." He began crying at bedtime and having toileting accidents. He continues to ask every day when he is going to sleep in "my bed." The behaviors that Beth wants to begin to work on are his morning tantrums and his refusal to go to bed at night.

Beth is concerned about the effects of all the changes on Jonathan and feels guilty that they cannot provide for their children as they would like. David requires so much time that there is not much time left for Jonathan. He has been forced to give up the things he enjoys. Beth has not talked to Jonathan about how he feels because she is afraid of upsetting him by dwelling on things that cannot be changed. Besides, he never talks about his school or his old friends.

For the next visit, Carrie comes in the morning and just observes the morning routine. Jonathan is a very verbal and imaginative 4-year-old. He enjoys pretend play with his cars and trucks. He is particularly interested in a game with the cars where one car drives away and does not come home.

David is a happy and quiet baby, but he does require a lot of time. He enjoys watching his brother play and "talking" with an adult. Carrie and Beth begin to explore ways of rearranging care times when someone can help with David or be available for Jonathan. Although Beth has been hesitant to burden other family members, she notes that her in-laws like to hold and play with David in the evening and that maybe she can ask for some assistance at that time.

Carrie and Beth continue to meet weekly during Jonathan's nap times so they can freely discuss the situation. There are several interruptions: David gets sick, and Scott has doctors' appointments. One strategy they identify is to capitalize on Jonathan's pride in being a competent "big brother." Beth makes a conscious effort to include Jonathan in caregiving tasks with David and tells him what a "good helper" he is. She also finds some inexpensive activities for Jonathan, such as playing with playdough and paint-with-water books, that he can do because he is "older"—activities that "big brothers" do and babies are not ready to do. When possible, Beth joins Jonathan, or at least is available to talk to him, while he is engaged in these special activities. For example, she gets out the playdough for Jonathan while she is feeding David. Beth also discovers that giving Jonathan extra time in the evening to make the transition to bed is helpful. Beth's in-laws are happy to take on one evening feeding so that Beth can have time with Jonathan at bedtime. They read books or make up stories. Beth finds books at the library with themes about loss, moving, or having a new sibling. She becomes very creative in storytelling and helped Jonathan tell stories to help him with his feelings about all of the changes in the family. After Jonathan is settled in bed, Beth then does colostomy care. This means she is not able to relax as early as she would like, but at least Jonathan does not interrupt and feel ignored.

Another strategy to help Jonathan cope with the losses is for Beth to spend a few minutes whenever possible joining him in his play and helping him put his feelings into words. For example, when Jonathan pretended that his toy car would drive away and not be able to come home, Beth would say something such as, "It must be sad that it can't go back home." Beth is excellent at listening to Jonathan and helping him to verbalize his feelings.

In addition to extra time with Jonathan, Beth institutes a time-out procedure for Jonathan when he has a tantrum. She finds a small chair at a yard sale and uses it as a place for Jonathan to calm himself and end his tantrum. With firm limits on his behavior, Jonathan begins to have fewer tantrums.

Carrie and Beth also explore ways for Jonathan to find some friends his own age. Someone at Carrie's office tells her about a local church that has a mother's morning-out program. She contacts that program to get information for Beth about fees, times, and other logistics.

Over the course of 6 weeks, Jonathan's behavior begins to improve. The family begins to understand, and to help him understand, how he is feeling about his new situation. As Jonathan's behavior improves, other family issues begin to arise. Beth comments about her own feelings of frustration at not being able to live in her own house and about her fatigue from taking care of both boys and her husband.

As the time for David's surgery approaches, Carrie's involvement with the Barnes family is coming to an end. Beth and Carrie review their work together concerning Jonathan and David. Carrie comments on Beth's ability to manage David's medical care and how well she understands Jonathan. Carrie is especially impressed with Beth's ability to organize and arrange her schedule to accommodate so many needs. Beth notes how much calmer things are now that Jonathan is not constantly having tantrums or whining. He still has his moments, but she feels she has some good strategies for assisting him.

They discuss David's upcoming surgery and Scott's continuing health needs. Together they talk about the ongoing stress in the family. Carrie asks if it would be helpful for her to check in periodically by telephone, even though she would no longer be visiting David at home. While leaving the door open, she also wants to connect Beth with other resources. She asks if it would be helpful for Beth to talk to another family in a similar situation.

As Carrie leaves, she feels a sense of loss. What a nice family this has been to work with! She hopes David does well with the surgery. She decides to check into a new resource she has recently heard about, "The Family Friend" program. The program matches senior citizen volunteers with a family with a child with special health or developmental needs.

Case Study II
The Martínez Family

Sandra Newcomb
and Jennifer Smith Stepanek

Ana Martínez is 8 months old. She was born at 24 weeks' gestational age with a Grade IV intraventricular hemorrhage. She also had retinopathy of prematurity with retinal detachment in both eyes. She has severe bronchopulmonary dysplasia and has a tracheotomy tube. She was on oxygen, but this has recently been discontinued. She is at a long-term chronic care facility. Plans are being made for her to be transferred to her home. The referral to the local Infant/ Toddler Program (ITP) comes from the chronic-care facility. As part of her transition plan, staff at the chronic care facility want her to be involved in early intervention services when she goes home. During diagnostic assessment, Ana was relatively quiet and scored at or below the 3-month level in all developmental domains. After 20 minutes, she began to fuss and cry, was calmed by rocking and holding, and fell asleep. She did not seek toys or initiate interactions, although she would hold and shake objects placed in her hands. These behaviors seem typical of Ana's behavior in other contexts. She responds to sounds by becoming still. She likes various textures, such as smooth, rough, hard, soft, and fuzzy.

Ana is usually quiet. She occasionally makes a smacking sound with her lips. She communicates her needs by crying. She attends to voices, but does not vocalize in return. She recognizes familiar caregivers and responds to them by crying less and by eating better. When upset, she can usually be calmed by rocking and holding. Ana drinks from a bottle and is beginning to take baby food from a spoon, although she does not like textures in her mouth and refuses junior or mashed table foods. She refuses something by crying and arching away. Ana can raise her head and prop herself on her arms when she is on her stomach. She kicks her feet when placed on her back. She has increased tone in her arms and legs. She arches her back, retracts her shoulders (holds them back), and hyperextends her head (throws it back) when she does not like something. She does not roll in either direction.

Gail, the service coordinator from the ITP, makes a home visit to see Ana's mother, Rosa Martínez. Rosa works for the government in a large metropolitan area. Her husband, Ramón, works two jobs, making it difficult for him to spend much time with the family. She also has a 9-year-old daughter, Carmen. Ramón, Rosa, Carmen, and Ana live in an apartment with Rosa's father, José López. Mr. López works in construction and is often gone for weeks at a time, depending on when and where work is available. Although Rosa's mother ordinarily lives with them as well, she recently returned to Mexico for several months to care for a relative who was ill. Rosa meets Gail at home late in the evening because she likes to visit with Ana at the hospital on her way home from work. Both Ramón and Mr. López are out, but Carmen is present and seems very interested in the information Gail is describing and in talking about her younger sister.

Gail explains the local infant program, her role, eligibility requirements, and types of available services. Rosa has a question about what early interventionists can actually do, but agrees to be involved with the program and signs the consent form. Rosa also signs consent forms for release of medical records and asks if "there are any other parents who have a child with a trach." She says that she hopes to eventually get Ana's tracheotomy tube out and that she wants her to "be normal." She says that Ana is a special, loving baby and that she wants her to say "mama" and to play with her sister, walk, and go to school with other children. Rosa also says that her government job carries a health maintenance organization insurance plan. However, a Medicaid Model Waiver program would have to help cover the cost of the 12 hours a day of home nursing that Ana needs.

When Carmen leaves the room, Rosa also expresses concern that Carmen is not doing well at school. Rosa says that she is unable to spend much time with Carmen, because she spends so much time after work at the hospital. Because of age restrictions, Carmen is rarely allowed to see Ana. She wishes there were something she could do for Carmen.

To address Rosa's concerns about Carmen, Gail asks some additional questions as she gets to know Rosa. She discovers that Carmen has just finished the third grade. Before this year, she did very well in school, with no particular concerns on the part of her teachers. She had several friends and joined in fairly easily in group activities. Before- and after-school care is at a child care center connected to the elementary school, and several of her friends and classmates also attend this center. At the beginning of third grade, Carmen was excited that her mother was having a baby and that she would have a brother or sister. But many things changed for her when Ana was born so early. For most of November and December, Carmen stayed with her grandfather if he was able to be home or with other relatives and family friends when he was gone. Both Thanksgiving and Christmas were difficult because Ana's health had not stabilized yet and Rosa's mother was still away. Carmen had to give up her dance lessons on Saturdays because Rosa was either at the hospital or too exhausted to take Carmen anywhere. The school was very supportive and helpful during this time and checked on Carmen to see how she was doing.

By mid-January, Ana had been transferred to the chronic care facility, and life settled down somewhat. Carmen could stay at home all of the time because Rosa no longer had to be out so much. Rosa went back to work regularly. The dance lessons never began again, because both time and money were now very limited. By early spring, the school realized that Carmen was doing poorly in most of her academics and that she had stopped playing in groups at recess. Although Carmen was never a real problem, she often would not comply with her teacher's directions, simply not doing what was expected of her and her classmates.

Rosa began to notice how much television Carmen watched and how little she spoke of her day. Rosa also discovered that Carmen was not telling her the truth. Carmen said she never had homework, although the teacher said this was not true and that Carmen had not been turning in work for a while. The teacher had not called, thinking she could handle this problem without burdening Rosa, who had so many other concerns right now. One evening in late May while Carmen and Rosa were watching television together, Carmen burst into tears and ran from the room. Rosa learned that Carmen thought her sister was never going to get better and was dying because Rosa had not spoken much about her recently and because Ana had been in the hospital so long. Rosa reassured Carmen that Ana was not only all right but was getting healthier and was going to come home soon.

As the time has come closer for Ana to come home, Carmen has become more demanding and defiant. This is frightening Rosa, who wonders how she can meet both her daughters' needs, how Carmen will be affected by actually having Ana home, and what reactions

Carmen will have to her sister's disabilities. Gail tells Rosa that she will look into local programs or services for siblings and also will gather some information to share with Rosa.

When Gail meets to plan the individualized family service plan, Rosa has some questions about the services. She agrees with the strengths and needs that have been identified, but is confused because, even though the doctors said Ana should have physical therapy daily, the ITP has recommended it only once a week. Someone else told her that Model Waiver funding can provide it twice a week. Rosa also says that, although she wants everything she can get to help her daughter get better, she wants Ana to have a regular playtime. Rosa also worries that all of the people coming to the house will disturb her father, who sometimes sleeps during the day.

The ITP has recommended vision therapy as a consult only twice a year. Rosa wonders why a child who is blind would not get more vision services. She says the home nursing would start at 16 hours a day at discharge, but would decrease to 12 hours a day after 1 month. Although this may be enough when Rosa's mother is home, she is worried about evenings and weekends and about having time for Carmen. (The nursing is for weekdays only.) Rosa says that she cannot afford to quit work, and she has no more leave. She is worried about bringing Ana home, but she does not have the time or energy to go to a support group. She just wants to know what she can do for both of her daughters and who can help her accomplish it.

Case Study III
The Winger Family

**Jennifer Smith Stepanek
and Sandra Newcomb**

Chris Winger was a full-term infant whose medical history was significant for frequent colds. At 2½ years, he was referred to the Infant/Toddler Program (ITP) for concerns about speech-language development by a community nurse at the local health department. The nurse met him when his mother brought Chris's 6-year-old brother for immunizations.

Chris was tested at a developmental evaluation clinic. When he came into the testing room, he seemed uninterested in the toys. He looked at the examiner but did not smile. He played with toys that were handed to him, but he did not fuss if toys were taken away and did not try to get the toys. He looked to his mother for her approval before taking a toy. He warmed up after about a half hour. During testing, he enjoyed the gross motor items most. He jumped off the small steps repeatedly. He was congested, and his mother reported that this was common for him. However, he was not on any medications. His developmental age in the area of cognition was 14 months; in receptive language, 12 months; in expressive language, 9 months; in social, 9 months; in fine motor, 12 months; and in gross motor, 24 months.

The service coordinator, Jeanette, meets with Tanya Winger at the Wingers' home and explains the ITP, her role, the evaluation process, eligibility, services, and the individualized family service plan. Tanya says that she is 22, has five children, and is pregnant. The oldest is age 7 and in the second grade, and the 6-year-old is in first grade; both are in school during the meeting. Tanya says she does not know if she can cope with "having them home all summer." She says her 4-year-old is still in bed because he "stays up late to watch TV." Chris sits quietly on the floor without toys, and the 1-year-old is lying on the floor nearby. He is also without toys and does not smile. Both children are wearing only diapers, which appear to be soiled. Tanya says that she can change their diapers only a few times a day because of how expensive they are. She says that the baby does not crawl or sit yet and that he is "a real good baby—he doesn't bother anybody, never cries, not like his two oldest brothers."

Jeanette has concerns about the living environment, which appears dirty. Chris has thick nasal secretions and audible wheezing. Although Tanya says he is "like this all the time," she says that he has not seen a doctor and that he has not had his immunizations yet. She says that they have no health insurance, she does not work, and they do not have a phone. She also says that the only financial help she has for food and clothes is the little bit of money her boyfriend sometimes gives her when he comes over. He is paying for the one-bedroom apartment in which she lives.

At one point in the conversation, she changes the 1-year-old's diaper. He has a severe diaper rash and Tanya tells Jeanette that "he has that a lot." When Tanya gets a bottle out of the refrigerator for Chris, Jeanette notices that there is no food, only four half-full bottles. After drinking from the bottle for several minutes, Chris hands the bottle to his younger brother, who begins drinking it. Tanya says that "they always share nicely like that." She says that Chris is a good boy and quiet like his little brother. Tanya thinks Chris is doing just fine, but that if the nurse thinks the infant program is a good idea, he can be in it because "I want whatever is best for my boys." She says that she would like Chris to "start talking and maybe playing a little bit more," but she is concerned about a child so young "going to school." She says she wants him to catch up on his shots, but that she has no money and that she would like to be able to feed the boys more, but food is expensive. She wants Chris to be smart and grow up to get a good job. She would like to find the boys' fathers so that she can get some child support and give her children a better life, because she loves them.

Case Study IV
The Miller Family

**Jennifer Smith Stepanek
and Sandra Newcomb**

Paul Miller, Jr., called "P.J.," was one of the most beautiful children his teacher, Sheila, had ever seen. His eyes sparkled and he had the longest, thickest eyelashes of any child she had ever worked with. P.J. lived with his mother, Jackie, his maternal grandmother, Ms. Case, and his older half-brother, Charles. Charles was a 10-year-old who adored his baby brother. He wanted so much to help and protect his brother in any way he could. P.J. had his fourth birthday party recently in class—a birthday no one had believed he would ever see. Much like his mother and her mother before her, P.J. was quite a fighter! Sheila had witnessed such positive attitudes in this family even as they struggled with many complicated and sometimes overwhelming problems.

Shortly after birth, P.J. was diagnosed with acquired immunodeficiency syndrome (AIDS). Jackie also discovered at the same time that she had human immunodeficiency virus (HIV). Jackie and Charles had been living with P.J.'s father, Paul, at the time. The details about exactly what followed were never clear, but, when Paul found out P.J.'s diagnosis, he disappeared. Jackie also had not heard from Charles's father in 8 years. With no source of income and a very sick baby, Jackie, Charles, and P.J. moved in with her mother.

P.J.'s early months were spent mostly in the hospital. He was sick frequently. Many times they did not expect him to survive. He not only survived but also began to flourish with the dedicated care and love he received. Although infected with HIV, his mother had not yet developed symptoms and was able to care for him. His grandmother and brother doted on him day and night. Ms. Case stated on more than one occasion, "P.J.'s going to fool them all. You just wait and see. This kid may grow up to be a doctor himself! With lots of love and prayer, ain't a thing God can't do!"

P.J. received home-based early intervention services until he was 3. Despite multiple hospitalizations, which often interrupted his developmental progress, he learned to walk and feed himself. He began to communicate what he wanted with single words. He exhibited some developmental delays, but his family, therapists, and teachers were all delighted with his progress. The decision to send him to preschool had been difficult. Would he get too sick being around many other children in the center? Finally, Jackie decided that, however long his life was, she wanted him to have the best opportunities and the most typical experience she could give him. So, with his new backpack and his family nervously watching, P.J. went to preschool, riding the bus with a big smile that said, "I have arrived! Where are the toys?"

P.J. loved school. He was an easygoing, engaging child who captured everyone's heart. His favorite activities were singing and playing in the housekeeping center. "Mere" (for "come here"), he would say, pointing to a chair for "Miss She-lee" to sit in and enjoy whatever delicious playdough treat he had prepared. They practiced making playdough birthday cakes for a month. P.J. was going to be 4 years old and understood well the concepts of cake, goodies, and presents for the celebration. Jackie asked if Charles and her mother could come to school that day to share in P.J.'s special occasion. "We want it to be special," she said. "We don't know how many more birthdays he will have."

The party went well. Sheila and the staff decorated the room with balloons, mostly red because that was P.J.'s favorite color. Jackie brought in cake and ice cream (also P.J.'s favorite foods). Linda, the occupational therapist, brought a camera and took many pictures. There were pictures of P.J. and each friend, P.J. and each teacher, P.J. and his family, P.J. and his brother, P.J. with balloons, P.J. eating, and so forth. His classmates made a special birthday card decorated with each person's handprint.

Less than a week after the party, P.J. came to school one day and did not seem to be himself. He was tired and cranky. Nothing seemed to cheer him. Sheila noticed a slight cough. When P.J. wasn't in school the next day, she was immediately worried. After the children left, she called P.J.'s house. Ms. Case answered and told her that P.J. had a really bad night and coughed a lot. Jackie had taken him to the doctor, and she was waiting to hear from his office. Later that evening Sheila called P.J.'s home again. P.J. had been admitted to the hospital with pneumonia. Sheila knew from P.J.'s prognosis that pneumonia could be fatal. She also knew from his history that he could come home again. She decided to visit P.J. the next day after school.

P.J. remained in the hospital in critical condition for weeks. It was hard to see him all alone in such a big bed with so many tubes and wires. Sheila and several other staff members from school visited several times a week. Occasionally, he felt better. Sheila always brought a small toy, Play-Doh, or markers and paper just in case P.J. felt well enough to play. She also brought some of his favorite books and tapes from school. Mostly, he liked having her hold and rock him or sit beside his bed and read him a book. Jackie or Ms. Case was usually there. Sheila's visits gave them the opportunity to leave the room for a break or to talk with her about how things were going. Charles came on the weekends. P.J. always seemed better when his big brother was with him.

Slowly, P.J. improved. When he was well enough to eat by mouth and enjoy playing for short periods, his mother decided to bring him home. However, P.J. was not able to continue in school. He had successfully battled this pneumonia, but his immune system was significantly weakened. A new teacher and therapist were assigned to work with P.J. at home.

Sheila, Linda (his occupational therapist), and Jean (teaching assistant) met with the new teacher and therapist and the family to plan educational activities for P.J. at home. Linda volunteered to spend time in Sheila's room videotaping some typical activities. The tape was then used at home with P.J. She taped music time, language circle, and some special messages from the children. The new teacher used the tape to help P.J. with the transition back to home-based services. Jackie asked if P.J. could come back and visit the class when the weather was warmer and P.J. was feeling stronger. Everyone agreed this was an excellent idea. P.J. had been such a vital member of his class that it would be good for P.J. and for his classmates to be able to visit occasionally. Jackie also shared that she had agreed to participate in a hospice program from the hospital. The last hospital stay had been hard for P.J. He missed his home and his family, and Jackie and her mother made a decision to keep him home from now on, no matter what.

P.J. continued to receive home-based services. He enjoyed the videotapes made by Linda and his class. His health fluctuated. Sheila and Linda continued to visit him occasionally. About 3 months later he developed pneumonia again. Jackie called the school and told Sheila and Linda that his prognosis was very poor this time. Sheila and Linda went to visit P.J. Knowing this might be their last visit, they decided to bring a red balloon and ice cream. He was unable to eat the ice cream, but he did smile at the balloon. They visited with P.J. and talked with his family. Charles decided to eat the ice cream in P.J.'s honor. It was really hard to leave the house, but they said their good-byes and went home.

Two days later the hospice worker called the school and told Sheila that P.J. died early that morning. He was cremated the next day. The family decided to officially receive guests at the funeral home, just before his memorial service. The rest of the day was a blur for Sheila. Nothing seemed real. She looked at the picture of his smiling face on the bulletin board behind her desk, thinking, "Sometimes life just isn't fair."

Case Study V
The Singh Family

Monimalika Day
and Deirdre A. Barnwell

Puja Singh is the first child of Amit and Anita. They are from India and have been in the United States for 3 years. Amit is a computer programmer, and Anita works at a local grocery store. Puja's grandparents have come to the United States to take care of the child. Amit speaks English fluently, even though it is his second language. Anita speaks English but is more comfortable in Hindi, which is her first language. Puja's grandmother does not speak any English. Puja is referred to the early intervention program by the pediatrician within 2 days after her birth. The pediatrician refers her for services because Puja has been diagnosed with Down syndrome.

When the service coordinator visits the family, she is greeted and offered a drink. Amit informs the service coordinator that they were told about the diagnosis at birth. He said he has heard the term *Down syndrome* before, but has no other information. Anita says she has never heard of Down syndrome before, and no one in her family has had this problem. She adds that her mother-in-law takes care of the baby most of the time. Anita says that her mother-in-law thinks Puja's muscles are not very good and gives her an oil massage every day. She adds that Puja's grandmother thinks she will be okay when she grows up. Amit explains that he thinks the grandmother does not understand that it is a genetic problem.

At one point, Amit asks the service coordinator if she knows whether there are any services for kids like Puja in India. When asked if they are planning to return to India, they say they are not sure. Anita takes the service coordinator to the child's bedroom. There is a double bed on one side of the room. Anita explains that Puja sleeps with her grandmother in this room. Puja's grandmother is sitting on the floor and is massaging Puja, who is lying prone on her grandmother's legs. Anita speaks to her mother-in-law in an Indian language, but she does not formally introduce her to the service coordinator. Later she tells the service coordinator that it would be impolite for her to address her mother-in-law directly by her name. When the service coordinator asks how long the grandparents are visiting, Anita says, "Well, they may decide to live with us." Asked what goals they have for Puja, Anita says, "We would like her to walk and talk like other children." She adds, "We don't know anything about Down syndrome. You have to tell us what to do."

Case Study VI
The Parent Group

Nancy Frank
and Sandra Newcomb

PARTICIPANTS

Dee and Malcolm have two boys, ages 4 and 2½. The 2-year-old has a significant language delay. He does not talk or play with toys and has frequent tantrums related to changes in routines or interference from his brother. The family is in the process of getting services and a complete evaluation, including genetic, developmental, and neurological testing. His hearing test is normal. He has not yet received early intervention services. The 4-year-old has no delays and is in preschool. Both parents are employed full-time.

Neyla and Tom and their 18-month-old daughter are a military family that relocated because of their daughter's medical needs. They are waiting for the results of testing at a large local military hospital to help establish a diagnosis. This is their first child. She has significant problems related to her prematurity, including delays in feeding, motor skills, and language acquisition. She receives physical therapy once a week through the local Infant/Toddler Program.

Keesha has three children, two sons ages 6 and 3 and a 9-month-old daughter. Her 3-year-old son has fragile X syndrome and has been receiving services for approximately 1 year. He initially received home-based services and recently made the transition to a toddler group that meets three times a week and provides speech-language intervention in the group. Keesha was unable to attend an earlier parent group because of the new baby. Her husband is not interested in participating.

Maria is a single mother with one 10-month-old son who was born premature. He is currently receiving scores on developmental tests at about the 4½-month age level, but no one is sure if he will have permanent problems.

Ann lives with her mother and does not work. Her son has many medical clinics involved with his care. He receives home-based special instruction and physical therapy once a week.

Marlene and Ed have four children, two daughters ages 15 and 9, a 12-year-old son, and a 22-month-old daughter with Down syndrome. Their daughter with Down syndrome has had heart difficulties, which were surgically repaired at 12 months. She is not walking yet, does minimal babbling, has low tone, and continues to have chronic ear infections. She is small for her age but is growing at an acceptable rate, given her prior medical condition. None of the older children have had any special education needs. Their youngest child receives home-based special instruction once each week and physical therapy twice a month.

These families are participating in an 8-week voluntary parent support group that meets for 1½ hours in the evening at a local school. There are two group facilitators: a special educator and a social worker with experience in both group facilitation and special education. Child care services are provided for all children of group members. Transportation is also available, although no one in this group has expressed a need for it.

FIRST MEETING

The group is scheduled to meet at 7:30 P.M. At the first meeting, families are greeted in the child care room and introduced to both group facilitators and child care providers. At 7:50 P.M., the parents move to the group room, get tea and coffee, and make name tags for themselves. The meeting actually starts at 8 P.M.

The facilitators introduce themselves, explain their background, and describe the purpose of the group. This is followed by a discussion of procedures and ground rules. There are no questions or comments at this point from any parents. The facilitators suggest that the rest of the meeting be spent with introductions and brainstorming topics for subsequent meetings. The parents are asked to introduce themselves and describe their family and their child with special needs.

Ed begins by introducing himself and his wife, Marlene. He briefly states that they have four children and the youngest has Down syndrome. He says that they really do not have any problems with their daughter's disability now that her medical condition is stabilized. Marlene then talks about how sick their daughter was and the extensive medical procedures she has been through. Neyla speaks up, saying she can really understand what Marlene is talking about, and she begins to describe the medical history of her daughter. She becomes upset and somewhat teary and her husband comforts her. He states that they hope things will be better now that they have moved to this area and can really find out what the long-term implications will be. Keesha then introduces herself and comments on the genetic testing she has been through with her son who has fragile X syndrome. She explains this disorder but says she is quite optimistic about her son, stating that he is now walking and starting to say single words. Maria seems uncomfortable about speaking up and simply states that she has a son who is a little behind but doing well now. Dee introduces herself and immediately states that her son has significantly different problems from the other children. He is very healthy and active and has no motor delays, but he has really difficult behavior problems. She would like information about behavior management so that she can handle her son's tantrums better. Malcolm comments that they have been lucky not to have had any serious medical problems with either of their children.

The facilitators jot down Dee's stated need for information about behavior management on some newsprint hanging on the wall. They comment that they have heard a lot of other concerns mentioned as well and wonder which are important to discuss in group. There is a silence. The facilitator points out one issue, dealing with professionals, and this opens up considerable discussion. By the end of the meeting, the group has generated a list of topics, including dealing with difficult behaviors, figuring out what services are important, dealing with the range of feelings they have experienced, dealing with the professionals, reconciling what professionals tell them with their own knowledge, getting help with day-to-day coping, dealing with fatigue, and learning more about communication and behavior management. The group agrees to review these topics the next week and to prioritize them.

SECOND MEETING

At the second meeting, group members arrive between 7:30 P.M. and 7:45 P.M., dropping their children off and entering the group room. Parents socialize with one another, picking up conversations from the previous week. At 7:45 P.M., the group gets started, with Maria and Marlene and Ed not there yet. After about 10 minutes, Marlene and Ed arrive and join the group. The facilitators review the previous week's discussion, asking if there are any questions about the information presented last week. Dee asks how members were selected for the group. The facilitator explains that the group is voluntary and that the key criterion is having a young child with special needs. Dee continues to ask about membership. In an effort to clarify her question, the facilitator asks if Dee is concerned that each child has quite different needs. She nods and states that her son seems so different—healthy and active. She says that people do not notice that there is anything wrong, because he looks so "normal." The facilitator asks if it is difficult for others to have such a different view of her family. Dee starts to say that things are not really as bad as she may have indicated. Keesha joins in, saying she understands how hard it is when other people react without understanding and often are critical of the parents. This begins an involved discussion of how parents manage the reactions and responses of other people to their children. Several parents describe ways in which the perceptions of others are not consistent with what their children are like. They talk at length about their concerns that their children will not be treated as children first.

The facilitators let the group know that time is almost up and ask parents what topic they might like to focus on next week. Parents want to continue their discussion about ways to handle people's different reactions to their child and to them as parents.

THIRD MEETING

Parents arrive at the third meeting between 7:30 P.M. and 7:45 P.M. and seek each other out to talk and visit. Group begins by 7:45 P.M., and everyone is present. Because Maria was not there the previous week, one of the facilitators reviews the discussion and the topic they decided on for tonight. Neyla comments that they have difficulty explaining their daughter's delays to other people because they do not have a diagnosis. Malcolm agrees and expresses anger about having to go here and there without learning anything new about their son's difficulties. He believes that if they understood the problem, they could start getting their son the right help. Keesha understands Malcolm's frustration and says that she felt the same way before she knew what was wrong. She knew that he was different in some way, but that doctors dismissed her concerns. Dee excitedly agrees and describes her struggles to be taken seriously when she began to share her concerns about her son. She comments that she might understand if this were her first child, but points out that she knew what a "normal" baby was like. Neyla looks upset, and Marlene comments that it must be hard to have your first and only child have problems. Neyla says that she never even had the opportunity to think her daughter was fine, because she had so many struggles just to survive. Maria nods but remains quiet. The other parents seem somewhat uncomfortable with Neyla's strong feelings, and the facilitator points out that several parents have dealt with frightening medical situations. Marlene cries quietly as she describes her fear that her daughter would not make it to her first birthday and through the open heart surgery. Keesha says she feels lucky that her son has had only the routine medical problems of childhood. However, she understands the impact of "bad" news, remembering all the testing and then the meeting to tell them "the bad news." She then says that you need to take 1 day at a time. One of the facilitators notes that Keesha has found a way to get through difficult periods and that everyone probably comes up with their own unique way to cope. Keesha agrees and says that, for her, things get better with time and that she can get back to treating her son like she would any other child.

One of the facilitators gently asks Maria about her son's medical status and she replies that he is healthy now. She adds that the doctors have all been very nice to her and tell her he is going to be fine, maybe just a little slow. She has to take her son to several medical appointments because everyone wants to make sure he is growing well. Sometimes, she says, it is hard to keep track of all the appointments and things she is supposed to do that the doctors or clinics tell her. Neyla agrees, stating she needs a separate calendar for her daughter's appointments alone, and other parents laugh. The facilitators mention that the meeting is almost over and ask what topic parents want to discuss the following week. There is no consensus, and the agenda is left open. The facilitators also indicate that they have been able to arrange to have speakers on managing behavior and understanding communication at a later date.

FOURTH MEETING

At the fourth meeting, parents are slow to arrive, and the meeting begins with only Keesha and Dee and Malcolm. Neyla had called and said their daughter was running a high fever, and they had taken her to the hospital for tests. Marlene and Ed arrive late. Maria is not there. The group seems somewhat disorganized and slow to begin, so the facilitator asks what has happened to everyone during the week. Dee replies that it has been a bad week. Her son started a toddler group, but has been having tantrums every day about getting on the bus. The teachers have called Dee to explain that he is having trouble with the entire daily routine, and she feels terrible. She does not know when to force her son to do things or when it is too hard for him. Deciding when to use discipline is very hard for her. Keesha agrees and comments that her son's refusal to do certain things is hard, especially when his refusal is accompanied by aggression.

The parents talk about how to determine which behaviors need discipline and which are related to the child's special needs. The discussion is low-key, but everyone has the opportunity to talk about their own unique situation. Marlene says that her older children let her daughter get away with things that she herself would not, such as scratching when she does not get her way. The discussion then moves to how siblings handle their brother's or sister's disability. The parents talk about juggling the needs of everyone in the family; it can be difficult not to focus all the attention on the child with special needs. They describe their other children, with Keesha and Dee swapping stories about their older sons. Parents share some ways in which they have handled sibling issues. The facilitators have to gently interrupt the discussion to end the meeting. They indicate that, in 2 weeks, there will be a speaker.

FIFTH MEETING

Parents arrive at the fifth meeting more promptly than they did at the fourth and are busy talking with each other when the facilitators attempt to start the group. The facilitators comment that everyone seems to have a great deal to discuss. Dee summarizes what happened the previous week for the parents who had missed that week. She asks Neyla and Tom how their daughter is doing. Neyla replies that her daughter had a mild case of pneumonia but is better now. However, one of the professionals who tested her last week used the diagnosis of cerebral palsy. Tom comments that their doctor was not willing to commit to this diagnosis, but clearly the people evaluating their daughter are considering it. Tom sounds angry and frustrated and says he wishes the professionals would just make up their minds and agree on a diagnosis so that he could then decide what he needed to do for his daughter. Neyla said she has had trouble thinking about anything else this week and has been upset all week. The other parents are quiet, just listening to Neyla. This is not an awkward silence, just a natural pause after something important has been said.

Dee is the first to speak, and it is clear she is quite upset as well. Their son had a neurology workup, and the neurologist had told her that he thought her son had pervasive developmental disorder. Dee smiles when she sees all the puzzled faces and comments that the other parents look just like she felt when the doctor said this. She did not know what this term meant, having never heard it before. The neurologist said that children with pervasive developmental disorder have delays in their language, social, and often cognitive development. He also described some unusual behaviors that children with this disorder sometimes have. Dee believes the neurologist is right because the odd behaviors described were very similar to ones they see at home. Malcolm says that at least now he can read something about what might be wrong. He agrees with Tom that the doctors should not say anything if they are going to be wishy-washy about a diagnosis. What they still do not know is whether their son will have mental retardation. He then glances at Keesha and looks uncomfortable about having said this.

Keesha laughs and assures Malcolm that it is all right that he made the comment about being "retarded." She has adjusted to the idea that her son has mental retardation, although it is still hard for her to say those words. Her husband does not accept this. She adds that he does work in the evenings, but she also thinks that one reason why he will not come to this group is that he is uncomfortable and ashamed of their son. Keesha believes her son will be in special schools all his life and will always need to live with some family members. She is afraid that he will develop some really unacceptable habits and will not be able to participate in regular church and social activities. Marlene shares similar fears and also has difficulty saying that her daughter has mental retardation, even though she has accepted the diagnosis. She copes by trying to concentrate on the things her daughter *can* do and what she is learning.

Maria has been quiet throughout this discussion, and one of the facilitators asks her how she feels about the uncertainty around her child's future. She replies that she does not think about it much. Her son is still such a baby that she does not think past his growing and getting strong. She is looking forward to when he can walk and talk, but is not sure when he will start doing these things, because he seems a little behind. The doctors keep saying that her baby "will be fine." Her mother, who helps her with child care, also thinks he will be all right, and she has raised several children.

As the group pauses, the facilitators remind parents that next week there will be a speaker on behavior management and understanding communication. The facilitators wonder if the group would like to brainstorm some questions for the speaker. They spend the last 15 minutes developing a list of questions.

SIXTH MEETING

The facilitators have called the speaker during the week prior to the sixth meeting to tell her what questions the parents want addressed.

The speaker arrives first, with lots of materials she sets out for the parents. One of the facilitators takes the speaker to the child care room to meet the parents and see their children briefly before she begins talking. Dee and Malcolm are the first to arrive. Dee immediately introduces herself and begins to describe their son. The other parents arrive within the next few minutes, and then they walk the speaker back to the group room. Maria had telephoned, saying she was unable to come because of a conflict with an activity at her church.

The speaker describes her training and orientation and then discusses some of the developmental markers she considers important. She then moves to an open discussion format, and parents eagerly ask their questions and voice their concerns. She notes that the children vary considerably and that she has quite a job addressing such a range of concerns. She then laughs and states that she will try to be both specific and general at the same time. She asks the group to be patient with her so that she can try to answer everyone's questions. The group settles down into an involved give-and-take between the parents and the speaker about a range of topics. It is hard to end because everyone continues to have questions and reactions to the topics being discussed. The speaker agrees to stay a few minutes after group to talk with those parents who have other questions or concerns.

SEVENTH MEETING

The seventh meeting begins by discussing reactions to the speaker the previous week. The parents felt very supported and appreciated her ideas and suggestions. Dee has thought a great deal about the speaker's point that behavior is a form of communication. She has tried harder to understand what her son is trying to say. She reports that, for the first time, their son sat at the table with them for a meal and actually pointed to something he wanted to eat. Malcolm sees that as a big achievement, but he cannot tell anyone at work, because they would not understand. He is glad that everyone in the group understands how much such "little things" mean.

Neyla speaks up next, wondering whether the doctors could be wrong about her daughter. She is doing many more things than the doctors predicted. Tom is sure she is looking at things and pointing. He is not sure whether he trusts the professionals, because he does not think his child is as delayed as they all say she is. Keesha responds, supporting Tom in his view of his daughter. They know their child better than anyone, and she will believe their reports

over any professional's. She's heard all the "doom and gloom" predictions about her son, but he continues to prove everybody wrong.
She last counted 20 or more words that he uses, and that goes
against the doctors who said he would not talk for a long time.
Keesha then smiles and says it is really great that Neyla and Tom's
daughter is looking at them and letting them know what she wants,
and Tom and Neyla nod and smile, too. Keesha adds that you just
have to keep treating her like your baby, not like a child with cerebral palsy.

Maria speaks up for the first time and agrees with Keesha. She
finds it hard to just be a mother and treat your child like a "regular"
baby when everyone else is looking for something wrong. She begins
to worry that every behavior is a sign of a problem. Sometimes she
just stops listening to others so that she can treat her child normally.
Marlene agrees, commenting that it is hard never to be allowed to
forget that her daughter has Down syndrome. She thinks having
older children is an advantage because she can remember each of
her babies doing the same thing.

The facilitators take advantage of a break in the discussion to
remind the parents that next week will be the last meeting. Several
parents comment that time has gone by fast, and they cannot believe
that the 8 weeks are almost over. Dee wonders where she will brag
when her son starts using a spoon and fork. One of the facilitators
acknowledges that the group has shared a lot and that it may be
hard not to have such a group. The other facilitator then mentions
that there is another ongoing group parents can join that meets less
frequently. She will bring more information at the next group. The
facilitators also ask if the parents want to do anything special for
their last group, such as have a potluck supper or bring desserts to
share. The parents discuss options and decide to bring desserts to
share for their last meeting.

EIGHTH MEETING

Parents come to the eighth meeting at different times, and the group
does not get started until almost 8 P.M. Maria has not arrived, and
no one has heard from her. The facilitators begin the group by saying
that it is the last meeting, and there are a few things they need to
do. First, they present information about other ongoing parent
groups, including times, dates, and locations. They give out sheets
with this information. They also give each parent a list with the
telephone numbers and addresses of group members (having sought
permission in advance). The facilitators acknowledge that they are

sorry Maria is not there for the last group. Then they comment on how much they have appreciated this group and their willingness to talk with one another so openly. They indicate that they will miss all of the members and thank them for having shared their experiences. They also ask about the parents' reactions to the group. The parents listen quietly, but do not comment. The silence is broken by Dee, who mentions that they took their son for additional testing, this time by a psychologist. He agreed with the diagnosis of pervasive developmental disorder. Several other parents ask them questions about the testing and the diagnosis.

After pursuing this discussion, the facilitators ask if anyone has anything to say in closing. Marlene responds that she has enjoyed the group and that it has been helpful to her. Dee remembers that at first she really did not think she was going to fit in, because her son's disability was different from the others. She is glad she came, but worries that the group is ending just as they are beginning to get a diagnosis and wonders with whom she will talk over her concerns. The facilitators point out that parents may continue to have things they want to talk through with others. Neyla says that she thinks she is going to try another group. Dee is not sure. Although she wants to, it was hard for her to come to this one, and she is not sure she can join another group. She worries that the next group may not be as nice as this one. Keesha is not sure what her plans are. She does know that she will probably have to go alone to another group, but has not decided if she wants to do this. She wishes her husband would feel comfortable coming, but is afraid this will not happen. Marlene and Ed are clear that they will not be attending any other group, but they might go hear a speaker if the topic is relevant. With three other children, their lives are too busy to commit more time. The facilitators comment that each family has to decide for themselves not only what is useful but also when they have the time and energy to invest in different activities. The facilitators reiterate how special this group has been. After a silence, Dee wonders where the delicious desserts are and, more important, when they are going to eat!

The parents, facilitators, children, and child care providers join together for dessert. Individuals talk with each other, and the group facilitators make it a point to speak to each parent individually, wishing them luck and saying good-bye. The meeting breaks up, with all the parents agreeing to stay in touch and Dee and Malcolm and Neyla and Tom agreeing to go to the new group together.

Index

Page numbers followed by "t" indicate tables.